A GUIDE TO THE NEW TESTAMENT

In grateful memory of
George Caird

A Guide To The New Testament

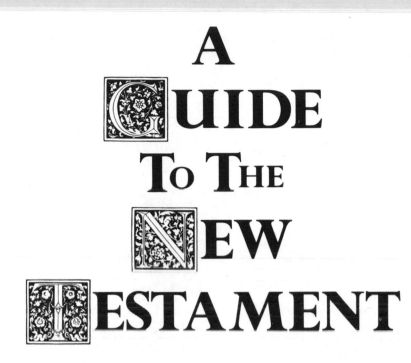

Francis Watson

B. T. Batsford Ltd · London

ISBN 0 7134 5398 2

Photoset by Deltatype Ltd, Ellesmere Port, Cheshire
and printed in Great Britain by
Anchor Brendon Ltd
Tiptree, Essex

for the publishers
B. T. Batsford Ltd
4 Fitzhardinge Street
London W1H 0AH

Contents

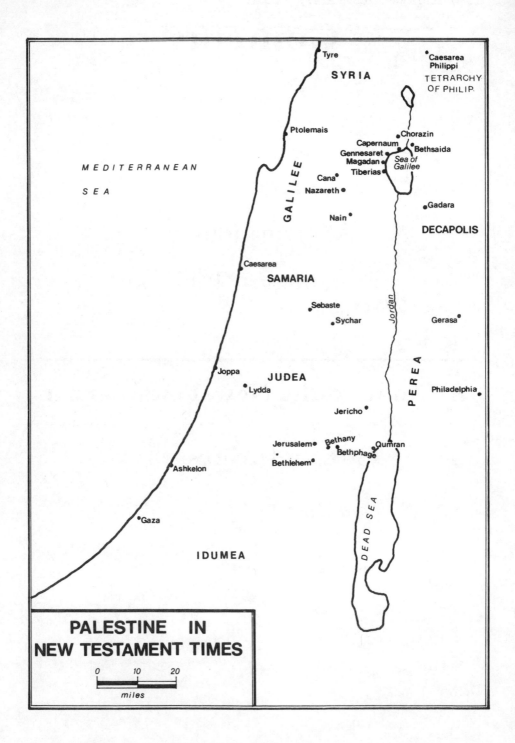

Tyre

SYRIA

Caesarea
Philippi

TETRARCHY
OF PHILIP.

Ptolemais

Chorazin

Capernaum

Bethsaida

Gennesaret

MEDITERRANEAN

Magadan

*Sea of
Galilee*

SEA

Tiberias

GALILEE

Cana

Nazareth

Nain

Gadara

DECAPOLIS

Caesarea

SAMARIA

Sebaste

Sychar

Gerasa

Joppa

JUDEA

Lydda

PEREA

Philadelphia

Jericho

Jerusalem

Bethany

Bethphage

Qumran

Bethlehem

Ashkelon

Gaza

DEAD SEA

IDUMEA

**PALESTINE   IN
NEW TESTAMENT TIMES**

0   10   20

miles

Preface

This *Guide to the New Testament* is intended to fulfil much the same purpose as any other guidebook. A guidebook is not absolutely essential for appreciating a visit to, for example, a historic building, and reading one can never be an adequate substitute for the visit itself. Yet a guidebook is often helpful. It can point to important features of the place that might otherwise be completely overlooked. It can provide explanations for the place's quirks and oddities, which would otherwise seem meaningless. It can give depth and insight to our experience by recounting the place's history, which will not just be a series of dull facts and dates but a story created by real people.

The purpose of the analogy is not to identify the New Testament with an ancient monument – and certainly not with an ancient ruin. Yet our appreciation and understanding of the New Testament too may be increased with the aid of a guidebook. The 27 books in it spring from a society and culture in many ways very different from our own, and they therefore use ideas, words and images with which we are no longer familiar. Most of their authors were not conscious of writing 'Holy Scripture', eternally and universally valid; they were writing to meet specific and often urgent needs in a particular historical situation, which we must reconstruct from the often fragmentary evidence they provide. The situation is further complicated by the centuries of Christian interpretation of these texts, which has sometimes hindered rather than helped a real understanding. At a deeper level, the content of these texts is often so strange and so novel – as it was even for the first century world they addressed – that great care is needed in order to understand them correctly.

But not all guidebooks are helpful. They can be frustratingly simplistic, and so fail to provide the range of information required. Alternatively, they can be far too specialized, and overwhelm one with a mass of irrelevant detail that is only really of interest to scholars. No writer of a guidebook can avoid seeming too simplistic to some and too specialized to others, but I have at least tried to be aware of both dangers in planning the layout and content of the book.

In order to avoid being too simplistic, I have restricted the number of entries so as to make space for adequate discussion. The alternative was to include a comprehensive range of entries with space only for a few brief remarks and long strings of verse references. The result would have been a New Testament *Dictionary*, possibly useful for some purposes but not particularly interesting or readable. Restricting the number of entries inevitably has the disadvantage that there are gaps. Why, some readers may complain, are there no entries for such important topics as 'poverty', or 'righteousness', or even 'the Trinity'? The answer is that these and many other missing entries are listed in a section at the back of the book entitled *Cross-References*, with guidance about where in the book relevant material can be found. Cross-references for each actual entry are also to be found in this section, and they correspond to the system of numbers in the text itself. The purpose of this system is to enable readers to follow up a subject in more detail if they wish, and also to avoid repeating material when discussing two related subjects.

In order to avoid being too specialized, I have not attempted to summarize the complete range of issues which preoccupy scholars in connection with each topic. Instead, I have concentrated on those points which seem to me to be most interesting and relevant, and this of course means that aspects which for others are crucially important have had to be ignored. I have also tried to avoid the jargon which afflicts New Testament studies like every other academic discipline. Those familiar with academic theology will no doubt be surprised by the absence of such well-worn terms as 'form-criticism', 'parousia' and 'eschatology' – terms which are indispensable within their proper context, but off-putting and confusing for those without a formal theological training. This book is not intended to be a guide to the academic study of the New Testament, although it may still be of some use to those engaged in such study; it is a guide to the New Testament itself, written from the standpoint of academic study. The two things are obviously related, but are not identical.

But what is this 'standpoint of academic study' from which the book is written? New Testament scholars describe their approach (somewhat forbiddingly) as 'the historical-critical method'. In fact, it is not really a method or technique at all, but a particular outlook, a particular range of questions which is brought to a text. This outlook is 'historical'. It does not ask questions such as: How does this passage help our own awareness of God? How can this text be applied to our own circumstances? It is not in principle hostile to such questions – indeed it may serve as a preliminary to answering them appropriately. But it does not ask or answer them itself. Instead it asks questions such as: In what circumstances did this text come to be written? What did its author mean by it? Did the events he may describe take place in the way he says they did? Are there perhaps other views expressed elsewhere about the events or ideas in question? To what extent has the contemporary non-Christian world influenced the language and ideas of New Testament writers?

This approach is also 'critical' in the sense that it does not simply accept traditional beliefs and opinions as authoritative and beyond question. It is not – or rather, it is not supposed to be – a form of propaganda for any particular religious outlook. It claims the right to a free investigation of the object in question, and is thus bound by the same principles of open and honest inquiry that govern other disciplines. How these principles work out in practice is another matter, and the fact that one tries to follow them is certainly no guarantee of success. Other qualities are needed too, including imagination, sympathy and insight. But the fundamental principle is that scholars should be able to weigh conflicting opinions calmly and dispassionately, resisting the temptation to prescribe in advance what the truth must be.

But this approach is not without its critics, who claim with varying degrees of emphasis that the New Testament should be studied neither historically nor critically. It is important not simply to dismiss this criticism out of hand because the problems it raises are often genuine.

Firstly, the *historical* emphasis of this outlook may be regarded as inappropriate. No-one will deny that the New Testament books were written in particular historical contexts, or that understanding those contexts can sometimes be helpful. But a legitimate objection can be raised when the New Testament is understood to belong so firmly to its original context that it cannot possibly be relevant or significant for later generations. A text may be understood as addressed *only* to the concerns of, for example, first century Christians in Asia Minor, and *in no sense* to universal human concerns, and in this way a barrier is set up between ourselves and the New Testament. The New Testament comes to resemble a collection of ancient artefacts in a museum, a mildly interesting testimony to customs and beliefs which are now quite alien to us.

It is true that the historical approach often has to treat the New Testament like this, but this is not the whole picture. There is no law of historical study that forbids interpreting a text in the widest possible context, so long as the original context is not neglected in doing so. Sympathy and imagination will naturally lead the reader to interpret the text in as much depth as possible, rather than treating it superficially with a clinical detachment which refuses to become involved. There is of course a risk in allowing too much scope for subjectivity, but risks cannot and should not always be avoided.

Secondly, the *critical* emphasis of this approach may be questioned. This is a much more emotive matter as some claim that criticism of this sort is destructive to Christian faith. It finds inconsistencies and contradictions between different parts of the New Testament; it points out differences between orthodox Christian belief and what the New Testament writers themselves believed; and it poses radical questions about the central claims of the New Testament, such as the incarnation, the virgin birth, and the resurrection. It is not surprising that there are many who regard New Testament scholarship as a kind of Trojan Horse within the Church, whose purpose is to destroy traditional Christian faith.

Historical criticism does indeed oppose the literalism which insists, for example, on the historical truth of every statement in the Gospels. The reason for this is not hostility towards traditional Christian faith as such, but the straight-forward observation that in countless instances the evangelists present the same incident or saying in different and incompatible ways. There are often good theological reasons for this, but they cannot all be correct from a historical viewpoint. The historical and critical approach inevitably leads to the conclusion that the relation between the texts and the events they describe is not so simple as was once thought.

In stories of secondary significance, this hardly matters. Christian faith has never depended on whether, for example, Mark's story of Jesus' 'cleansing of the temple' can successfully be harmonized with John's. But this approach may also affect areas of the New Testament which are much more central to Christian life and thought, and it is these areas – notably the incarnation, virgin birth and resurrection – where controversy is sharpest and where opinions diverge the most. Some scholars think that historical and critical study does indeed make it hard or impossible to affirm such beliefs with intellectual integrity. Others totally reject such a view: they argue that the alleged historical reasons against traditional beliefs are not nearly as strong as their proponents claim, and that they are frequently based on conjecture and hypothesis rather than fact. Neither side can necessarily claim any greater degree of 'objectivity' than the other, for those who oppose traditional beliefs may be motivated by personal reasons just as much as those who defend them.

It is not the purpose of this book to argue for either a 'liberal' or a 'conservative' theological stance. Its task is more modest: to discuss various features of the New Testament as objectively as possible, leaving individual readers to draw their own conclusions. Historical study in itself neither imposes nor precludes any theological position, and genuinely open and constructive historical work has been carried out by scholars holding a great variety of different views. Individual interpreters will rightly and inevitably be influenced by their own total understanding of the world, but what is important is that this element of personal involvement should enhance and not diminish the value of historical work.

I am most grateful to Miss Rachel Wright, of B. T. Batsford Ltd, for inviting me to write this book, and for her helpful comments and suggestions. I would also like to express my gratitude to Mrs Mollie Caird for allowing me to dedicate this book to the memory of her late husband, George Caird. Professor Caird was Dean Ireland's Professor of the Exegesis of Holy Scripture at the University of Oxford from 1977 until his sudden death at Easter 1984, shortly before he was due to retire. In his teaching and writing he combined the highest standards of scholarship with a desire to communicate to the widest possible audience, believing as he did that the contents of the New Testament actually mattered.

Francis Watson
King's College London
1987

List of Abbreviations

Genesis	Gen.	II Corinthians	II Cor.
Exodus	Exod.	Galatians	Gal.
Leviticus	Lev.	Ephesians	Eph.
Deuteronomy	Deut.	Philippians	Phil.
1 Samuel	1 Samuel	Colossians	Col.
Psalms	Ps.	I Thessalonians	I Thess.
Proverbs	Prov.	II Thessalonians	II Thess.
Isaiah	Isa.	I Timothy	I Tim.
Jeremiah	Jer.	II Timothy	II Tim.
Daniel	Dan.	Titus	Titus
Micah	Micah	Philemon	Philem.
Zechariah	Zech.	Hebrews	Heb.
Malachi	Mal.	James	James
Matthew	Matt.	I Peter	I Peter
Mark	Mark	II Peter	II Peter
Luke	Luke	I John	I John
John	John	II John	II John
Acts	Acts	III John	III John
Romans	Rom.	Jude	Jude
I Corinthians	I Cor.	Revelation	Rev.

Chronological Table

The Roman Emperors	Jewish History	The Early Church
Octavian (Augustus) 30 BC–AD 14	Herod the Great 37–4 BC Archelaus 4 BC–AD 6 Herod Antipas 4 BC–AD 39 Philip 4 BC–AD 34 Quirinius governor of Syria, AD 6–11 Revolt of Judas the Galilean AD 6 Annas high priest AD 6–15	Birth of Jesus c. 5 BC
Tiberius AD 14–37	Caiaphas high priest AD 18–36 Pontius Pilate governor of Judaea AD 26–36	Ministry of John the Baptist, c. AD 28–9 Ministry of Jesus, c. AD 29–30 Conversion of Paul c. AD 33
Caligula AD 37–41	Herod Agrippa I AD 37–44 Caligula's attempt to install statue of himself in Jerusalem Temple AD 40–1	Arrival of Christianity in Rome, c. AD 40
Claudius AD 41–54	Theudas' revolt c. AD 45 Agrippa II AD 50–c. 100 Felix governor of Judaea, AD 52–60	Martyrdom of James son of Zebedee c. AD 43 Paul at Corinth c. AD 50–1: I, II Thess., ?Gal.

CHRONOLOGICAL TABLE

The Roman Emperors	Jewish History	The Early Church
Nero AD 54–68		Paul based at Ephesus c. AD 53–6: I Cor., II Cor., ?Phil., ?Philem., Rom.
		Paul arrested in Jerusalem AD 57
		Paul in prison in Caesarea AD 57–60
	Festus governor of Judaea AD 60–2	Paul's imprisonment and martyrdom in Rome AD 60–2
		Martyrdom of James brother of Jesus AD 62
		Persecution in Rome under Nero, AD 64; martyrdom of Peter
	Jewish revolt, concluding with fall of Jerusalem and destruction of Temple, AD 66–70	
Galba, Otho, Vitellius AD 68–9		
Vespasian AD 69–79		Mark c. AD 75, ?Col., ?Eph.
Titus AD 79–81		
Domitian AD 91–6		c. AD 80–100 Matt., Luke–Acts, John; I, II, Tim., Titus, Heb., I, II Peter, James, I, II, III John, Jude, Rev.

ABBA An Aramaic word meaning 'father' – Aramaic was the language spoken by Jesus and the first disciples. It occurs (together with a Greek translation) in Mark's version of Jesus' prayer in Gethsemane: 'Abba, Father, all things are possible to thee; remove this cup from me . . .' (Mark 14.36). Paul twice speaks of the cry, 'Abba, Father!', as inspired by the Spirit (Rom. 8.15–16, Gal. 4.6), and this shows that this Aramaic word was used in the worship of Greek-speaking congregations.[1] Luke's version of the Lord's Prayer begins with the word 'Father' (Luke 11.2), and in the Aramaic original *Abba* will have been used here.[2] The use of *Abba* in addressing God is unprecedented in Jewish sources, but it is at the heart of Jesus' message of child-like trust in God.[3]

ACTS OF THE APOSTLES

The second volume of a two volume work, the first of which is the Gospel of Luke. Both are dedicated to the 'most excellent Theophilus' (Luke 1.3, Acts 1.1), and together they are intended to give a historical account of the origins of Christianity, from the birth of John the Baptist to Paul's preaching the gospel in Rome.

1 Contents The contents of the book of Acts may be roughly divided into four main sections. (*i*) The origins of the Jerusalem Church (Acts 1–5): Jesus' ascension, the coming of the Spirit on the Day of Pentecost, Peter's preaching and miracle-working activity, and the opposition of the Jewish leaders are among the main themes here.[1] (*ii*) Persecution leads to missionary activity among the Samaritans and the Gentiles (Acts 6–12). The martyrdom of Stephen causes Christians to flee from Jerusalem and to preach the gospel elsewhere; the main instigator of the persecution, Saul (i.e. Paul) is converted, and Cornelius, a Gentile centurion, is converted through the preaching of Peter.[2] (*iii*) Paul's great missionary journeys in Asia Minor and Greece (Acts 13–19) are described. Again and again, Paul's preaching is rejected by the Jews, so that he preaches to the Gentiles instead; in Acts 15, the legitimacy of accepting Gentiles into the Church is decided once and for all.[3] (*iv*) Paul's final journey to Jerusalem leads to his being taken into protective custody by the Romans and to a prolonged legal process that culminates in his appeal to Caesar and his journey to Rome (Acts 20–28).[4]

2 Authorship The use of 'we' in several sections suggests that the author may have been a companion of Paul (16.10–17, 20.5–21.18, 27.1–28.16). From the second half of the second century onwards it was believed that the author was

Luke, who is mentioned as a 'fellow-worker' of Paul in Philem. 24, and as 'the beloved physician' in Col. 4.14 (*see also* 2 Tim. 4.11; however, only the first of these three passages occurs in a letter certainly by Paul).[5] It is possible that this traditional view is correct, but more likely that it is simply a guess based on Paul's references to companions and fellow-workers. It is not even certain that the author really was a companion of Paul because the 'we sections' could be merely a literary device.

3 Date Because Acts ends without describing the outcome of Paul's trial, it has been suggested that the book was written prior to the hearing before Caesar took place – that is, in about AD 62.[6] But this is very unlikely; Acts ends as it does because its main aim is to describe how Paul fulfilled his ambition to preach the gospel in Rome, and probably also because his trial ended with his condemnation and execution. The author stresses the former at the expense of the latter to show how God's providence was still at work even in a gross miscarriage of justice. The date of Acts is dependent on the date of Luke, which in turn depends on the date of Mark, the main source for Luke. As Mark and Luke give clear evidence of having been written after the destruction of Jerusalem in AD 70,[7] Acts was probably written between AD 80 and 100.

4 Historical Value Acts is a historical source of great value for our knowledge of early Christian history, but it must always be used critically, as it is sometimes at variance with information provided by the (much earlier) letters of Paul. For example, Acts claims that Paul had persecuted the Church in Jerusalem, whereas Paul states that the Christians of Judaea had never even set eyes on him (Gal. 1.22–24). Acts presents Paul as a Pharisee whose conversion made no difference to his attitude to the Jewish Law (e.g. 22.6, 25.8, 26.5), whereas for Paul his life as a law-observant Jew is a thing of the past (e.g. Phil. 3.4–9).[8] In addition, the speeches ascribed to Peter, Stephen and Paul are probably the composition of the author.[9]

5 Purpose In one sense, the author's purpose is simply to describe the progress of the gospel from Jerusalem to Rome (*see* 1.8). But the way that he presents the history shows that he had at least two important subordinate aims. Firstly, he seeks to minimize conflict within the early Church. For example, Paul's letter to the Galatians gives evidence of a long-standing controversy between Paul and the leaders of the Jerusalem church about whether Gentiles should be accepted into the Church without submitting to the Jewish law; this culminated in a clash with Peter and Barnabas (his former fellow-worker) at Antioch (Gal. 2.11–21), when Paul vehemently but apparently unsuccessfully defended the rights of Gentiles within the Church. Acts tells us nothing of this; there is a quarrel with Barnabas, but only over a trivial matter (Acts 15.36–40).[10] Here and elsewhere, the author of Acts presents an idealized view of the apostolic age as a time of near perfect harmony.

Secondly, Acts appears to have a political aim in its remarkably favourable view of Roman authority. The first Gentile convert is a Roman soldier (10.1); the Roman governor of Cyprus is 'a man of intelligence' who believes the Christian message (13.7–12); the Roman governor of Achaia (southern Greece) dismisses the Jews' charges against Paul (18.12–17); above all, in 21.27–27.44 the Roman authorities repeatedly save Paul's life and so ensure that he is able to preach the gospel in Rome. The author's purpose is probably to oppose both Christian hostility towards the Roman state and Roman hostility towards the Church. Acts thus implies that the Roman state is ordained by the providence of God to further the gospel, and that the Church should not be seen as a political threat.[11]

ADAM

In Luke 3.23–38, Jesus' genealogy is traced back not just to Abraham, as in Matthew, but to Adam. In this way, the evangelist stresses that he is significant not just for the Jewish people but for the whole world.[1]

Paul too uses the figure of Adam to stress the universality of Jesus.[2] In Rom. 5.12–21, Jesus Christ is seen as the answer to the world-wide problem of the sin and death which have come into the world through Adam. In I Cor. 15.45–49, Paul again contrasts Adam with Christ, but here he does not have in mind Adam's sin but the earthly body bestowed on him at his creation. Adam was a 'man of dust', and at present we still share his likeness. Paul thus makes use of two rather different aspects of the story of Adam in Gen. 2–3.

In I Tim. 2.12–15, the author (writing under the name of Paul)[3] uses Adam and Eve to support his ban on women teaching or exercising authority in the Church; man is inherently superior to woman because Adam was created first and Eve was deceived by the serpent, not Adam.[4]

AGRIPPA

King Herod Agrippa II was the son of Herod Agrippa I; Acts refers to the former as 'Agrippa' and the latter as 'Herod', whose death as a divine punishment for his treatment of the apostles is described in 12.20–23.[1] Agrippa II is seen in a more positive light. His visit to Caesarea gives the imprisoned Paul another opportunity to defend himself, and Agrippa's response is favourable: he could have been set free if he had not appealed to Caesar (Acts 26.32). Agrippa is known to have remained loyal to the Romans even during the Jewish revolt of AD 66–70, and Luke's purpose in introducing him into his narrative is probably to show that a respected ally of Rome had asserted the legality of Paul's activity and, by implication, the legality of the whole Christian movement.[2]

ANDREW

In the lists of the twelve apostles, Andrew is either placed second, after his brother Simon Peter (Matt. 10.2, Luke 6.14, Acts 1.13), or fourth, after Peter, James and John (Mark 3.18).[1] In the Synoptic Gospels, he plays virtually no independent part, but in John he is more important[2]: he is one of the two disciples of John the Baptist to believe in Jesus, and he introduces his brother Simon to Jesus (1.40–42; contrast Mark 1.16–18, where a different account of the call of Simon and Andrew is given).[3] He is also mentioned at the feeding of the five thousand (John 6.8), and with Philip tells Jesus of the interest he has aroused among some Greeks (John 12.22).

ANGELS

Angels are mentioned in about two thirds of the books of the New Testament, in some cases repeatedly; the early Christians adopted a belief in angels from the Old Testament and from inter-testamental Jewish literature, especially apocalyptic texts. Angels were envisaged as 'men in dazzling apparel' (Luke 24.4) and as 'ministering spirits sent forth to serve, for the sake of those who are to obtain salvation' (Heb. 2.14).

(*i*) According to New Testament narrative, angels are sent from time to time by God to guide and instruct people.[1] In the nativity stories in Matthew and Luke, angels play a prominent part. Joseph is told by an angel in a dream that Mary has conceived by the power of the Holy Spirit (Matt. 1.20), and later an angel warns him to flee to Egypt and tells him when it is safe to return (Matt. 2.13,19). In Luke 1 an angel announces to Zechariah and Mary the birth of the holy children, and in Luke 2.8–12 it is an angel who announces the birth of the Messiah to the shepherds. Angels interpret the meaning of the empty tomb (Luke 24.4–7) and the ascension (Acts 1.10–11), and they guide and encourage the preachers of the gospel (Acts 8.26, 27.23). Belief in angels is therefore a form of belief in God's providential care for his people (*see* Rom. 8.28).

(*ii*) The angels are, however, first and foremost the inhabitants of the heavenly world. According to Rev. 5.11–12, God's throne is surrounded by 'myriads of myriads and thousands of thousands' of angels, all praising him with a loud voice. It is the destiny of human beings to share the life of the angels in heaven (Mark 12.25).

(*iii*) As the inhabitants of heaven, the angels are to be involved in the return of Christ when the heavenly world will break into the present world.[2] Matt. 16.27 is typical of this belief: 'The Son of man is to come with his holy angels in the glory of his Father, and then he will repay every man for what he has done'. In Revelation, the angels are responsible for the preordained series of catastrophes which will precede the end of the world; here, they have a punitive role.

(*iv*) There are, however, several attempts in the New Testament to diminish the status of angels. Paul claims that 'we are to judge angels' (I Cor. 6.3), and that Christ has now freed us from the law of Moses given by angels (Gal. 3.19–24). Heb. 1.5–2.9 declares the superiority of Christ to the angels who gave the law (2.2),[3] and Col. 2.18 condemns the worship of angels.

ANNAS[1] High priest, AD 6–15. It is strange that he is referred to in Luke 3.2, Acts 4.6, and John 18.13–24 as though he were still high priest, either alongside Caiaphas (the actual high priest at this time) or instead of him. In John's passion narrative, Jesus is brought after his arrest first to Annas, and it is at his house that Peter's denials take place; after Annas has examined Jesus, he sends him to Caiaphas. In the Synoptics, Jesus is brought only to 'the high priest' – that is, Caiaphas (Matt. 26.3,57).

ANTICHRIST The term 'Antichrist' occurs in the New Testament only in the letters of John (I John 2.18,22, 4.3, II John 7). The author takes up a traditional belief ('You have heard that Antichrist is coming') and applies it to Christians who have broken away from his church because they understand the person of Christ in a different way.[1] The traditional belief is evident in II Thess. 2.1–12: before Jesus returns to bring his reign to an end, 'the man of lawlessness' will lead a final rebellion against God.[2] In Rev. 13 he is portrayed as a 'beast' who is given authority over the world by 'the dragon' – Satan. The beast blasphemes against God and conquers his saints, but is eventually defeated and thrown into the lake of fire (19.20).[3] Belief in the Antichrist stems from the book of Daniel, in which the Syrian king, Antiochus Epiphanes (175–164 BC) is described in mysterious language as a persecutor and a blasphemer whose overthrow would mark the inauguration of God's kingdom on earth. Belief in the Antichrist, however, was not universal, and the earliest form of Christian expectation held that Christ would return suddenly, without any signs preceding him (see I Thess. 5.2–3).

ANTIOCH (SYRIAN) Antioch, the capital of the Roman province of Syria, was the third largest city in the empire (after Rome and Alexandria). Acts 11.19–26 tells us that it was the birthplace of Gentile Christianity, and that it was there that the followers of Jesus were first called 'Christians'. According to Acts 13.1–3, it was the Church of Antioch that sent Paul and Barnabas on their first missionary journey; Antioch is the home to which Paul always returns after his travels (Acts 14.26–28, 15.30–35, 18.22–23). Galatians 2.11–14 shows that Gentile converts at Antioch originally did not have to observe the Jewish food-laws, but that in response to pressure from the Jerusalem church, this liberal attitude was abandoned – to Paul's disgust. This passage suggests a less happy relationship between Paul and the Church at Antioch than Acts implies.[1]

APOLLOS Acts 18.24–19.1 describes Apollos as a preacher from Alexandria whose understanding of the gospel was corrected by Priscilla and Aquilla, colleagues of Paul, when he came to Ephesus.[1] He then crossed over to Corinth, where he encouraged the Church by his vigorous defence of the gospel in the synagogue. Paul's first letter to the Corinthians (written soon after this) confirms that Apollos had been in Corinth. Paul, however, was not very happy about the effects of his visit as some of the Corinthians had been much more impressed with Apollos's preaching than with Paul's own. In I Cor. 1, Paul opposes the view that the gospel is compatible with 'wisdom' (probably meaning from Greek philosophy), and this view may well have been advocated by Apollos.[2]

APOSTLE The traditional Christian understanding of the term 'apostle' is fairly straightforward. The apostles were the twelve disciples appointed by Jesus to accompany him during his earthly ministry and to preach the gospel to all nations after his resurrection. We may therefore speak of 'the twelve apostles' (Rev. 21.14). The New Testament usage, however, is rather more complicated than this.

1 The Gospels The word 'apostle' is used here only infrequently; we instead hear of 'the disciples' or 'the twelve'.[1] In Mark 6.30 the twelve are described as apostles on their return from a preaching tour, and the twelve and the apostles are also identified in Matt. 10.2 and Luke 6.13. Luke uses the term more frequently than the other evangelists: 'The apostles said to the Lord . . .' (Luke 17.5); 'he sat at table, and the apostles with him' (Luke 22.14); see also Luke 24.10. As apostle comes from the Greek word for 'to send', it is generally linked with the idea of mission, and this is perhaps the reason why it is so rare in the Gospels – missionary activity by the twelve not being prominent in Jesus' ministry.

2 Paul As the earliest writings in the New Testament, Paul's letters give valuable historical evidence about the primitive Christian understanding of apostleship,

(i) In a list of appearances of the risen Jesus, Paul speaks of one appearance to 'the twelve' and of another to 'all the apostles' (I Cor. 15.5,7). This suggests that for him the two groups are not identical. As I Cor. 15.11 sees preaching as the essential function of the apostle, Paul's meaning is presumably that out of the five hundred or more people to whom the risen Christ appeared (15.6), some (including the twelve) were sent out to preach the gospel and so to found churches. Seeing the risen Lord and founding churches are referred to in I Cor. 9.1–2 as the indispensable marks of the apostle. Paul can therefore describe Andronicus and Junia as 'people of note among the apostles' (Rom. 16.7), although they were obviously not members of 'the twelve'. They were perhaps the founders of the Church at Rome, and Paul's statement that 'they were in Christ before me' suggests that they may have been among the earliest Jewish Christian congregation at the time of the resurrection appearances. Further references to 'the apostles' as a fixed group of Jewish Christian missionaries are found in Gal. 1.17,19 and I Cor. 9.5, where they are apparently differentiated from Jesus' brothers (notably James), who also played a prominent role in the early Church.

(ii) As the risen Christ had appeared to him and sent him to preach, Paul considers himself to be an apostle (I Cor. 15.8–10); indeed, he is the only apostle to be sent to Gentiles rather than Jews (Rom. 11.13, see also Gal. 1.15–16, Rom. 1.5, 15.15–21). He acknowledges, however, that not everyone accepts him as a true apostle (I Cor. 9.2), and in Gal. 1–2 engages in a furious controversy with Jewish Christians who claim that he derives his limited authority merely from the Jerusalem apostles and not directly from Christ.[2] What was at issue was essentially whether the apostles were a fixed group from among the earliest Jerusalem congregation, or whether anyone who regarded himself as commissioned by the risen Lord could call himself an apostle. It was not only Paul who posed this problem: in II Cor. 10–12, Paul refers to a group, apparently independent of Jerusalem, who regard themselves as apostles and who seek to exercise apostolic authority at Corinth.[3] Paul disputes their claim, describing them as 'false apostles' who 'disguise themselves as apostles of Christ' (11.13).

3 Acts According to Acts 1.21–22, it is necessary to have accompanied Jesus during the whole of his ministry in order to become an apostle; as this passage concerns the appointment of a replacement for Judas among the twelve, it is clear that for Luke the twelve and the apostles are identical. By both these criteria, Paul could not be an apostle, and Acts does not usually describe him as such (14.4,14 are the only exceptions).[4] It is strange that, with the exception of Peter and John, Acts seems to portray the twelve apostles as confined to Jerusalem (see 8.1), despite the fact that the risen Lord had commissioned them to be his witnesses to the end of the earth (1.8). Luke thought that the Jerusalem Church had the authority to make binding decisions (notably over the question of the admission of Gentiles to the Church), and it is probably for this reason that he refers to the apostles in connection with Jerusalem.

Although there is much that remains obscure, the earliest Christian view of apostleship seems to have developed as follows:

(*i*) The term 'apostle' was probably used rarely, if at all, in the ministry of Jesus. (*ii*) The 'apostles' were a fixed group within the Jerusalem Church who were recognized as commissioned by the risen Christ to preach and to found churches. This group was not confined to 'the twelve' appointed by Jesus. (*iii*) Missionaries independent of this group also claimed to be apostles – for example, Paul and his opponents in II Corinthians. The legitimacy of such claims was denied by the Jerusalem Church. (*iv*) The later Church identified the apostles with the twelve, and denied all claims to an independent apostleship. Although Paul's authority was generally accepted, his claim to be an apostle in his own right was often ignored or treated with caution.

ARCHELAUS

After the death of King Herod the Great in 4 BC, his territories were divided between three of his surviving sons, Archelaus, Antipas and Philip.[1] Archelaus ruled over Judea until AD 6, when the Romans sent him into exile in Gaul. He is mentioned in Matt. 2.22: the reason why Joseph decided to settle in Galilee was that he was afraid of Archelaus, and Galilee was outside his dominion. Matthew (unlike Luke) assumes that Joseph and Mary originally *lived* in Bethlehem in Judaea (rather than merely being temporarily resident there).[2] Archelaus thus becomes the reason why Jesus was brought up in Nazareth and not Bethlehem.

ASCENSION

The only accounts of the ascension in the New Testament are in the writings of Luke (but *see also* John 20.7). In Luke 24.50–1, the risen Jesus was 'carried up into heaven' on the same day as his resurrection. Yet according to Acts 1 the risen Jesus remained on earth for 40 days (v. 3) before being taken up to heaven in a cloud (v. 9), thus prefiguring his future return from heaven with the clouds (v. 11). In Luke the ascension takes place at Bethany; in Acts, on the Mount of Olives. It is clear that Luke intends this story to be taken literally from his reference to the disciples gazing upwards as Jesus ascends (Acts 1.10). The author, together with most early Christians, shares the views of Jewish apocalyptic writings that there are a series of heavens above the earth; the visible heaven containing the stars is the lowest, and the highest is the dwelling-place of God. Jesus therefore ascended 'through the heavens' (Heb. 4.14) until he arrived at the highest heaven, where he sat down at God's right hand.[1]

The point is often made that this (obviously outdated) view of the universe does not affect the underlying meaning of the story. Although this is true, it does not mean that the apparent objectivity of the story is unimportant and that it is based upon purely subjective experiences. The early Christians all believed that after the resurrection Jesus appeared to his disciples, that the time of those appearances was now ended, and that he was now in heaven with his Father. Thus, some form of belief in the ascension was required, and the fact that only Luke tells an ascension story does not mean that it was unimportant in the early Church.[2]

ATHENS[1] Paul's visit to Athens in Acts 17.15–34 is one of the highpoints of the narrative. With great literary and dramatic skill, the author portrays this event as the first encounter between the gospel and the culture and philosophy of the classical world, of which Athens remained the symbol. Luke is not impressed by the pretensions of Athens: the masterpieces of sculpture of which the city was full are contemptuously dismissed as 'idols' (v. 16), and the philosophers there are said to be concerned only with the frivolous pursuit of novelties (v. 21). And yet the speech which Luke ascribes to Paul in vv. 22–31 is heavily influenced by Greek philosophy, and even quotes from Greek poets to confirm a point about God (v. 28). Paul's doctrine of the resurrection is mocked (v. 32), but Luke has shown that there is a considerable overlap between the gospel and the best of Greek thought.[2] The ambivalent attitude towards classical culture which was typical of later Christians is already present here.

ATONEMENT[1] The crucifixion of Jesus was a serious problem for the success of early Christian preaching; Paul admits that it is 'a stumbling block to Jews and folly to Gentiles' (I Cor. 1.23). It seemed incredible that God should permit Jesus to be crucified if he really was the Messiah and the Son of God, as Christians claimed. Christians responded by claiming that the sufferings of the Messiah were predicted in detail by the Scriptures; but they also argued that the death of Jesus was of positive value in the divine plan to save the world.

1 The death of Christ as a sacrifice The earliest known statement about Christ's death is that he 'died for our sins according to the scriptures' (I Cor. 15.3). There are similar statements elsewhere about Christ dying 'for us' (e.g. Rom. 5.8) or 'for the ungodly' (Rom. 5.6). The language here reflects the Jewish idea of the sin-offering (alluded to in Rom. 8.3): in this sacrificial rite, the sins of the guilty person are transferred on to an animal, which is then slaughtered. The animal dies instead of the sinner, and so the sinner is freed from his or her sin. References to the blood of Christ (e.g. Rom. 3.25, 5.9) show that the idea of sacrifice is in mind. This is worked out in great detail in the Epistle to the Hebrews, in which Jesus is seen as both high priest and sacrificial victim (e.g. Heb. 7.26–27). The ritual for the Day of Atonement and for the inauguration of the old covenant at Mount Sinai is used to explain what Jesus has done (Heb. 9).[2]

2 Dying and rising with Christ Although Paul makes use of sacrificial language, he also develops a view of the death of Christ which links it very closely with the resurrection. He contrasts this world, which is under the rule of hostile, anti-divine and anti-human powers, with the world above, and sees the death and resurrection of Christ as the means by which Christ left the former realm and entered the latter. In baptism, the Christian dies with Christ (Rom. 6.2–8, Gal. 2.20) and rises with him (Rom. 6.4, 11, Gal. 2.19) – although the resurrection of the dead also remains a future reality and is not wholly realized in the present (Rom. 6.5, 8).[3] In other words, the Christian follows the pattern established by Christ. One's old life is put to death and a new life within the Christian community begins. The New Testament writers did not all ascribe a positive value to the death of Jesus. In Luke and Acts, for example, the cross is seen primarily as a terrible mistake by the Jews which God rectified in the resurrection (Acts 2.23–24, 3.14–18, 4.10–11, 5.30, etc.).[4] Such passages also stress that the Jews' error was ordained in advance by God, but there is no explanation of why this should have been necessary.

AUGUSTUS The reign of the first of the Roman emperors lasted from 31 BC to AD 14. He is mentioned in the New Testament only in Luke 2.1: 'In those days a decree went out from Caesar Augustus that all the world should be enrolled'. This statement raises major historical problems: first, no such world-wide decree is known from other historical sources; secondly, there was indeed a decree that the inhabitants of Judaea should be enrolled for tax purposes, and this took place 'when Quirinius was governor of Syria' (Luke 2.2). However, this was in AD 6, at least ten years after 'the days of Herod' (1.5) during which the annunciation took place. It seems that here as elsewhere, Luke's attempts to set the Christian story in a world-historical perspective are inaccurate.[1] However, the reference to Augustus serves his theological purpose, which is to argue that the Roman state should be regarded as a friend of the gospel and not as its enemy.[2] It is the Roman emperor who unwittingly ensures that the Christ is born in Bethlehem in accordance with prophecy.

BAPTISM The early Christians were apparently united in seeing baptism as a rite of passage in which an old way of life comes to an end and in which one enters a new social environment – the Church.

1 John the Baptist[1] The New Testament traces the origins of the rite of baptism to John the Baptist, who saw it as a sign of repentance in the face of the divine judgment that would shortly be unleashed upon the world. According to Mark, the Baptist preached a baptism of 'repentance for the forgiveness of sins' (Mark 1.6), and this suggests that baptism was regarded as instrumental in procuring forgiveness. However, Christians regarded John's baptism as deficient in that it was not accompanied by the gift of the Holy Spirit (Acts 19.1–7).[2]

2 The Baptism of Jesus The fact that Jesus himself had submitted to a baptism involving repentance and the forgiveness of sins was somewhat embarrassing for the early Church as it appeared to contradict belief in his sinlessness. Matt. 3.14–15 solves this problem by appealing to the inscrutable divine will; the Gospel of John does not refer to Jesus' baptism at all.[3] Yet the baptism of Jesus was important for the early Church in providing the model for Christian baptism: after being baptized, Jesus immediately receives the Holy

Spirit, and it was the general early Christian belief that the two things were closely connected (Acts 2.38, I Cor. 12.13, John 3.5).

3 *The Origins of Christian Baptism* The Synoptic Gospels give no indication that Jesus followed John the Baptist's example and baptized people. John 3.22–26 suggests that he did do so, but this is contradicted by 4.2 (probably an insertion into the text). According to Matt. 28.19, it was not the earthly Jesus but the risen Lord who instituted Christian baptism, and this reflects an awareness that this rite was not a feature of Jesus' ministry. Because Paul and Acts imply that baptism was the universal custom of all churches, it must be assumed that in the earliest days of the Jerusalem Church the baptism instituted by John the Baptist was revived, though with a characteristically Christian stress on the Holy Spirit.

4 *Early Christian Views of Baptism* Baptism is invariably seen as the rite of entry into the Church (and therefore unrepeatable) and as the occasion for receiving the Holy Spirit.[4] In baptism, the old life of sin and death is annulled, and a new life begins; hence it can be said that 'baptism . . . now saves you' (I Peter 3.21). Various metaphors are associated with the rite. Paul links the convert's descent into the water, his immersion and his re-emergence with the death, burial and resurrection of Jesus (Rom. 6.2–4). Elsewhere, he relates it to entry into the body of Christ (I Cor. 12.13). In John 3.5 and Titus 3.5, baptism is seen as a new birth. For the early Christians, these dramatic metaphors signified something quite concrete: the abandonment of many of the features of their previous social environment, and the adoption of new beliefs and patterns of conduct within small communities often subject to persecution.

BARABBAS All four Gospels state that Pilate wished to release Jesus and that he offered the crowds a choice between him and Barabbas; to his chagrin, the crowds chose Barabbas,[1] 'a man who had been thrown into prison for an insurrection started in the city, and for murder' (Luke 23.19). The existence of Jewish rebels and their occasional release from prison is attested to during the chaotic years preceding the great revolt of AD 66–70, but the story of Barabbas as presented in the gospels is historically problematic. Pilate's behaviour is extraordinary: wishing to release Jesus, he treats him as though he has already been found guilty, and then leaves his fate to the whim of the crowd. There is no evidence from Palestine or elsewhere of the annual release of a single prisoner of the people's choice. Finally, the name 'Barabbas' is strange: it simply means 'son of the father', and there is no other evidence for its use. The development of the story was perhaps influenced by the Jewish war of AD 66–70: the point would then be that in choosing Barabbas the rebel rather than Jesus, the crowd chose the way of rebellion, with its later disastrous consequences.

BARNABAS The earliest references to Barnabas are in Galatians, where Paul refers to the part he played in the development of the early Christian mission to the Gentiles.[1] When controversy arose over this issue, Barnabas accompanied Paul to Jerusalem to try to reach an agreement with the leaders of the Church there. Paul tells us that those leaders 'gave to me and Barnabas the right hand of fellowship, that we should go to the Gentiles . . .' (Gal. 2.9) – that is, they recognized the legitimacy of the mission to the Gentiles. However, Paul complains that a little while later 'even Barnabas' succumbed to pressure from Jerusalem to impose the Jewish Law on Gentile converts (2.13), an act which Paul sees as a deviation from 'the truth of the gospel' (2.14).[2] Yet despite the quarrel, there are still favourable references to Barnabas in I Cor. 9.6 and Col. 4.10.

There are further references to Barnabas in Acts. He is said to have been a Levite from Cyprus and a member of the earliest Jerusalem Church (4.36–7) who was sent to Antioch to investigate the entry of the first Gentiles into the Church (11.22); it was he who was responsible for bringing Paul from Tarsus to Antioch (11.25–26). Acts has a notable tendency to make all the main participants in the Gentile mission originate in Jerusalem, and so it is impossible to be sure that it is historically accurate here.[3] The same is true of its account of Barnabas and Paul's visit to Jerusalem in 11.30 and 12.25; Paul's own narrative in Gal. 1–2 seems to allow no room for any such visit. However, Gal. 2.9 confirms that Acts 13–15 is correct in making Barnabas Paul's main fellow-worker in his early missionary activity among Gentiles.

BEATITUDES The nine blessings that open Matthew's 'Sermon on the Mount' are generally referred to as 'the beatitudes'. Four of them (the blessings for the poor, those who mourn, the hungry and the persecuted) also occur with somewhat different wording in Luke's 'Sermon on the Plain' (Luke 6). It is generally held that when Matthew and Luke have material in common, they derive this from a lost source known as 'Q' (from the German, *Quelle*, source).[1] Two of the beatitudes provide instructive examples of the way in which the early Church reinterpreted Jesus' teaching. In Luke 6.20–21, blessings are pronounced on 'you poor' and on 'you that hunger now', but the equivalent passage in Matthew refers to 'the poor *in spirit*' and 'those who hunger and thirst *for righteousness*' (Matt. 5.3,6). It seems that sayings which originally referred to a state of deprivation (Luke's version) were reinterpreted to apply to ethical qualities (Matthew's version). Luke's form fits the circumstances of Jesus' ministry, whereas Matthew's seems to reflect the situation of a Church in which physical poverty and hunger were no longer problems.[2]

BETHANY This village lies at the foot of the Mount of Olives, only a short way from Jerusalem. According to Mark, it is the village where Jesus acquires the colt for his triumphal entry into Jerusalem (11.1), where he stays the night after this event (11.11) and where, two days before his arrest, he is anointed by a woman 'in the house of Simon the Leper' (14.3). Matthew and Luke have nothing to add to Mark at this point, except that Luke 24.50 makes Bethany the site of Jesus' ascension.[1] In John, Bethany is the village of Mary and Martha (also mentioned in Luke 10.38–42, though with no reference to Bethany) and their brother Lazarus (11.1), and it is here that Lazarus is raised from the dead.[2] In John, the anointing takes place five days before Jesus' arrest, the day before the triumphal entry, and is performed by Mary in her own home (12.1–3). This illustrates the early Christians' lack of concern about the precise details of the stories they handed on.

BETHLEHEM This village is mentioned in the New Testament only in connection with Jesus' birth. It was the birthplace of King David, and is therefore referred to in Luke 2.4,11 as 'the city of David'. As many Jews expected that the Messiah was to be a descendant of David, the belief emerged that he was to be born in Bethlehem. This belief is expressed in Micah 5.2 (quoted in Matt. 2.6): 'But you, O Bethlehem Ephrathah, who are little to be among the clans of Judah, from you shall come forth for me one who is to be ruler in Israel, whose origin is from old, from ancient days'. It was a problem for the early Christian proclamation of Jesus as Messiah that he was known to have come from Nazareth in Galilee rather than from Bethlehem (see John 7.41–42). Additionally, Matthew and Luke give two rather different explanations of this fact.[1] In Luke's version, Joseph and Mary are only temporarily resident in Bethlehem because of the decree of Caesar Augustus[2]; Nazareth is their home town to which they return after Jesus' birth (Luke 2). However, Matthew assumes that Joseph and Mary originally *lived* in Bethlehem; hence, the magi visit them not in a stable or an inn, but in a house (2.11). They leave Bethlehem not because it is not their home but because they are warned of Herod's murderous plans. After the period in Egypt, Joseph does not return home to Bethlehem but moves to Nazareth because of his fear of Archelaus (2.22).[3] So, in their different ways, the two nativity narratives both attempt to reconcile the fact of Jesus' origins in Nazareth with the prophecy about Bethlehem.

BISHOP Since the second century the term 'bishop' has been applied to an individual who holds authority over all the churches in a particular area, usually a city and the surrounding countryside. This usage has no basis in the New Testament, where the term translated 'bishop' (*episkopos*, overseer) is synonymous with 'elder'. According to Acts, the 'elders' of the Church at Ephesus were 'overseers' or 'bishops' whose function was 'to care for the church of God' (20.17,28). In a letter attributed to Paul, Titus is told to 'appoint elders in every town', and a description is immediately given of the character necessary for these 'bishops' or 'overseers' (Tit. 1.5–9). The function of these 'overseers' is 'to give instruction in sound doctrine and also to confute those who contradict it' (v. 9). Paul addresses his letter to the Philippians to 'all the saints in Christ Jesus who are at Philippi, with the bishops and deacons', and this too indicates that the idea of a single bishop exercising authority over a church or a group of churches is unknown to the New Testament. In general, Paul's letters do not suggest that he appointed 'elders' or 'bishops' in every church he founded; he himself continued to care for his churches, but individual church members still enjoyed a considerable degree of freedom. It is probable that a more organized system of 'elders' or 'bishops' originated from a desire to curb some of the excesses to which this freedom had led.[1]

BODY OF CHRIST In addition to its literal meaning (Jesus' physical body), the phrase 'body of Christ' is used by Paul in two distinct senses: the bread of the Eucharist is identified with the body of Christ, but so too is the Church. The two uses come together in I Cor. 10.16–17: 'The bread which we break, is it not a participation in the body of Christ? Because there is one bread, we who are many are one body, for we all partake of the one bread' (*see also* I Cor. 11.27–29 for the same twofold usage). The body of Christ is identified first with 'the bread which we break', and second with 'we who are many'. The first view derives from the traditional account of the institution of the Eucharist (quoted in I Cor. 11.23–25), in which Jesus takes bread, breaks it and says, 'This is my body which is for you'.[1] The second view is probably quite separate from this and derives from Paul's own reflections about the nature of the individual Christian congregation: in the local church a diverse group of people can still be a unity, for as the body has 'many members, and all the members do not have the same function' (Rom. 12.4), so it is with the Church. In his most famous exposition of this theme (I Cor. 12), Paul uses the metaphor of the body to oppose the elitist and hierarchical tendencies of those who claim a special relationship with God (manifested in speaking in tongues) from which others are excluded.[2]

In Colossians and Ephesians (which many scholars now regard as the work of later disciples of Paul) the idea of the Church as the body of Christ is expounded in a rather different way.[3] In an attempt to explain how 'the body' relates to the exalted, heavenly Christ, Christ is now seen as 'the head' of the body (Col. 1.18, 2.19, Eph. 1.22–23, 4.15–16, 5.23). 'The body' is no longer the local church (which is where the emphasis lies in I Corinthians) but the universal Church.[4] In Eph. 5.23,29–30, the relationship between 'head' (Christ) and 'body' (the Church) is rather confusingly compared with the relationship between husband and wife.[5]

CAESAREA The port of Caesarea, built in 12–9 BC, was one of the many architectural achievements of Herod the Great,[1] and from AD 6 it was the official residence of the Roman governors of Palestine. Thus, Caesarea and not Jerusalem was Pontius Pilate's normal place of residence. According to Acts, Caesarea was also the home of Philip the evangelist (8.40) and of Cornelius the centurion, the first Gentile convert (10.1). But Caesarea becomes especially important at a later point of the narrative in Acts, as the place of Paul's imprisonment. The author sees this imprisonment as a kind of protective custody: Paul was rescued in Jerusalem from fanatical Jewish extremists by Roman power (21.27–23.35), and his custody at Caesarea is at least better than the certain death which would await him in Jerusalem (25.1–22).[2] Here, Jerusalem is seen as the symbol of mob rule, fanaticism and injustice, whereas Caesarea symbolizes Roman law and order.

CAESAREA PHILIPPI At the death of Herod the Great in 4 BC, the northern part of his territories was handed over to his son Philip, who built Caesarea Philippi in 2–1 BC at the source of the Jordan at the foot of Mount Hermon – the site of a shrine to the god Pan.[1] Caesarea Philippi is mentioned in the gospels only in connection with Peter's confession of Jesus as the Christ (Mark 8.27, Matt. 16.13). In Mark, this event represents the turning-point that brings to an end the period of miracles in Galilee and that inaugurates the long journey south towards Jerusalem and the crucifixion.[2] It is interesting that Mark locates this event in predominantly Gentile territory; he may be making the point that Jesus is not merely the Messiah of the Jews but the Saviour of the world.[3]

CAIAPHAS[1] The high priesthood of Caiaphas lasted from AD 18 to 36. Between AD 15 and 65, no less than 17 high priests were appointed by the Roman governors, and 16 of these held office for a total of 32 years between them – an average of just two years each. As Caiaphas's high priesthood lasted for no less than 18 years (including the ten years of Pilate's term of office), it seems that he must have shown an exceptional subservience to the two governors under whom he served. When Pilate was recalled to Rome in disgrace, Caiaphas was dismissed, presumably as a concession to Jews who resented his pro-Roman attitude. Luke 3.2, Acts 4.6 and John 18.13–24 strangely state that Caiaphas shared the high priesthood with his father-in-law Annas (high priest from AD 6 to 15); and John 11.49 and 18.13 speak of him as 'high priest that year', as though the high priesthood were an annual appointment. The writers' lack of knowledge of Jewish institutions presumably explains these inaccuracies.

CALL At the beginning of his ministry, Jesus is said to have 'called' the first disciples to himself (Mark 1.20), and in one saying he regards 'calling' people as the main purpose of his coming: 'I came not to call the righteous, but sinners' (Mark 2.17). Paul in particular takes up this idea of a divine call; conversion from paganism to Christianity is seen as a response to the call of God which sounds forth in the preaching of the gospel. Christians are therefore described as 'the called' (Rom. 1.6,7, I Cor. 1.2), and God is frequently described as 'he who called you' (Gal. 1.6, 5.8, I Thess. 2.12, 5.24; this usage is taken up in I Peter 1.15, 5.10, II Peter 1.3). For Paul, this means that life as a Christian rests not on one's own arbitrary decision but on the will of God; this is especially clear in Rom. 8.30, where God's call is the manifestation in time of his eternal decree to save his elect.[1] In one respect, Paul's view of God's call is rather different from Jesus': whereas Jesus called people to give up their old way of life to follow him, Paul insists that Christians should remain in the position in which they were called by God (I Cor. 7.17–24). Christian discipleship is to be worked out within one's old sphere of life.

CANA According to John 2.1–11, this village – about nine miles north-east of Nazareth – was the site of Jesus' first miracle, his changing of water into wine. This is seen by the evangelist as a manifestation of Jesus' glory ('glory as of the only Son from the Father', 1.14), which led his disciples to believe in him (2.11). Verse 6 links the water with 'Jewish rites of purification', and the point of the story may therefore be that Jesus transforms the old religion of Judaism. A similar point is made in the parables of Mark 2.18–22.[1]

CAPERNAUM This village at the northern end of the Sea of Galilee is associated in all four Gospels with Jesus' miracle-working activity – for example, in the stories of the healing of the centurion's servant (Matt. 8.5, Luke 7.1, *see also* John 4.46) and of the healing of the paralysed man who is let down through the roof (Mark 2.1).[1] More significantly, Capernaum rather than Nazareth is seen as Jesus' home during his public ministry. When he returns there, he is reported to be 'at home' (Mark 2.1), and his family is also to be found there (Mark 3.21,31, John 2.12). It is therefore at Capernaum that Jesus pays his taxes (Matt. 17.24) and there too that he and his family are known to the residents (John 6.42,59). Matthew 4.13–16 claims that this move from Nazareth to Capernaum was the fulfilment of prophecy, which spoke of the shining of the light 'beside the sea' – Capernaum is on the 'sea' of Galilee whereas Nazareth is not.[2] Despite these close links with Capernaum, Matt. 11.23 (*see* Luke 10.15) suggests that Jesus' ministry there was not particularly successful.

CHILDREN In the best-known New Testament reference to children, Jesus is indignant at his disciples' refusal to allow children access to him: 'Let the children come to me, do not hinder them; for to such belongs the kingdom of God' (Mark 10.14). Such stories were preserved by the early Church not simply because of their intrinsic value, but because they met particular needs in the Church's life – in this case, the need to define the position of children within the Church. Children are to play a full part in the life of the Church, and are not to be excluded on the grounds that they are too young to understand; this seems to be the point of the story. As the word 'prevent' elsewhere occurs in the context of baptism (Acts 8.36), it is possible that the story also asserts the legitimacy of the baptism of children.

Elsewhere in the New Testament, the place of children within the family is briefly discussed (Col. 3.20–1, Eph. 6.1–4): in accordance with the Fifth Commandment, children are to honour and obey their parents, and fathers are not to discipline them too harshly. There is also a strong tendency to use the idea of childhood metaphorically, as an illustration of the relationship between the believer and God the Father (e.g. Mark 10.15, Rom. 8.15–16, John 1.12).[1]

CHRIST The Greek word, *Christos* comes from the verb meaning 'to anoint', and is a translation of the Hebrew and Aramaic term usually transliterated, *Messiah*, meaning 'Anointed One'. The application of this term to Jesus can only be understood against the background of its use in the Old Testament and the Judaism of the inter-testamental period.

1 The Jewish Background The term 'anointed one' is generally applied in the Old Testament to the king – David or one of his descendants. It was believed that God had appointed David and his descendants to rule over his people, and that he had promised to be with them always: 'His line shall endure for ever, his throne as long as the sun before me' (Ps. 89.36). Extravagant expectations were fastened on the king: 'I will crush his foes before him and strike down those who hate him . . . And I will make him the first-born, the highest of the kings of the earth' (Ps. 89.23,27); 'Ask of me, and I will make the nations your heritage, and the ends of the earth your possession' (Ps. 2.8). Throughout the centuries following David, during which time Judah's political fortunes were often at a low ebb, the accession of each new king seems to have revived these expectations: 'Of the increase of his government and of peace there will be no end, upon the throne of David and over his kingdom, to establish it, and to uphold it with justice and with righteousness from this time forth and for evermore' (Is. 9.7).

Such hopes did not die out with the destruction of the Davidic monarchy by the Babylonian capture of Jerusalem in 586 BC. It was still hoped that the time would come when a descendant of David would be restored to the throne of his fathers and enjoy the power and peace that they had failed to maintain. In the first century BC the author of the so-called 'Psalms of Solomon' still remembers God's promise to David and his descendants, and prays for its fulfilment: 'Raise up for them their king, the Son of David, to rule over your servant Israel . . . Undergird him with the strength to destroy the unrighteous rulers, to purge Jerusalem from Gentiles who trample her to destruction' (17.21–2). The Messiah is to be a righteous king over Israel, and even the other nations will benefit from the justice of his world-wide rule.[1]

The Jewish hope for the Messiah thus arises from the tension between belief in the greatness and faithfulness of the God of Israel and the experience of oppression at the hands of heathen nations. The Jews look forward to the time when this tension will be resolved – when God through his Messiah destroys the power of evil over his world and establishes his reign of righteousness and peace. The Messiah is thus *the bringer of the new age*. Although it is part of his work to break the power of the Gentiles, he is not necessarily a military figure, since it is widely held that his supernatural powers make normal warfare unnecessary.

2 Did Jesus regard himself as the Messiah?
The early Christians used a number of traditional Jewish concepts to explain the significance of Jesus as they understood it; 'Messiah' was one such concept. However, in the Synoptic Gospels Jesus hardly ever speaks of himself as Messiah, and on the rare occasions when he does so (e.g. in Mark 14.61–62) this may well be the confession of early Christian faith rather than an authentic historical fact.

Jesus seems to have regarded himself as the agent through whom God was already inaugurating his reign upon earth – that is, 'the kingdom of God'. He claims that his exorcisms show that 'the kingdom of God has come upon you' (Matt. 12.28 = Luke 11.20).[2] His ministry was oriented towards healing the sick and recalling 'tax-collectors and sinners' to fellowship with the heavenly Father[3]; thus the inauguration of the kingdom of God is seen in the conquest of sickness and sin rather than in the destruction of the Gentiles.[4] Although Jesus did see himself as the bringer of the new age, his view is strikingly different from the Jewish messianic hope: the new age is paradoxically present in the midst of the old, and nationalistic connotations seem absent. His comparative lack of interest in the title

'Messiah' makes his claims more significant rather than less; they cannot be tied down by any previously existing conceptions.

3 The Title 'Christ' in the New Testament If the preceding suggestions are correct, then the title 'Messiah' was first definitely applied to Jesus by the earliest Jewish Christian congregations. As none of the New Testament writings come from this context, we cannot be sure about the exact sense in which these Jewish Christians used the title, but the disciples' question in Acts 1.6 may well be an accurate reflection of it: 'Lord, will you at this time restore the kingdom to Israel?' It was expected that Jesus would shortly return in messianic glory to exalt Israel over the Gentiles. However, in the New Testament writings this understanding of messiahship has faded into the background (except perhaps in the Book of Revelation).

(*i*) Paul regards Jesus as the bringer of the new age, but sets this against the universal background of the sin and death which Adam has brought into the world, rather than the specific problem of the oppression of the Jewish people.[5] The title 'Christ' thus loses its original meaning, and indeed virtually becomes a name – an alternative to 'Jesus' – rather than a title. For example, in II Cor. 4.10–14, Paul mentions 'Jesus' six times, and in 5.14–20, 'Christ' seven times; but there is no appreciable difference of meaning between the two.

(*ii*) In Mark 8.27–33, Peter's confession of Jesus as the Christ is immediately followed by the announcement of his forthcoming sufferings – to Peter's dismay. Here and throughout his gospel, Mark sets forth the great paradox which transforms the Jewish idea of the Messiah: that the bearer of the new age is overcome by the powers of the old age.[6]

(*iii*) In Luke 1.32–33 the traditional Jewish understanding of messiahship is expressed: 'The Lord God will give to him the throne of his father David, and he will reign over the house of Jacob for ever; and of his kingdom there will be no end.' However, as the story of Luke and Acts proceeds, this traditional idea is transformed, first by Jesus' death and resurrection, and then by the persistent Jewish refusal to believe that he really is the Messiah, which leads to salvation being offered to the Gentiles instead.

CHRISTIAN The word occurs only three times in the New Testament. According to Acts 11.26, it was during the early days of the Church at Antioch that the disciples were first called Christians. In Acts 26.28, Agrippa's response to Paul's appeal is, 'In a short time you think to make me a Christian!' The author of I Peter exhorts his readers not to be ashamed of suffering as a Christian (4.16).[1] These passages all suggest that 'Christian' was a name first bestowed by outsiders; the early Christians preferred to designate themselves with some such term as 'the elect' or 'the saints'.

CHURCH The Greek word *ekklesia* means 'assembly'; it never refers to a building and need not have a religious sense. For example, it is used in Acts 19.32 of an assembly of the citizens of Ephesus. In the Gospels, the word 'church' is found only in Matt. 16.18 ('Upon this rock I will build my church') and 18.17, and both of these passages are generally thought not to be authentic sayings of Jesus.[1] Paul uses the word frequently, generally with reference to the individual, local congregation: for example 'the church of God which is at Corinth' (I Cor. 1.2), 'the church which meets in their house' (Rom. 16.5). He therefore speaks about 'churches' or 'assemblies' in the plural: 'the churches of Galatia', 'the churches of Judaea which are in Christ' (Gal. 1.2,22). Rarely if ever does Paul use 'the church' to refer to all Christians everywhere; he speaks instead of 'the churches of God' (I Cor. 11.16).[2] In Acts and Revelation, which use the word 'church' frequently, the meaning is again generally the local congregation. Only in Colossians and Ephesians (the work probably of later disciples of Paul) is 'church' used to refer to the universal Church. In Col. 1.18, Christ is said to be 'the head of the body, the church' (see also Eph. 1.22–3), and in Eph. 5.23–32, Christ is seen as the Church's husband.[3] Here, the authors have in mind a universal community, 'built upon the foundation of the apostles and prophets' (Eph. 2.20).

CIRCUMCISION[1] According to Gen. 17, the sign of God's covenant with Abraham and his descendants was to be circumcision. In New Testament times, circumcision had long been regarded as a sign of the unique relationship with God which differentiated the Jewish people from the Gentiles[2]; conversely, it was regarded by non-Jews with derision, and was a considerable barrier to conversion to Judaism. When Paul and others began preaching the gospel to Gentiles, it was inevitable that there should be disagreement about whether or not they should submit to circumcision.[3] Paul argued strongly that 'neither circumcision counts for anything nor uncircumcision, but a new creation' (Gal. 6.15), and by this he meant not only that circumcision itself was unimportant but also that the barrier between Jews and Gentiles (of which circumcision was the symbol) had been broken down. This matter first became an issue at Antioch, where there were both Jewish and Gentile Christians together in the same congregation. In Gal. 2, Paul tells us how he went to Jerusalem to consult the leaders of the Church there, but although he claims in vv. 1–10 (*see also* Acts 15) to have received a favourable response, he tells in the remainder of the chapter of an attempt by the Jerusalem authorities to compel Gentiles to adopt the Jewish way of life.[4] The whole letter to the Galatians is a violent protest against a similar attempt to impose circumcision and the Jewish law on Paul's Gentile converts in Galatia. In Rom. 2.25–29 and 4.9–12, Paul again discusses the subject of circumcision, this time in a less critical situation, and argues that it is quite possible to obey God and to imitate the example of Abraham's faith without submission to circumcision. What was at issue in all this was the question of whether the Church was to live within the confines of the Jewish community, sharing its way of life, or whether it was to separate itself from that community and adopt a more universalistic outlook.

CLAUDIUS Acts refers twice to the emperor Claudius, who reigned from AD 41 to 54. Acts 11.28 speaks of 'a great famine over all the world' which 'took place in the days of Claudius'. During this period, there were indeed local famines in various places (including Judaea, AD 46–8) but none of these was universal. As in

Luke 2.1, Luke has made a local event universal.[1] In Acts 18.2, he refers to Claudius' expulsion of all the Jews from Rome, and the Roman historian Suetonius informs us that this took place because of rioting in the Jewish quarter 'at the instigation of Chrestus' – that is, as the result of the preaching of the Christian gospel. The most likely date for the expulsion is AD 49.

COLLECTION In Gal. 2.10 the request of the leaders of the Jerusalem church for financial support for impoverished members of their congregation is mentioned. Paul accepted this proposal, but for some time the projected collection seems to have fallen into abeyance, owing to the poor relations between Paul and Jerusalem. Cor. I (16.1–4) indicates that when Paul revived the idea, he commanded members of the churches of Galatia and Corinth to set aside money each week for this collection. But the project was again jeopardized, this time by a serious dispute between Paul and the Corinthian congregation.[1] It seems that, among other things, they questioned his honesty in financial matters (see II Cor. 12.16–18), and in II Cor. 8–9 Paul has to plead with them to get their offering ready in time, in language that is both flattering and anxious. At the time of the writing of Romans, Paul has successfully completed the collection – he mentions only the churches of 'Macedonia and Achaia' (Rom. 15.26), but it seems that others were involved too. He is about to take it to Jerusalem (v. 25), after which he hopes to come to Rome (vv. 23–4). He also requests prayer 'that I may be delivered from the unbelievers in Judaea, and that my service for Jerusalem may be acceptable to the saints' – a reference to his unpopularity among both non-Christian and Christian Jews because of his attitude towards the Law, which he refused to impose on Gentile converts.[2] Acts tells of this final visit to Jerusalem, during which Paul was arrested. The fact that the collection is not even mentioned here may suggest that Paul's worst fears were realized.

COLOSSIANS, PAUL'S LETTER TO Of the 13 letters that claim to have been written by Paul, up to six are regarded by many modern scholars as not genuine (Ephesians, Colossians, II Thessalonians, I and II Timothy, and Titus).[1] As large numbers of writings were produced by early Christians under the names of apostles, it would not be surprising if some of these had found their way into the canon. The value and significance of these canonical books would not necessarily be affected by the conclusion that Paul himself did not write them. They would then bear witness to a continuing tradition in which his ideas were developed by his followers and applied in new ways to new situations.

1 Situation Colossians is closely related to the brief and definitely genuine letter of Paul to Philemon, which was written to persuade Philemon to accept back a runaway slave by the name of Onesimus, who had just become a Christian under Paul's influence.[2] Onesimus's imminent return home is also mentioned in Col. 4.9, and Colossians therefore purports to have been written at the same time as Philemon. Almost all the individuals named in Col. 4.9–17 are also named in Philemon. One of them, Epaphras, is seen in Col. 1.7 as the founder of the Church at Colossae, and Paul is thus writing to people whom he has never met (2.1). In

1.15–20, Christ is seen in cosmic terms as both the creator and the reconciler,[3] and in 2.6–23 the conclusion is drawn from this that no human rules and regulations can add anything to what the Colossians already possess in Christ. Here, an ascetic philosophy which teaches, 'Do not handle, Do not taste, Do not touch' (2.21) is in mind.

2 Authorship There are historical, stylistic, and theological reasons for doubting that Paul himself could have written Colossians. According to Philem. 24, Epaphras is in prison with Paul, and greetings are sent from him and other individuals, including a certain Aristarchus. But in Col. 4.10–12, Aristarchus is the prisoner rather than Epaphras, who has arrived from Colossae with news of the church he has founded there (1.4,7–8). This small discrepancy may be significant. From a stylistic point of view, Colossians lacks the rhetorical vigour which is such a characteristic feature of Paul's style. More importantly, there are a number of theological themes in Colossians which seem foreign to Paul. For example, his identification of the 'church', the 'body of Christ', with the local community (I Cor. 12) is abandoned in Colossians, where 'church' and 'body of Christ' are universal in scope, and where Christ becomes the head of the body (1.18,24).[4] Col. 1.24–29 states that Paul's mission to the Gentiles springs from a revelation to the first Jewish Christians of God's intention to save the Gentiles; this agrees with Acts but conflicts with Paul's vehement insistence on his independence from Jerusalem.[5] 2.9–13 claims that through union with Christ salvation has already been attained in all its fulness, a view which Paul opposes (I Cor. 4.8–13, Rom. 8.18–25, etc.). All this does not mean that Paul himself *cannot* have written Colossians, but it does make it very doubtful.

3 The 'Colossian Heresy' Col. 2 seems to have particular opponents in mind. The Colossians are warned not to be taken in 'by philosophy and empty deceit, according to human tradition . . .'. This 'philosophy' seems to have comprised an ascetic way of life influenced by Judaism, with its commandments about observing certain days and abstaining from certain types of food and drink (vv. 16,21). In Romans and Galatians, Paul attacks the idea that Christians should have to practise Judaism, and if he is the author of Colossians, then Col. 2 marks a new phase in this attack. Here, a curious type of Judaism is opposed which does not stress Jewish national privileges and thinks that the ritual commandments of the law are of value in promoting asceticism. However, if Paul is not the author, the real author may simply be trying to give verisimilitude to his attack on asceticism by linking it to the historical Paul's conflict with Judaism.[6]

CORINTHIANS, PAUL'S FIRST LETTER TO
In addition to the important theological discussions in I Corinthians, this letter gives us a uniquely vivid picture of life within an early Christian congregation (although perhaps not a typical one).

1 The Founding of the Church at Corinth Paul arrived at Corinth at the end of his so-called 'second missionary journey', which took him from Antioch in Syria through Asia Minor, across to Macedonia (northern Greece) and south through Greece to Athens and Corinth (Acts 15.36–18.1). Acts 18.1–18 tells us of Paul's 18 month stay in Corinth: his work as a tentmaker alongside Aquila and Priscilla, his unsuccessful preaching to the Jews in the synagogue, his preaching to the Gentiles instead, and his appearance before Gallio, the proconsul of Achaia.[1] Paul states that his converts did not come from the higher social strata: 'Not many of you were wise according to worldly standards, not many were powerful, not many were of noble birth' (1.26). However, the words 'not many' imply that this description did not apply to all the Corinthian Christians. Rom. 16.23 speaks of one of them, Erastus, as the 'city treasurer'; a first century inscription has been found at Corinth ('Erastus, commissioner for public works, laid this pavement at his own expense'), which may refer to the same individual. The problems at the Eucharist discussed in 11.20–22 may suggest that there were tensions between rich and poor Christians at Corinth.

2 Later Developments at Corinth Paul appears to have written to the Corinthians fairly shortly after leaving Corinth, for in I Cor. 5.9–13 he mentions an earlier letter giving instructions about disciplining erring members of the congregation. It is possible that the apparently independent fragment inserted in II Cor. 6.14–7.1 is a part of this lost letter. When during his third journey Paul arrived at Ephesus (Acts 19.1, I Cor. 16.8), he received news from Corinth from three sources. First, Paul mentions in 16.12 that he is acquainted with Apollos, who (as I Cor. 1–4 and Acts 18.24–28 indicate) had just been to Corinth.[2] Secondly, he states that 'it has been reported to me by Chloe's people that there is quarreling among you, my brethren' – quarreling about the respective merits of Paul, Apollos and Peter (1.11–12). Thirdly, he says that an official delegation from the Corinthians, consisting of Stephanas, Fortunatus and Achaicus (16.17), have brought a letter from the Corinthians to him asking his advice about certain problems.

Paul addresses himself to this letter in 7.1 ('Now concerning the matters about which you wrote'), and wherever the formula 'Now concerning' recurs (7.25, 8.1, 12.1), he is touching on matters raised in the Corinthians' letter. Some of the Corinthians, zealous to imitate Paul's example, are proclaiming that Christians ought not to marry and that married Christians should abstain from sexual intercourse (chapter 7).[3] Some consider that as the gods of their pagan neighbours do not really exist, it is all right for Christians to participate in social gatherings in pagan temples, and so to play a full part in the life of the non-Christian community (chapters 8–10). Some consider that ecstatic speech ('speaking in tongues') is an indispensable hallmark of possessing the Spirit (chapters 12–14).[4] Other problems that Paul has to deal with include the man living with his (possibly widowed) stepmother (5.1–13), lawsuits between Christians (6.1–8), and people who find the doctrine of the future resurrection of the body incredible (15.12–58).

3 Paul's Response In I Corinthians, Paul shows that he is unhappy about many of the beliefs, attitudes and practices which have sprung up in the Corinthian church.

(*i*) **Wisdom** After criticizing the Corinthians for the divisions between them (1.10–17), Paul embarks on a long attack on 'the wisdom of the world', which regards the cross as 'foolishness' but which has itself been made foolish by 'Christ crucified', who is 'the wisdom of God'. It is not immediately clear how this attack on 'wisdom' is related to the problem of divisions at Corinth, as the context suggests that it ought to be. In I Cor. 1–4 as a whole, the frequent mention of Apollos suggests that it is those who say 'I belong to Apollos' (I Cor. 1.12) whom Paul is particularly concerned about; although he is not personally hostile to Apollos, he seems to regret the effects of his visit. The attack on 'wisdom' is therefore an attack on a view probably taught by Apollos, that 'wisdom' (Greek philosophy) and the gospel are compatible. It would not be surprising if as a native of Alexandria (Acts 18.24) Apollos taught this, because a form of Judaism strongly influenced by Greek philosophy had long been associated with Alexandria.

(ii) **Freedom** In his response to problems of conduct and worship, Paul would have seemed surprisingly conservative to some of his converts, who felt that their views were consistent with his gospel of freedom. He rejects the radicalism of those who regard Christian freedom as grounds for sexual license (chapters 5–6), and of those who feel free to participate in social gatherings in pagan temples (chapters 8–10). As regards worship, Paul seeks to limit the spontaneity of Corinthian worship, which was attributed to the free working of the Spirit, by insisting that 'all things should be done decently and in order' (14.40).

(iii) **The Church** The disorders at Corinth led Paul to some profound theological reflection about the nature of the *church* (i.e. the individual, local congregation). The key is to be found in the idea of unity in diversity and diversity in unity. The differing teaching of Paul, Apollos and Cephas is not a reason for splitting into groups, but a sign of the rich resources available to the Christian (3.21–23). The fact that only a minority possess the gift of speaking in tongues does not mean a split between those who possess the gift and those who do not, for they are all alike part of the body of Christ (12.12–31), which should be characterized by love rather than discord (chapter 13).[5]

(iv) **The Resurrection** In chapter 15, the denial of the doctrine of the resurrection of the body by some of the Corinthians gives Paul the opportunity of presenting his most extended discussion of that subject. He links this doctrine very closely to the resurrection of Jesus. If there is no resurrection of the dead, then Jesus was not raised and Christian faith is futile (vv. 12–19); conversely, Jesus' resurrection from the dead is the beginning of the general resurrection (vv. 20–28). However, Paul does make some concessions to those who find the resurrection of the dead incredible; he argues in vv. 42–50 that the body which is buried is not identical with the body which is to be raised because 'flesh and blood cannot inherit the kingdom of God' (v. 50).[6]

CORINTHIANS, PAUL'S SECOND LETTER TO

In some ways, II Corinthians is the hardest of all Paul's letters for us to understand. It is written throughout in a highly emotional tone which suggests that there have been great upheavals in Paul's relationship with the Corinthians since the writing of I Corinthians. Paul refers to these upheavals, but never explains precisely what had happened, as the original recipients were already well aware of this.

1 Situation In II Cor. 8.10 Paul mentions that the Corinthians first expressed a desire to participate in his collection for the Jerusalem Church 'a year ago'.

I Corinthians was written shortly after this first expression of interest (I Cor. 16.1–4), and the events to which II Corinthians alludes must therefore have taken place during the year following the writing of I Corinthians.

(*i*) **Paul's Second Visit to Corinth** In I Cor. 16.3–9 Paul announces his intention of paying the Corinthians a second visit, after completing his work in Ephesus and revisiting the churches of Macedonia (notably the Philippians and the Thessalonians). When he comes, he will make arrangements for the conveyance of the Corinthians' gift to Jerusalem.[1] Later, he changed his mind: he would visit Corinth first, then Macedonia, and then return to Corinth, from where he would begin the journey to Judaea (II Cor. 1.16). But when he arrived in Corinth, the visit was a disaster, and Paul seems to have temporarily abandoned the plan and returned to Ephesus. He refers in II Cor. 2.1 to a 'painful visit'. One person in particular had challenged his authority (2.5–10, 7.12), and the Corinthians had not taken Paul's side as they should have done.

(*ii*) **The Severe Letter** Immediately after this visit, Paul wrote a letter to the Corinthians which is alluded to in II Cor. 2.3–9, 'out of much affliction and anguish of heart and with many tears' (v. 4). Here and elsewhere, Paul seems to be defending himself against the charge of having been over-severe. In 7.8, he admits that at one point he had regretted sending this letter, and 7.9–12 implies that the Corinthians felt that it was unnecessarily harsh.

(*iii*) **Reconciliation** The letter was conveyed to Corinth by Titus (7.14–15),[2] and Paul then faced an agonizing wait for his return with news about the Corinthians' response. In a state of great anxiety, he went to Troas to await Titus, but did not find him there and crossed over to Macedonia (2.12–13). There too he had to wait; but Titus eventually arrived with the good news of the Corinthians' repentance (7.5–16). Paul shortly afterwards despatched him to Corinth again, bearing a letter of reconciliation. This situation accounts for the conciliatory tone of II Cor. 1–9.

(*iv*) **II Cor. 10–13 and Paul's Severe Letter** In chapter 10, the mood changes abruptly. Paul writes with almost unparalleled bitterness and sarcasm against those Corinthians who deny his authority, comparing him unfavourably with certain visitors whom Paul denounces as false apostles (11.13–15). It is likely that II Cor. 10–13 is to be identified with the severe letter alluded to in 2.3–4, etc. This would mean that II Corinthians comprises not one letter but two: II Cor. 10–13 is the earlier, and was written in response to Paul's disastrous second visit to Corinth, and II Cor. 1–9 is the letter of reconciliation written after Titus' return. A later editor has united the two.

2 *Some Theological Themes* It is typical of Paul that the tensions between himself and the Corinthians call forth profound theological reflection.

(*i*) **Boasting** In the 'Severe Letter' (II Cor. 10–13), Paul accuses the visitors who have arrived at Corinth of arrogance. They 'commend themselves' and 'boast beyond limit' (10.12–18), regarding themselves as 'superlative apostles' (11.5,13, 12.11), impressing the Corinthians by their authority (11.20) and claiming visions and revelations (12.1). Some of the Corinthians think that Paul compares unfavourably with the visitors. In response, Paul denies the legitimacy of this 'boasting', quoting from Jer. 9.24, 'Let him who boasts, boast of the Lord' (10.17). Yet because the Corinthians wish him to, he is prepared to boast of himself, although in doing so he will be speaking 'not with the Lord's authority but as a fool' (11.17). He has endured far more hardships in the service of the gospel than his opponents (11.21–29). And yet, since they boast of their power and authority, Paul will boast only of his weakness: he once had the humiliation of being let down from the city walls in a basket to escape his enemies, and he is plagued by a 'thorn in the flesh' (some sort of physical disability) through which the Lord taught him that 'my grace is sufficient for you, for my power is made perfect in weakness' (11.30–12.10). Although like his opponents Paul claims to have received visions, he distances himself from them (12.1–7). These reflections seem to spring from Paul's conviction that the cross, as well as the resurrection, determines the character of Christian life in this world (*see also* I Cor. 4.8–13).[3]

(*ii*) **The Resurrection** In the 'Letter of Reconciliation' (II Cor. 1–9), Paul continues this discussion of power and weakness, although with much more stress on the hope of the resurrection (4.17–18). The important section on the resurrection in 5.1–10 continues the discussion begun in I Cor. 15.[4] In the earlier passage, the resurrection is understood in a cosmic sense, as the culmination of Christ's reign over the universe: 'The last enemy to be destroyed is death' (v. 26). In II Cor. 5.1–10, the resurrection is seen as the fulfilment of one's individual destiny, which one anxiously longs for throughout this mortal life. We yearn for the time when we may leave this 'tent' (i.e. the mortal body, our temporary dwelling-place) and exchange it for our eternal, heavenly 'house' (i.e. the resurrection body). It is characteristic of this period of exile from our true home that 'we walk by faith, not by sight' (v. 7).

(*iii*) **Law and Spirit**[5] In II Cor. 1–9, Paul is concerned to avoid giving the impression that he is engaging in the same 'boasting' that he undertook in the 'Severe Letter'; in 3.1 and 5.12, he denies that he is beginning to commend himself again. But since the problems at Corinth had arisen because the Corinthians no longer trusted him fully, he devotes a considerable amount of space to explaining his understanding of his apostolic activity. In II Cor. 3, he compares his own work as a minister of the new covenant with the work of Moses as the minister of the old. The law was given to Israel through Moses at Mount Sinai; the Spirit is given to Gentile converts through the preaching of Paul. The law brought death (since it was an absolute demand which no-one could fulfil); but the Spirit brings life (v. 6). The divine glory which illumined Moses' face at the giving of the law is as nothing to the glory which accompanies the giving of the Spirit (vv. 7–11).

CORNELIUS In Acts 10, the conversion of Cornelius through Peter's preaching marks the beginning of the mission to the Gentiles. Great stress is laid on the fact that it is God who brings about this turning-point: for example, the Holy Spirit is 'poured out' upon Cornelius and his friends before they are baptized (vv. 44–6) to indicate that it is God's will that they should receive baptism (vv. 47–8).[1] Peter's lengthy recapitulation of the story in response to criticism (11.1–17) emphasizes that the initiative has been God's throughout, and it is this that finally silences criticism (11.18). Later, Luke will use this story to justify Paul's mission to the Gentiles (15.7–11). One of the main concerns of Acts is the legitimacy of Gentile Christianity, and it is important for Luke to base this upon the unquestioned authority of Peter, and not simply on Paul, whose status remained controversial.

COVENANT[1] In Jewish theology, the 'covenant' refers to God's special relationship with Israel, founded upon the choice of Abraham and his descendants and upon the giving of the law through Moses at Sinai. This posed a problem for the early Church, especially for Gentile congregations which were entirely separate from the synagogue and the Jewish community. It was undeniable that Scripture emphatically taught that God had entered into covenant with the Jewish people; as Paul says of his fellow countrymen, 'They are Israelites, and to them belong . . . the covenants' (Rom. 9.4). But how then could the position of Gentile Christians be justified, without abandoning Scripture altogether? One answer was found in Jeremiah's prophecy of the new covenant: 'Behold, the days are coming, says the Lord, when I will make a new covenant with the house of Israel and the house of Jacob, not like the covenant which I made with their fathers . . . I will put my law within them, and I will write it upon their hearts' (Jer. 31.31–3). The earliest Christian reference to the 'new covenant' is found in the narrative of the institution of the Eucharist, in Paul's version: 'This cup is the new covenant in my blood' (I Cor. 11.25).[2] This enables Paul to contrast himself as a 'minister of a new covenant' with Moses, and his congregations with the Jewish community in which the 'old covenant' is read (II Cor. 3.4–18).[3] The contrast between the two covenants is worked out in detail in Heb. 8–9. The advantage of this theory was that it enabled the early Christians to believe both that the Jewish Scriptures were authoritative and that God's covenant with the Jewish people had been superseded.

CREATION There are in the New Testament no hymns of praise to God for the created order such as are found in the Old Testament (e.g. Ps. 104). Indeed, one may feel that sometimes the New Testament writers are so concerned with salvation from a world that is utterly corrupt that they have lost sight of the Jewish belief in a world that is created by God and fundamentally good. Yet this would be a misunderstanding: it is precisely because the New Testament holds that the world is fundamentally good that the evils which defile it are regarded as intolerable.

1 Jesus The teaching ascribed to Jesus in the Synoptic Gospels everywhere presupposes the dependence of the created order on God as its creator and sustainer. It is God who 'makes his sun rise on the evil and on the good, and sends rain on the just and on the unjust' (Matt. 5.45). Jesus teaches his disciples to take the created order more seriously, not less: 'Consider the lilies of the field, how they grow; they neither toil nor spin; yet I tell you, even Solomon in all his glory was not arrayed like one of these' (Matt. 6.28–29). In his parables a sense of wonder at the mystery of natural processes is to be found: for example, the growth of the seed in the earth (Mark 4), and even the homely process of bread-making (Matt. 13.33). It is consistent with this that his preaching of the kingdom of God is concerned with God's rule over *this* world, not some other-worldly realm.[1]

2 Paul As a city-dweller Paul shows less appreciation for the natural order than Jesus does (*see* I Cor. 9.8–10), but he does believe that the creation makes known God's power (Rom. 1.19–20). Paul sometimes speaks as though the second coming of Christ will result in the destruction of this present world order: 'The form of this world is passing away' (I Cor. 7.31). Elsewhere, however, he argues that far from being destroyed, creation is moving towards its goal – its liberation from the decay and death that have corrupted it (Rom. 8.18–25). In I Cor. 15 Paul's insistence on the resurrection of the body (rather than the immortality of the soul) shows the continuing influence of the Jewish belief in the goodness of the created order.[2]

3 Creation through Christ In a number of passages it is said that creation took place through Christ, who was believed to have existed in a discarnate, heavenly state even before his earthly life (I Cor. 8.6, Col. 1.16–17, Heb. 1.2, John 1.1–3).[3] This belief may have been influenced by the portrayal of Wisdom as accompanying and assisting God in creating the world in passages such as Prov. 8.22–31. The point is that it is natural for God to save the world through Christ because in the beginning he created the world through Christ. The salvation attained through Christ is the way in which the created order reaches its destiny; it is not regarded as wholly evil and beyond redemption.

CRUCIFIXION[1] This barbaric form of execution was extremely widespread throughout the ancient world, especially (although not exclusively) for political crimes. For example, Josephus, the historian of the Jewish revolt of AD 66–70, tells of the fate of Jews who escaped from besieged Jerusalem and were caught: 'The soldiers, out of the rage and hatred they bore the prisoners, nailed those they caught, in different postures, to the crosses, by way of jest, and their number was so great that there was not enough room for the crosses and not enough crosses for the bodies'. Flogging generally preceded crucifixion, and nails were normally used to fasten the hands and the feet; the weight of the body was born by a wooden peg. Death sometimes took several days, and the bodies were often left on the cross to serve as a deterrent to others. In general, Roman citizens were exempted from crucifixion, which was regarded with horror as the ultimate punishment. Yet no protests are to be found against its use; its necessity in extreme cases was generally accepted.

DAMASCUS This important city was (and is) situated in southern Syria, north-east of the Sea of Galilee. In New Testament times, it was a member of the federation of cities known as the Decapolis (*see* Mark 5.20, 7.31, Matt. 4.25), and had a sizable Jewish community.[1] Damascus is especially associated with Paul's conversion (Acts 9, 22, 26); Paul's own reference to his return to Damascus confirms that his conversion indeed took place there (Gal. 1.17). However, Acts' claim that Paul was sent to Damascus by the high priest to arrest and bring to Jerusalem any Christians he found there (Acts 9.1–2) is problematic, because the high priest did not have any such powers beyond Judaea.[2] Damascus is also the scene of Paul's early missionary activity in Acts 9.20–25, and this is partially confirmed by II Cor. 11.32 and Gal. 1.17.[3]

DAVID[1] In one strand of Jewish messianic belief, the Messiah was to be a descendant of David,[2] and early Jewish Christianity adopted this belief. In order to prove that Jesus was 'the son of David' or 'of the seed of David', genealogies were constructed (Matt. 1.1–16, Luke 3.23–38). However, in both of them it is Joseph (and not Mary) who is said to be descended from David, despite the story of the Virgin Birth; in addition, they have hardly any names in common between Joseph and David.[3] Of the four evangelists, John shows the least interest in affirming Jesus' Davidic descent (*see* 7.42). In Mark, Jesus is addressed as 'son of David' by blind Bartimaeus (10.47–48, *see also* 11.10); yet in 12.35–37, Jesus specifically denies the appropriateness of this title for the Messiah ('How can the scribes say that the Christ is the son of David?'). Matthew and Luke reproduce this narrative but elsewhere stress the importance of Jesus' descent from David, and this is an important theme in early Christian preaching according to Acts (2.25–36, 13.22–23,32–37). Paul is aware of this theme (Rom. 1.3), but makes no real use of it. In general, Jesus' descent from David was regarded as extremely important by those Christians who retained links with the Jewish community, but as much less so by others.

DEATH Throughout much of the Old Testament, death is seen as part of the natural order. At least in the case of the righteous who lived a normal span of life, death was perceived as an occasion for mourning but not as a fundamental challenge to belief in the goodness of God. Human beings are in the same position as all living creatures: 'When thou takest away their breath, they die and return to their dust' (Ps. 104.29); 'Dust thou art, and unto dust shalt thou return' (Gen. 3.19). The New Testament takes a different view: death is no longer seen as part of the natural order, but as an enemy to be overcome. This perception is already present in the gospel stories in which Jesus raises people from the dead: Jairus's daughter (Mark 5.21–43), the son of the widow of Nain (Luke 7.11–17), and Lazarus (John 11). In Mark 12.18–27, Jesus is portrayed as arguing in favour of the popular belief in resurrection. The real reason, however, for the New Testament view of death is to be found in belief in the resurrection of Jesus. Because of this, death is seen as an enemy whose conquest has already begun and is shortly to be completed. As Paul puts it in I Cor. 15.26, 'The last enemy to be destroyed is death'. Following the story in Gen. 2–3, Paul sees death as the result both of the human physical constitution (I Cor. 15.47–49) and as the result of sin (Rom. 5.12). Yet despite its awesome power, the whole created order will ultimately be liberated from it (Rom. 8.18–25).[1] According to John 11.26, Jesus promises that even now, 'Whoever lives and believes in me shall never die'.[2]

DECAPOLIS The 'Decapolis' was a federation of ten cities (from the Greek *deka*, ten and *polis*, city), situated east of the Jordan (with one exception, Scythopolis), which had accepted the Greek way of life. There would probably have been a sizable Jewish community in all of them. The New Testament refers to three of these cities by name: Damascus, Gadara (Matt. 8.28) and Gerasa (Mark 5.1).[1] The Decapolis is mentioned three times in Matthew and Mark, and the function of these references is to stress that Jesus' sphere of influence was not confined to Galilee. In Matt. 4.25, crowds come to Jesus from Syria and the Decapolis; in Mark 5.20, the man from whom the legion of demons has been cast out proclaims the good news in the Decapolis; and in Mark 7.31, Jesus himself travels through 'the region of the Decapolis'. In the same context, Mark mentions a journey to Tyre and Sidon (7.24,31), and in 8.27, a journey to Caesarea Philippi; in all these passages he is emphasizing that Jesus is the Saviour of the Gentiles.

DEMONS[1] Various mental and physical disabilities were popularly ascribed in Jesus' day to the activity of 'demons' – spiritual entities with the power to become embodied in human beings (*see* Matt. 12.43–45) and to speak through them (Mark 5.7–12). Demons were associated above all with madness. Mark 5.2–5 gives a graphic description of the effects of demonic possession: the man with the unclean spirit lived among the tombs, possessed superhuman strength, and continually cried out and cut himself with stones. Madness and possession are explicitly linked in John 10.20: 'He has a demon and he is mad'. Elsewhere, we read of 'a blind and dumb demoniac' (Matt. 12.22): here, blindness and dumbness are explained as the result of demonic possession. Faced with alarming mental and physical disabilities, popular thought explained them by means of the theory of demonic possession.

Outside the Synoptic Gospels, the pagan gods are identified as demons (I Cor. 10.20–21, Rev. 9.20), and demons are blamed for false teaching within the Church (I Tim. 4.1). In John, Jesus' claim to be Son of God is regarded as either true or the mad self-assertion of one possessed by a demon (7.20, 8.48–52, 10.20–21).

DESCENT INTO HELL Between its affirmations of the crucifixion and resurrection of Jesus, the so-called Apostles' Creed inserts a reference to Jesus' 'descent into hell'. 'Hell' here translates the Greek word, *hades*; it refers not to a place of punishment and hell-fire, which in Jewish and early Christian thought will only come into operation after the end of the world,[1] but to a great underground cavern to which the soul descends at death. It is often said that the New Testament hardly ever refers to Jesus' descent into Hades, but this is only partially correct, for in the phrase 'resurrection from the dead', 'from the dead' means 'from among the dead people'. Jesus' descent to the realm of the dead is not emphasized, but it is presupposed in the proclamation of his resurrection (*see* Rom. 10.7, Eph. 4.9–10). However, it is true to say that the New Testament does not generally ascribe any significance to Jesus' descent into Hades independent of his death and resurrection. The one exception is I Peter 3.18–20: Jesus was 'put to death in the flesh but made alive in the spirit, in which he went and preached to the spirits in prison, who formerly did not obey, when God's patience waited in the days of Noah . . .'. The author returns to this subject in 4.6: 'This is why the gospel was preached even to the dead, that though judged in the flesh like men, they might live in the spirit like God'. According to these passages, Jesus descended to Hades to secure the salvation of at least some of those who had lived, sinned and died before his coming.

DEVIL[1] The Greek *diabolos*, 'slanderer', is a translation of the Hebrew, *satan*. Christian theology has generally assumed that the devil was created as an archangel, but that his pride led to his fall, turning him into God's most implacable enemy. There is perhaps an allusion to this theory in I Tim. 3.6, where it is said of the bishop that 'he must not be a recent convert, or he may be puffed up with conceit and fall into the condemnation of the devil'. The New Testament assumes that the devil is 'the ruler of this world' (John 12.31, 14.30, 16.11), and that 'the whole world is in the power of the evil one' (I John 5.19)[2]; when tempting Jesus, the devil quite legitimately claims that all the kingdoms of the world are his to give to whomever he wishes (Luke 4.6).[3] There is never any attempt to explain why God temporarily entrusted the rule of his world to this evil being. The devil functions as a negative form of providence: he is continually directing the course of events so as to cause harm to God's people, and although the Son of God has already overcome him in principle, he remains a formidable enemy. In addition, the devil stirs up persecution (Mark 4.15, I Thess. 3.5, I Peter 5.8), in an attempt to force people into apostasy and causes dissension within the Christian fellowship (II Cor. 2.11), promulgating false doctrine (II Cor. 11.14–15, II Tim. 2.26). In Rev. 12–13 in the time immediately before the end the devil is cast down to earth and raises up the two beasts (antichrist figures) to make war on the saints and to deceive all the peoples of the earth (*see also* II Thess. 2.9).[4] Yet all his malevolent activity is still subject to the control of God, whose purpose is to test and refine his people's faith. The devil is in fact much less powerful than he seems: he is like a strong man who has been bound by one stronger than himself, and already his goods are being plundered (Mark 3.27, *see* John 12.31). His fate is to be 'thrown into the lake of fire and sulphur', where he will be 'tormented day and night for ever' (Rev. 20.10, *see also* Matt. 25.41).

The function of these varied references to the devil is to stress that evil is not merely a matter of individual human actions or unfortunate events but an awesome supernatural power. Paradoxically, the New Testament both recognizes the reality of this power and declares that it has already been utterly vanquished by Christ.

DISCIPLE[1] In all four Gospels, those who accompany Jesus are generally described as 'the disciples' or 'his disciples'. This phrase is usually synonymous with 'the twelve' (used in Mark 4.10, 6.7, 9.35, and so on), and so Matthew can refer to 'the twelve disciples' (10.1, 11.1, 20.17). This suggests that the early Church in general identified 'the disciples' exclusively with the twelve apostles, and used the two terms for the periods before and after the death and resurrection of Jesus. Thus Paul never speaks of Christians of his own day as 'disciples'. However, in Luke, Acts and John, there are signs of a broader usage. Luke speaks of 'a great crowd of his disciples' (Luke 6.17), and 'the whole multitude of the disciples' (19.37). In Acts, it is much the most common designation for Christians, and it is therefore specifically differentiated from 'the twelve' in 6.2 ('And the twelve summoned the body of the disciples . . .'). John 4.1 and 6.60–66 likewise show this broader usage, as do the sayings concerning discipleship (e.g. Luke 14.26–33, John 8.31, 15.8), which cannot have been understood by the early church to refer only to the twelve. Underlying this inconsistency of usage is the twofold early Christian attitude towards the twelve: they are both in a class of their own and the typical representatives of all Christians.

DIVORCE[1] The question of the grounds for divorce was debated by the rabbis, and Matthew's version of Jesus' teaching on divorce picks up this debate. Jesus is asked, 'Is it lawful to divorce one's wife for any cause?' (Matt. 19.3) – that is, is a man free to divorce his wife whenever he wishes, or does he need specific grounds? Jesus' answer is that marriage is binding except when the wife commits adultery; that is the only legitimate grounds for divorce (v. 9, *see* 5.32). However, in Mark 10.2–12 the debate is not about the grounds for divorce but about the legitimacy of divorce in *any* circumstances. In response to the question, 'Is it lawful for a man to divorce his wife?', Jesus answers that it is not, and that remarriage after divorce is always adultery. His answer involves a contrast between Moses' allowing of divorce and the original institution of marriage in Gen. 3: laws which do not reflect the original goodness of the created order are not a true expression of the will of God, however necessary they may be for the good of society.[2]

As regards the identification of remarriage after divorce with adultery, Mark 10.11–12 applies this to the woman who divorces her husband, as well as to the man who divorces his wife. Because Jewish law permits only the man to obtain a divorce, the saying has clearly been adapted to conform to Roman law, in which either partner could obtain a divorce. Matthew preserves a form of the saying which is more Jewish and probably closer to the original: 'Whoever divorces his wife . . . and marries another commits adultery' (Matt. 19.9). It is possible that this was intended to prohibit a man divorcing his wife in order to marry someone else, thus giving the wife some protection against the shame and economic hardship of divorce. Paul takes the discussion further in I Cor. 7.10–16: despite Jesus' prohibition of divorce, it is recognized that divorce will still occur among Christians (although they are forbidden to remarry); Christians, therefore, should not stand in the way of an unbelieving husband or wife who wishes for a divorce.

ELISABETH[1] In all four gospels there is a close relationship between John the Baptist and Jesus, and in Luke this is traced back to the circumstances of their birth.[2] The miraculous birth of Jesus to Mary is paralleled by the miraculous birth of John to Mary's relative, Elisabeth, who was 'barren' and 'advanced in years' (v. 7). The story is perhaps modelled on the Genesis narrative of the miraculous birth of Isaac to Sarah, who like Elisabeth was 'barren' and 'advanced in years'. Elisabeth is regarded by Luke as a representative of the righteous remnant in Israel who keep God's commandments (1.6) and long for his promised redemption.[3] Her barrenness is a symbol of Israel's inability to procure this redemption for itself, and the miraculous birth of a son shows that salvation begins in the activity of God.

EMMAUS[1] According to Luke 24.13, this village was situated 60 stadia (about 7 miles) from Jerusalem. A village with a similar name (Amwas) is in fact located about 19 miles from Jerusalem, and perhaps because of this some manuscripts of Luke read, 'a hundred and sixty stadia'. However, the story requires the village to be closer to Jerusalem than this. In Luke 24.13–35, the journey to Emmaus serves as the backdrop to the resolution of a theological problem. The two disciples begin the story in a state of confusion, unable to understand the crucifixion of the one whom they had expected to redeem Israel, or the women's report of a vision of angels announcing his resurrection. The resolution of this confusion occurs first through the perception that the Scriptures speak of a suffering and resurrected Messiah, and secondly through the moment of recognition 'in the breaking of the bread'.

EMPTY TOMB In I Cor. 15.1–11, Paul gives the earliest account we possess of Christian belief in the resurrection of Jesus. His references to Jesus' burial and resurrection suggest that he must have believed that Jesus' tomb was empty. However, he says nothing here about the 'story of the empty tomb' (Mark 16.1–8, etc.), which is strictly speaking a story about the miraculous manifestation of the fact that the tomb was empty.

1 The Versions of the Empty Tomb Story Each of the evangelists narrates a version of the story, and there are a number of differences between them – mostly comparatively minor.

(*i*) **Mark** The oldest and best manuscripts of Mark end at 16.8, at the conclusion of the story of the empty tomb. The copies of Mark used by Matthew and Luke do not seem to have included any additional material, and it therefore seems likely that this was the original end of the gospel. Mark's testimony to the resurrection is thus a mere eight verses long. It is an enigmatic narrative, and lacks the note of incredulous joy found in the other gospels; the solemn rituals of mourning are suddenly thrown into confusion by an encounter with a young man dressed in a white robe, which causes the women to flee from the tomb in terror. Despite the instruction to tell the disciples, the women are too frightened to speak, and so the gospel ends on a note of dissonance.[1]

(*ii*) **Matthew** In Matt. 27.62–28.15 Mark's empty tomb story is developed in various ways. It is combined with the story of the guard, installed at the tomb to prevent Jesus' disciples stealing his body. Matthew is combating the Jewish claim that the disciples actually did this, and he claims that this slanderous assertion was first spread by the guards, who had been bribed to do so and to keep silent about their knowledge of Jesus' resurrection (28.11–15). In Matthew the women come to the tomb merely to 'see it', and not to anoint Jesus. An explanation is provided for the removal of the stone: there was an earthquake, and an angel descended from heaven, terrified the guards, rolled away the stone and sat on it. This is an expansion of Mark's reference to a young man in white.[2] The women leave the tomb not only in a state of fear (as in Mark), but with great joy; they do not keep silent (as in Mark), but immediately tell the disciples. Although the angel has told them that they will meet Jesus in Galilee, they in fact meet him on their way back into the city.[3]

(*iii*) **Luke** Two of Luke's alterations to Mark are comparatively minor. The women prepare the spices on the evening of the day on which Jesus was crucified, rather than buying them on the day on which he rose; and the young man in white is replaced by 'two men in dazzling apparel'. More significantly, Luke's account of the angels' message is different to Mark's. In Mark 16.7, the women are told: 'Go, tell his disciples and Peter that he is going before you to Galilee; there you will see him, as he told you'. Luke 24.6–7 has: 'Remember how he told you, while he was still in Galilee, that the Son of man must be delivered into the hands of sinful men, and be crucified, and on the third day rise'. Luke tells of resurrection appearances only in or near Jerusalem, and in this way he sets the scene for the beginning of his second volume, which opens in Jerusalem.[4] It is sometimes suggested that belief in appearances in Jerusalem was a later development in the tradition, which originally linked them only with Galilee; but because the earliest account of appearances (I Cor. 15.5–8) says nothing about their location, the suggestion remains hypothetical. Like Matthew, and contrary to Mark, Luke states that the women told the disciples what had happened; unlike Matthew, he adds that the disciples did not believe them. In some manuscripts of Luke, Peter visits the tomb, as in John (Luke 24.12, *see also* v. 24).

(*iv*) **John** In John 20.1 only Mary Magdalene goes to the tomb; she goes while it is still dark, and not at dawn; and because the body of Jesus was anointed at his burial (19.39–40), nothing is said about any further anointing.[5] As in Luke 24.12, Peter runs to the tomb in response to Mary's report, and sees the linen cloths lying there (John 20.2–10). Here, however, he is accompanied by the unnamed 'disciple whom Jesus loved', who sees the linen cloths and believes.[6] The point of this is probably to exclude the theory that the body had been taken by grave-robbers: no robber would take the corpse but leave behind the cloths together with their immensely valuable contents of 'myrrh and aloes' (19.39). Thus, the linen cloths lead the beloved disciple to conclude that the only possible explanation for the tomb being empty is that Jesus has risen. The encounter between Mary and the angel takes place after this, and is immediately followed by an appearance of Jesus, whom she at first takes to be the gardener who was perhaps responsible for moving the corpse. Here too, the possibility that the body may have been taken away by natural means is hinted at and then excluded (vv. 15–16).

2 The Significance of the Empty Tomb Story The four versions of the empty tomb story thus differ from one another in a number of ways, and it is impossible to harmonize them into a single, coherent narrative.[7] Yet they are agreed about the central issue: the empty tomb and its discovery is a sign of the objectivity of the resurrection of Jesus. The story implicitly opposes two alternative views of the resurrection that were put forward at an early date. The first is the response of those who reject the Christian claim altogether, and who assert that the disciples merely experienced subjective visions or dreams; the second is the response of *Christians* who seek to make the resurrection less 'physical' and more 'spiritual', because a truly physical resurrection seems too hard to believe. These responses were no doubt inevitable; but it is the purpose of the empty tomb story to oppose them, by stressing that the resurrection was an act of God preceding all subjective experience of it, and leaving behind an empty tomb as a sign of the inconceivable event that had taken place.

Like all signs, the empty tomb is ambiguous, and the later evangelists show that they are aware of a number of possible explanations for the disappearance of Jesus' body. Matthew answers the Jewish objection that the disciples had stolen the body with his elaborate story of the guard; John insists that the body could neither have been stolen by tomb-robbers nor removed by the gardener. It is possible that here and elsewhere legendary elements have crept into the tradition, but these too testify in their own way to the primitive understanding of Jesus' resurrection as an unprecedented and overwhelming act of God.

EPHESIANS, PAUL'S LETTER TO
Of the 13 letters ascribed to Paul, up to six are regarded by many scholars as unauthentic (Ephesians, Colossians, II Thessalonians, I and II Timothy, Titus).[1] If Ephesians was not written by Paul, then it provides evidence of the way in which his teaching was understood perhaps several decades after his death. An anonymous author writes what he thinks Paul would have said had he still been alive.

1 Situation Ephesians has less to say than any other Pauline or supposedly Pauline letter about the situation either of the author or of the recipients. Paul is allegedly writing from prison (3.1), where he is suffering for the sake of the gospel

(3.13), but where despite his chains there are still opportunities for preaching (6.19–20). As in Col. 4.7–8, Paul states that Tychicus (a companion of Paul referred to elsewhere, and presumably the bearer of the letter) will give the recipients further news. Nothing more is said about Paul's situation. As regards the recipients, the words 'at Ephesus' do not appear in 1.1 in some important manuscripts: the letter is simply addressed to 'the saints who are also faithful in Christ Jesus'. If this represents the original text, then Ephesians is intended to be taken as a general letter for all Christians, and this is confirmed by the very general nature of the contents, in which nothing is said about the circumstances of the recipients other than the fact that they are Gentiles (1.12–13, 2.17–22, 3.1).

   2 **Authorship** The style of Ephesians is calm and other-worldly, and lacks the vigorous rhetoric and argumentative style which is so characteristic of Paul. Also absent is his strong sense of a personal bond between himself and his readers. But the main reason why most scholars feel that Paul is unlikely to have written Ephesians himself is that much of its theology differs from his. The differences are particularly notable if Colossians is also assumed to be unauthentic, for Ephesians and Colossians have a number of themes in common: for example, the idea of the universal Church as the body of Christ, of which Christ is the head.[2] Like Col. 1.24–29, Eph. 3.1–13 states that the divine decision to incorporate Gentiles into the church was communicated to the earliest Jewish Christians, and that Paul as apostle to the Gentiles was acting in accordance with their wishes. That is also the view of Acts, but it appears to disregard the major differences of opinion between Paul and the Jerusalem authorities at this point (Gal. 2.11–21)[3]. The early Church is being idealized from the standpoint of a somewhat later age. The argument against the authenticity of Ephesians, however, is cumulative: at point after point, Ephesians seems both to develop Paul's ideas and to diverge from them, and several of these points will emerge in the following section.

   3 **Theological Themes** Ephesians is a free meditation on the privileges and responsibilities of being a Christian, and several characteristic themes are especially prominent.

   (i) **The Exalted Christ** In I Cor. 15, Paul stresses that the resurrection of Jesus is only the beginning of God's victory over his enemies; God's reign has not yet arrived in all its fulness. Ephesians places much more stress on the present reign of the exalted Christ, who has already overcome the hostile 'principalities and powers' in his resurrection (1.19–23). Christians have already been exalted with him to share his glorious position at the right hand of God (2.6); the suffering of Christ on the cross no longer determines the present life of Christians in the way that it does in Paul.[4]

   (ii) **Cosmic Reconciliation** The exaltation of Christ is at the heart of the author's vision of the reconciliation of the entire cosmos. He believes that the world has mysteriously fallen prey to hostile, anti-divine supernatural beings – the 'principalities and powers in the heavenly places' (3.10), the 'world rulers of this present darkness' (6.12). But God has now made known the hidden plan which he determined before the creation of the world: the plan 'to unite all things in him [Christ], things in heaven and things on earth' (1.10). God's love thus embraces all his enemies, whether human or angelic. This plan to reconcile all things is revealed in the Church, in which the old hostility between Jews and Gentiles has been abolished through the death of Christ, who thus 'created in himself one new man in place of the two, so making peace' (2.15). The accomplishment of reconciliation here foreshadows the reconciliation of all things.

(*iii*) **The Universal Church** The word 'church' no longer refers to the local congregation but to the whole Christian community, past and present. It is seen as a temple built on the foundation of 'the apostles and prophets' – that is, the leaders of the earliest Jewish Christian community (2.19–22). It is the agent of God's purposes in the world (3.10) and the object of Christ's love (5.23–33). The gifts of the exalted Christ are gifts to the whole Church (4.7–13), and not just to the local congregation, as in I Cor. 12. The author must have been aware of the great diversity among different groups of Christians, but nevertheless insists that 'there is one body' which finds its unity in the 'one Spirit', in 'the one hope that belongs to your call', and in 'one Lord, one faith, one baptism, one God and Father of us all' (4.4–6). However, this does not mean that every opinion which claims to be Christian is acceptable, for the author warns of the danger of being 'tossed to and fro and carried about by every wind of doctrine, by the cunning of men, by their craftiness in deceitful wiles' (4.14). He is evidently aware of the problem of heresy. We have here the beginnings of belief in 'one holy, catholic and apostolic church' whose task is to preserve both unity and truth.

EPHESUS This port on the western coast of Asia Minor (modern Turkey) was from 133 BC the capital of the Roman province of Asia, and the site of the temple of Artemis, one of the seven wonders of the world. The origins of the Church there are not entirely clear. According to Acts, Paul paid a brief visit to Ephesus at the close of his 'second missionary journey' (18.18–20); but nothing is said about any converts. However, 18.27 speaks of 'brethren' there, and in 19.1 Paul on his return to Ephesus meets 'disciples'. In the ensuing story (19.2–7), the author's point is that these people's conversion is only completed by the arrival of Paul[1]; but it is implicitly acknowledged that Christianity at Ephesus was originally independent of Paul. Presumably, Jewish Christian missionaries had already proclaimed in the synagogues of Ephesus that Jesus was the Messiah – as at Rome.

Paul's long stay at Ephesus is extremely important in Acts: first, it provides the occasion for vivid narratives about the encounter between the gospel and pagan magic and religious practice (19.11–41); and secondly, Paul's address to the elders of the Church at Ephesus (20.17–38) is intended as a farewell to all his Gentile churches. An extended stay at Ephesus is confirmed by Paul's letters (I Cor. 16.8–9, *see also* II Cor. 1.8–9). Both passages suggest that he experienced considerable opposition there; in I Cor. 15.32, he even contemplates the possibility that at Ephesus he will be thrown to the lions. If (as is likely) Paul wrote Philippians from Ephesus,[2] he must have been imprisoned there; Phil. 1.15–18 would then hint at divisions in the Ephesian Church between those who were for Paul and those who were against him.

II Tim. 1.15 suggests that in the post-Pauline period, the anti-Pauline group was victorious, and there is further evidence of this in the letter to the Ephesian Church in Rev. 2.1–7, where references to those who eat 'food sacrificed to idols' (v. 6, *see* vv. 14–15) and to 'those who call themselves apostles but are not' may relate to Paul. In later Christian tradition, the Church of Ephesus is linked not with Paul but with John.

EXORCISM[1] The Synoptic Gospels (unlike John) contain several stories relating to Jesus' activities as an exorcist: possessed individuals are cured in the synagogue at Capernaum (Mark 1.21–28), in the country of the Gerasenes (5.1–20), in the region of Tyre and Sidon (7.24–30), and at the foot of the Mount of Transfiguration (9.14–29). Exorcisms also feature prominently in the general summaries in 1.34, 3.11–12, etc., and in the mission of the disciples (6.7). There is no hard-and-fast distinction between exorcism and healing: deafness and dumbness may be attributed either to physical causes (7.31–37) or to demonic possession (9.25). However one regards the historical authenticity of the individual stories, it seems certain that Jesus did see himself as an exorcist as well as a preacher. In answer to the criticisms of the Pharisees, he sees his activities in this sphere as a sign that the kingdom of God is already beginning to dawn (Matt. 12.24–29),[2] even though v. 27 shows that Jesus as an exorcist was by no means unique.[3] Outside the Synoptic Gospels, exorcism is much less prominent; references to it are found only in Acts 5.16, 16.16–18 and 19.11–17. There is nothing in Paul's letters to suggest that he or any of his converts practised exorcism.

FAITH The New Testament places equal emphasis on the grace of God manifested in Jesus Christ and on the need for a genuine human response in order to appropriate this. That response may be seen as 'following Jesus' or 'obedience'; or it may be summarized in the word, 'faith'. Faith is here a matter of individual decision, and to some extent this differentiates the New Testament from the Old and from Judaism, where membership of the community and acceptance of its beliefs is an automatic result of being born a Jew. In the New Testament, however, faith is by no means a purely private decision because it is always linked with a change of life and with joining the community of the Church. Thus, it is linked with repentance in Mark 1.15 and elsewhere: 'Repent and believe the gospel'. Faith is not just belief but social reorientation.[1]

1 The Synoptic Gospels The view of faith in the Synoptic Gospels is somewhat different to the rest of the New Testament because they link faith so closely with the miracles of Jesus (and not, for example, with his identity). Mark 5.34 is a typical example of this: in the story of the healing of the woman with a flow of blood, Jesus says, 'Daughter, your faith has made you well; go in peace, and be healed of your disease'. It is faith on the part of the person requesting a miracle which enables Jesus to perform it. Thus, in Mark 9 the father of a possessed child asks Jesus for help, and is told that everything hinges on his own faith: All things are possible to him who believes' (v. 23). By his confession of faith ('I believe; help my unbelief!'), the father makes possible the healing of his son. Conversely, the unbelief of the people of Nazareth means that Jesus 'could do no mighty work there' (Mark 6.5–6). Commitment to Jesus means far more in the Synoptic Gospels than merely belief in his power to perform miracles, but the term 'faith' is not used in this broader sense; the idea of 'following' him is preferred (Mark 1.17, 8.34, Luke 9.57–62). Because the early Christians all seem to have understood their commitment in terms of faith, the synoptic usage was probably not their own invention, but goes back to Jesus himself.

2 John In John, faith is linked almost exclusively with the question of Jesus' identity. The purpose of the gospel is 'that you may believe that Jesus is the Christ, the Son of God . . .' (20.31). The crucial issue is whether one believes Jesus' statement, 'I am the Son of God', or rejects it as blasphemous (10.31–39), for 'you will die in your sins unless you believe that I am he' (8.24). This faith brings one eternal life here and now: 'He who hears my word and believes him who sent me has eternal life; he does not come into judgment, but has passed from death to life' (John 5.24). Thus, 'he who comes to me shall not hunger, and he who believes in me shall never thirst' (6.35).[2] Coming to Jesus and believing in him are seen in terms of divine predestination: 'No-one can come to me unless the Father who sent me draws him' (6.44, *see* v. 65).[3] Jesus himself as the divine Son of God is normally seen as the object of faith, but because his sonship implies total obedience to the Father, it can also be said that 'he who believes in me, believes not in me but in him who sent me' (12.44).

3 Paul Of all the New Testament writers, it is Paul who has most to say about the nature of faith.

(*i*) **The Object of Faith** In Paul, faith is faith 'in Jesus Christ' (Rom. 3.22) or 'in him that raised from the dead Jesus our Lord' – that is, God (Rom. 4.24). More commonly, 'faith' stands on its own with no explicit reference to its object: 'Since we are justified by faith . . .' (Rom. 5.1). In some contexts, Paul stresses that faith incurs accepting the truth of certain statements: for example, that Christ died for our sins, that he was raised from the dead, that he is Lord (I Cor. 15.1–4, Rom. 10.9).[4] In others, faith appears to have a rather more general content – especially where Paul is discussing Abraham, who is for him the great Old Testament exemplar of faith (Gal. 3, Rom. 4). Yet it would be a mistake to differentiate belief in doctrinal statements from the attitude of trust towards God for these are for Paul two sides of a single coin.

(*ii*) **Faith and Works** In Galatians and Romans, Paul stresses that we are justified (i.e. accepted by God) on the basis of faith and not works: 'We hold that a man is justified by faith apart from works of law' (Rom. 3.28). It is often held that

Paul is here denying that human moral effort ('works') has any part to play in attaining salvation, which must be received as a pure gift from God ('faith'), but this is a misunderstanding. Paul is asserting the right of Gentile Christians to remain separate from the Jewish community and its way of life based on the law; the denial that salvation is 'by works of the law' simply means that one does not have to 'live as a Jew' (Gal. 2.14) in order to attain it.[5] Faith for Paul is by no means effortlessly passive, for it necessitates the abandonment of an old way of life and the adoption of a new one.

(*iii*) **Faith and Hope** Although 'life' is in one sense for Paul a present reality, in another sense it remains future; faith is thus orientated towards the future as well as towards the past and present. Abraham believed the divine promise of the world to come (Rom. 4.13), and despite the element of fulfilment in the coming of Jesus Christ, Christian faith is still essentially directed towards the future, as Abraham's was. At this point, faith and hope are virtually identical: Paul can describe the Christian attitude towards the unseen future realities either as 'hope' (Rom. 8.24–25) or as 'faith' (II Cor. 5.7, *see* 4.18). Paul, unlike John, does not see faith as the unambiguous present possession of eternal life.[6]

4 Hebrews Paul's view of faith influenced other New Testament writers: the author to the Hebrews makes positive use of it, whereas James reacts against it. In an extended discussion in Heb. 11, Paul's stress on the future aspect of faith is applied to many of the great figures of the Old Testament: 'These all died in faith, not having received what was promised, but having seen it and greeted it from afar, and having acknowledged that they were strangers and exiles on the earth' (v. 13). Encouraged by the examples of this great 'cloud of witnesses' (12.1), Christians must imitate their faith and endurance rather than 'shrinking back' into unbelief (10.35–39).

5 James[7] In James 2.14–26, the author attacks the idea that we are justified by faith not by works, arguing that 'a man is justified by works and not by faith alone' (v. 24). This statement is clearly an explicit denial of Rom. 3.28 ('a man is justified by faith apart from works of law'). Elsewhere in this passage the author shows that he is directly countering Pauline arguments, notably in the quotation of Paul's favourite text about Abraham – 'Abraham believed God, and it was reckoned to him as righteousness' (Gen. 15.6) – to prove that Abraham was 'justified by works' (v. 21). The author understands by 'faith' a purely intellectual belief (e.g. 'that God is one', v. 19), and claims that this is incomplete without acts of obedience to God. However, Paul never denies this; the only point of his opposition to 'works of the law' is to reject the view that Gentile Christians must adopt the Jewish way of life and become members of the Jewish community. Faith is not contrasted with obedience in general; indeed, faith and obedience may be identified (Rom. 1.5). Thus, James has apparently misunderstood Paul.

FASTING According to Mark 2.18–22, Jesus was criticized for failing to teach his disciples to fast. No doubt he and they observed the general fast on the Day of Atonement, but they did not adopt the extra fasts that were regarded as an indispensable sign of true piety. His response to criticism is that fasting is inappropriate to the new age in which the kingdom of God is already beginning to dawn: 'Can the wedding guests fast while the bridegroom is with them?' (v. 19; see also Matt. 11.18–19 for Jesus' rejection of fasting).[1] In some respects, early Jewish Christianity adopted a more conservative attitude towards Jewish practices than did Jesus,[2] and fasting is a case in point. Mark 2.20 is probably a Jewish Christian addition designed to limit the abolition of fasting to the period of Jesus' earthly ministry: 'The days will come when the bridegroom is taken away from them, and then they will fast in that day'. The instructions on fasting in Matt. 6.16–18 may tell us more about Matthew's conservative Jewish piety than about Jesus himself. There is nothing in Paul's letters to suggest that he enjoined fasting on his converts or practised it himself. At this point, he seems closer to the spirit of Jesus than some of the other early Christians.

FEAR OF GOD For all its stress on the love of God, the New Testament constantly states that we should fear God: 'Fear him who can destroy both soul and body in hell' (Matt. 10.28) – 'If you invoke as Father him who judges each one impartially according to his deeds, conduct yourselves with fear . . .' (I Peter 1.17). Here and elsewhere, the fear of God is linked with the prospect of judgment. It is not to be understood as dread of an arbitrary and capricious tyrant, but as the recognition that life is lived in responsibility to God.[1] Fear of God is a corrective to excessive self-confidence: 'Do not boast, but fear' (Rom. 11.20). However, fear is seen by Paul and by the author of I John as a secondary element in the relationship between the individual and God. Paul states that 'you did not receive the spirit of slavery to fall back into fear, but you have received the Spirit of sonship' (Rom. 8.15). I John 4.18 asserts that 'perfect love casts out fear' for 'fear has to do with punishment, and he who fears is not perfected in love'.[2] Both writers hold that where there is love towards God, there is no room for fear of the day of judgment.

FEASTS[1] The annual Jewish feasts play a prominent part in New Testament narrative. This is true, above all, of the Passover, which inaugurated the seven days of unleavened bread and commemorated the Exodus from Egypt, because Jesus' crucifixion took place at Passover time. Two earlier Passovers are mentioned in John 2.13 and 6.4; these passages, together with the mistaken assumption that the unnamed feast of John 5.1 must have been a Passover, led to the traditional belief that Jesus' ministry lasted three years. Fifty days after the Passover, the feast of Pentecost (from the Greek word for fifty) took place, commemorating the beginning or 'first fruits' of the harvest. This is linked in Acts 2.1 with another great event in the Christian story, the descent of the Spirit. All the action of John 7.1–10.21 takes place at the Feast of Tabernacles (or Booths), which celebrated the completion of the harvest, and the following section (10.22–39) takes place at the winter Feast of Dedication, which commemorated the rededication of the temple in 164 BC. The Day of Atonement does not appear in the gospel narratives, but is discussed in Heb. 9.1–14: the high priest's annual entry into the holy of holics with sacrificial blood is compared and contrasted with Jesus' sacrifice of himself and his permanent presence in the heavenly holy of holies.[2]

However, a certain distancing from the Jewish feasts is noticeable. In John 6.4, 7.2, references to 'the feast of the Jews' suggest that the feasts have no real significance for the incarnate Son of God. Paul asserts that observing the Jewish feasts is a matter of individual decision, and should not be forced on Gentile Christians (Rom. 14.5–6); and Col. 2.16–17 proclaims Christian freedom from this aspect of the Jewish law. I Cor. 5.6–8 allegorizes the Passover: the Passover lamb represents the crucified Christ, the 'leaven' which must be removed represents 'malice and evil', and the 'unleavened bread' represents 'sincerity and truth'. Thus, the destruction of the temple in AD 70 (which made the traditional way of observing the feasts impossible) did not represent such a crisis for Christians as it did for Jews.

FELIX As a result of his brother Pallas' favour with the emperor Claudius, Felix received the procuratorship of Judaea, which he held from AD 52 to 60. He married the daughter of King Agrippa I,[1] Drusilla (mentioned in Acts 24.24). Despite the flattering reference in Acts 24.2 to the peace and prosperity he brought to Judaea, he in fact took harsh measures to suppress the growing liberation movement which culminated in the revolt of AD 66–70. Josephus blames him for the assassination of the high priest Jonathan, and Tacitus states that he indulged in every kind of barbarity and 'exercised the power of a king in the spirit of a slave'. He is portrayed in an ambiguous way in Acts 23.24–24.27 in connection with Paul's trial. Luke's very positive attitude towards Roman authority is present in the respectful opening of Paul's defence: 'Realizing that for many years you have been judge over this nation, I cheerfully make my defence' (24.10).[2] Yet Luke cannot ignore the fact that Felix did not release the innocent Paul as he should have done, and attributes this to his desire to learn more about Paul's teaching, his expectation of a bribe, and his fear of upsetting the Jews (24.24–27).

FESTUS Porcius Festus was appointed Felix's successor as procurator of Judaea in AD 60, and died there in AD 62. He appears in the third and fourth of the hearings recounted in Acts 23–26, in conjunction with Paul's Jewish accusers in Acts 25 and King Agrippa in Acts 26. Unlike the corrupt Felix, he is portrayed as the embodiment of Roman justice who protects Paul from the fanatical hostility of his accusers. In response to the Jews' request that Paul be brought to face trial in Jerusalem, Festus tells Agrippa, 'I answered them that it was not the custom of the Romans to give up any one before the accused . . . had opportunity to make his defence' (25.16). According to Luke, Festus found Paul innocent, and would presumably have released him had he not appealed to Caesar (25.18–19,25). Unlike Felix, who had 'a rather accurate knowledge of the Way' and enjoyed hearing Paul (24.22–26), Festus was bewildered by the Christian message (25.19–20) and even suspected that Paul was mad (26.24). Nevertheless, from Luke's point of view he represents the Roman law and order providentially ordained by God to further the spread of the gospel.[1]

FLESH The New Testament characteristically uses the word 'flesh' in an extended sense to refer not merely to the material from which the body is composed, but to human creaturely weakness. When John writes, 'That which is born of the flesh is flesh, and that which is born of the Spirit is Spirit' (John 3.6), he has in mind human incapacity for the divine truth Jesus has come into the world to reveal. But it is Paul who makes the most profound theological use of the idea of flesh. In I Cor. 15.42–50, 'flesh and blood' are perishable and weak, and as such excluded from the kingdom of God; God will replace the present earthly body with a new, glorious spiritual body.[1] Elsewhere, flesh is not merely weak but the source of evil: 'I know that nothing good dwells within me, that is, in my flesh' (Rom. 7.18).[2] Elsewhere, flesh represents the whole way of life of those who live for and from this visible, tangible world, rather than by faith in the unseen realities revealed in Jesus Christ. Thus, Paul's former life as an impeccable Jew was marked by false 'confidence in the flesh' (Phil. 3.3–6).[3] To reject the message of Jesus as the crucified Messiah is to think of him 'according to the flesh' (II Cor. 5.16). To have received a good Greek education is to be 'wise according to the flesh' (I Cor. 1.26).[4] Flesh thus refers to the outlook, values, beliefs and behaviour which those who stand outside the church regard as self-evidently correct and appropriate, and which Paul proclaims as overturned by the gospel.

FOOD LAWS One of the characteristics that separated Jews from their Gentile neighbours was their strict adherence to dietary laws – notably abstention from pork, the draining of the blood of the slaughtered animal, and the rejection of meat from animals slaughtered in pagan temples (which was regarded as tainted with idolatry). Most Jewish Christians would have continued to observe these laws without question because there was no immediately obvious reason why belief in Jesus as the Messiah should lead one to abandon the Jewish way of life. The subject became controversial, however, when Gentiles were accepted into the Church, and the New Testament contains several attempts to resolve the controversy.

1 Mark The Gospel of Mark seems to originate from a Gentile Christian community in which the Jewish food laws were not observed. The crucial passage is Mark 7.14–19, where the evangelist reports Jesus' saying, 'Whatever goes into a man from outside cannot defile him', and adds his own comment: 'Thus he declared all foods clean' (vv. 18–19). Here, Mark goes back to the teaching of Jesus to justify his community's abandonment of the food laws. Matthew, as a Jewish Christian, omits Mark's comment from his version of this teaching (Matt. 15.17–18).[1]

2 Acts Peter's vision in Acts 10.9–16 alludes to the food laws. In a trance, Peter sees a receptacle full of clean and unclean animals, and is told to 'kill and eat'. When he refuses on the grounds that 'I have never eaten anything that is common or unclean', he is told, 'What God has cleansed, you must not call common'. At first sight, this appears to suggest that the food laws have been abolished, but in fact the point is to justify the conversion of the first Gentiles: 'God has shown me that I should not call *any man* common or unclean' (10.28).[2] Acts takes a rather conservative view of the food laws, repeating three times the so-called 'Apostolic Decree' commanding abstinence from food offered to idols – that is, meat from animals slaughtered in pagan temples – and from meat from which the blood has not been drained (15.20,29, 21.25).

3 Paul Contrary to Acts' claim that he was responsible for enforcing the Apostolic Decree (15.22–31, 16.4), Paul vehemently opposed the imposition of food laws on Gentile converts as a distortion of the gospel, in which all such distinctions between Jew and Greek were abolished (Gal. 2.11–21).[3] Food laws are no longer an issue for Gentile Christians; they may 'eat whatever is sold in the meat market without raising any question on the ground of conscience', knowing that 'the earth is the Lord's, and everything in it' (I Cor. 10.25–26).

FORGIVENESS The whole New Testament is concerned with the restoration of the relationship between humanity and God, and to that extent forgiveness is at the heart of its message. However, it is perhaps surprising how rarely and how unsystematically the actual words 'forgive' and 'forgiveness' are used. They hardly occur at all in the letters of Paul or in the Gospel of John; the reason is perhaps that 'forgiveness' implies the restoration of an already existing relationship which has been temporarily marred, and this does not do justice to the radical nature of humanity's separation from God as portrayed by Paul and John.[1] In the Synoptic Gospels and Acts, varied views are expressed about how forgiveness is attained. Mark 1.4 states that responding to John the Baptist's preaching with repentance and baptism procured the forgiveness of sins. But Matthew omits this reference to forgiveness as for him forgiveness is inseparable from Jesus himself, and specifically his death. He therefore adds the phrase, 'for the forgiveness of sins' to Mark's version of Jesus' saying, 'This is my blood of the covenant which is poured out for many' (Matt. 26.28). Luke links forgiveness with belief in the name of Jesus, and not with his death (Luke 24.47, Acts 2.38, 10.43). In Mark 2.1–12, Jesus' healing of a paralysed man is intended to prove that 'the Son of man has authority on earth to forgive sins' (v. 10); again, there is no reference to his death.

FREEDOM[1] The institution of slavery was universal in the Graeco–Roman world, and it was therefore natural for New Testament writers to understand salvation metaphorically as 'freedom' after the 'slavery' of one's previous way of life. Freedom is always seen as a gift bestowed through Christ, and never as the natural condition of human beings. In John 8.31–36, committing sin is understood as slavery to sin, from which the Son sets one free. In Gal. 4.21–5.1, it is life under the Jewish law that is understood as slavery: Paul allegorizes the Genesis account of Abraham's having children by two women, the slave girl Hagar and the free woman Sarah, and identifies those who live under the law with the children of the former, and those who do not with the children of the latter. However, freedom might suggest the removal of all moral constraints, and both Paul and the author of I Peter are aware of this problem (Gal. 5.13, I Peter 2.16).[2] It also seems to conflict with the understanding of Christians as slaves of Christ, and Paul notes this paradox when he writes: 'He who was called in the Lord as a slave is a freedman of the Lord. Likewise he who was free when called is a slave of Christ' (I Cor. 7.22). Christian life is thus neither slavery to a new master, however benevolent, nor absolute self-determination; both sides of the paradox must be maintained.

GADARA This Hellenistic city was a member of the Decapolis group.[1] It was situated about 6 miles south-east of the Sea of Galilee but possessed land up to the edge of the lake. In the New Testament it is mentioned only in connection with the well-known story of the Gadarene swine. Although the manuscript evidence is not entirely clear, it seems that Mark 5.1 (followed by Luke 8.26, 37) links this story not with Gadara but with Gerasa, another city of the Decapolis 30 miles south-east of the Sea of Galilee. Gadara occurs only in Matt. 8.28, and the evangelist seems to have corrected Mark's reference to Gerasa in order to save the pigs a long run across country.

GALATIANS, PAUL'S LETTER TO THE

The importance of this letter for the study of early Church history is out of all proportion to its length. It also contains an uncompromising exposition of Paul's doctrine of justification by faith and not works of the law – a doctrine that, as interpreted by Luther, has been fundamental to Protestant theology.[1]

1 The Founding of the Galatian Churches There has been much discussion about the location of the churches to which Paul addresses his letter. 'Galatia' may refer either to the region in central Asia Minor invaded by Celtic invaders (Gauls) in the third century BC, or to the greatly enlarged Roman province of that name established in 25 BC and including some of the cities evangelized by Paul on his 'first missionary journey' (Acts 13–14). These alternatives are referred to as 'north Galatia' and 'south Galatia' respectively. Because Acts 16.4–4 clearly distinguishes 'Galatia' from the cities visited in Acts 13–14, it is likely that Paul does the same and that the 'north Galatian' theory is therefore correct.

Acts 16.6 and 18.23 imply that the Galatian churches were founded shortly after the council at Jerusalem and the quarrel with Barnabas narrated in chapter 15. In Gal. 2, Paul gives a first-hand account of these events.[2] Here, the quarrel implicates not only Barnabas but James, Peter and the whole of the Church of Antioch: it seems that at the instigation of James, the Antiochene Church rejected Paul's insistence that Gentile Christians were free from the Jewish law. The founding of the Galatian churches thus took place after this major setback for Paul. He has little to say about his first visit to Galatia, apart from a puzzling reference to a disease (possibly affecting his eyes) that delayed him there for a while (Gal. 4.12–15).

2 Paul's Opponents Omitting his usual polite thanksgiving for his readers' faith, Paul writes at the beginning of the letter, 'I am astonished that you are so quickly deserting him who called you in the grace of Christ and turning to a different gospel', and blames this desertion on 'some who trouble you and want to pervert the gospel of Christ' (1.6–7). These people 'would compel you to be circumcised' (6.12) – that is, they seek to impose the Jewish law on Paul's Gentile converts; they try to persuade them to submit first of all to circumcision, the rite of entry into the Jewish community, as the first step in adopting the Jewish way of life.[3] In 2.11–14, Paul indicates that much the same thing had already taken place in Antioch (although circumcision is not mentioned in that passage): Gentiles there were 'compelled' to 'live as Jews', and on that occasion the main culprits were the men sent by James to enforce this. Although the identity of Paul's opponents in Galatia has been much disputed, the most likely solution is that they were the 'men from James' who had already been successful in Antioch and were now seeking to extend their influence into the new Gentile churches founded by Paul. That would explain why Paul uses such harsh language not only about his opponents in Galatia, but also about James, Peter and John: they were 'reputed to be something (what they were makes no difference to me)', 'reputed to be pillars' (2.6,9). His quarrel is with the Jerusalem church itself.

3 The 'Other Gospel' Paul accuses his opponents of preaching 'a different gospel', 'another gospel' (1.6–7), and it is possible to reconstruct from his response the main outlines of their teaching. They would have stressed that Jesus was the Jewish Messiah, sent by God to fulfil the promises he had made to the Jewish people. Those who benefit from the Messiah's coming are those who live within God's covenant with Israel. This covenant was originally made with Abraham, and the promise of salvation was given to him and to his 'seed' (his descendants).[4] But physical descent from Abraham, though desirable, is not essential, because in Gen. 17 the crucial sign of whether one is a member of God's covenant with Abraham is circumcision. If the Galatians wish to participate in the salvation brought by Jesus the Messiah, they must therefore join the people of Abraham through circumcision, the rite of entry into the Jewish community. Circumcision is not an isolated action, but the beginning of a whole new life of observance of the Jewish law.

This 'gospel' was in direct opposition to Paul. His opponents told the Galatians that Paul had originally been accepted by the apostles as a true preacher of the gospel, before the full radicalism of his approach became apparent; he had been commissioned by them to preach to the Gentiles. But then it became clear that, in order to increase the success of his preaching, he was telling his converts not to concern themselves with inconvenient commandments like circumcision and the food laws. When James sought to remedy the situation, Paul violently opposed him, and by his insubordination forfeited the authority which had previously been bestowed upon him. If he disregarded some of the divine commandments in this cavalier fashion, what was there to stop him from dispensing with the rest of them? His converts would be able to do whatever they liked.[5]

4 Paul's Response These are the ideas and the accusations to which Paul responds in Galatians.

(*i*) **Apostleship** In Gal. 1–2, Paul denies that his authority derives from the Jerusalem apostles; he is an apostle in his own right, directly commissioned by the risen Christ, and his opposition to Peter and James at Antioch was therefore not an act of insubordination.

(*ii*) **Abraham** Paul argues that Abraham is to be seen as the founder member not of the Jewish community but of the community of faith in which the barrier between Jew and Gentile is broken down. The key text is Gen. 15.6, quoted in Gal. 3.6: Abraham 'believed God and it was reckoned to him as righteousness'. This is taken to be a legitimation of the position of Gentile Christians who 'believe God' without submitting to the Jewish Law. Abraham's 'seed' to whom the promise of salvation was given is identified not with the Jewish community but with Christ (3.16) and those who are in Christ (3.29). In response to his opponents' claim that the Galatians needed to become children of Abraham, Paul states: you are *already* the children of Abraham.

(*iii*) **Law** Paul's opponents claim that there can be no salvation for those who do not submit to the law, and Paul replies that there can be no salvation for those who do. The law pronounces a curse on all who do not keep it in its entirety, and only Christ can save us from this (3.10–13). If the Galatians submit to the law, they will put themselves under the rule of hostile, anti-divine powers (4.1–10) and lose their salvation (5.2–4).[6]

(*iv*) **Ethics** Paul indignantly repudiates the view that his teaching leads to moral license: freedom from the law is not to be used as 'an opportunity for the flesh' but as a call to mutual love and service (5.13). The gift of the Spirit prevents Christians from fulfilling their natural desires, and this makes the law superfluous (5.16–26).

GALILEE This region in the northern part of Palestine was only fully converted to Judaism in the second century BC, and was ruled by Herod Antipas (a son of Herod the Great) from 4 BC to AD 37; it was not subject to direct Roman rule until AD 44.[1] Its main geographical feature is of course the 'Sea of Galilee' (or 'Lake of Gennesaret', Luke 5.1, or 'Lake of Tiberias'). Its main cities were Tiberias, the new capital, and Sepphoris, the old, and it is remarkable that no visit of Jesus to either of these places is recorded. With the exception of Nazareth, Cana and Nain, the Galilean towns or villages mentioned in the Gospels are all on or near the lake: Capernaum, Gennesaret, Bethsaida, Chorazin, and the unidentified Magadan and Dalmanutha.[2] References to specific places are comparatively rare, and the evangelists sometimes seem to have only a hazy idea of the geography of the region (*see for example* Mark 5.1, 7.31, Luke 17.11). Jesus' Galilean origin is a problem in John because Scripture links the Messiah with Bethlehem in Judaea (7.41,52),[3] but Matthew solves this problem by quoting the well-known passage from Isa. 9 ('The people who sat in darkness have seen a great light . . .'), with its reference to 'Galilee of the Gentiles' (Matt. 4.15–16).

GALLIO The brother of the philosopher Seneca, Gallio was the proconsul of Achaia who dismissed Jewish charges against Paul at Corinth, according to Acts

18.12–17. He was later forced to commit suicide by Nero. A fragment of an inscription found at Delphi shows that his term of office as proconsul of Achaia must have run from May AD 51 to May AD 52, and this is therefore a very important point of reference for dating Paul's life and letters. In Acts, Gallio's importance is that he finds Paul not guilty of any crime against the Roman state, and dismisses the case as a religious disagreement over which the State has no jurisdiction. Like Claudius Lysias (23.28–29) and Festus (25.13–27), Gallio is thus a spokesman for Luke's conviction that the Empire and the Church can co-exist harmoniously.[1]

GAMALIEL[1] According to Acts 22.3, Paul was 'educated according to the strict manner of the law of our fathers' by Gamaliel in Jerusalem. Because he later asserts, 'I am a Pharisee, a son of Pharisees' (23.6), Luke must regard Gamaliel as a Pharisee; the references to him in rabbinic literature neither confirm nor disprove this. In Acts, Paul remains faithful to his Pharisaic upbringing (in contrast to Phil. 3.4–8),[2] and Gamaliel is therefore presented in a positive light. His wisdom is apparent in Acts 5.33–40, where he dissuades the Sanhedrin from putting the apostles to death: 'If this plan or this undertaking is of men, it will fail, but if it is of God, you will not be able to overthrow them. You might even be found opposing God!'[3] Luke no doubt holds that the subsequent success of the Christian movement is proof of its divine origin, and that the persecution of the church (in his day, probably by the Romans rather than by the Jews) is a dangerous act of rebellion against God.

GENTILES[1] In all four gospels Jesus' ministry is almost entirely confined to the Jews: as Matt. 15.24 puts it, 'I was sent only to the lost sheep of the house of Israel'. Encounters between Jesus and Gentiles are regarded as altogether exceptional, although there are sayings appreciative of the faith of Gentiles: 'Truly I say to you, not even in Israel have I found such faith' (Matt. 8.10, *see also* 15.28).

During the early years of the post-Easter period, it was regarded as self-evident that the gospel was to be preached by Jews to Jews; the essence of that gospel was that in Jesus the Messiah God was fulfilling his promises to the Jewish people. Judaism had long been a missionary religion, and Gentile conversions to Judaism were not uncommon. It was therefore natural that among those who responded to early Christian preaching there should have been some of these Gentiles ('proselytes'). But what was radically new about the preaching of Paul, who regarded himself as 'the apostle to the Gentiles', was that he exempted his Gentile converts from the Jewish law; one did not have to become a Jew in order to become a Christian, for in Christ there is neither Jew nor Gentile (*see* Gal. 3.28). This startling step may have been motivated not only by theological considerations but also by the fact that Jewish requirements such as circumcision and the food laws acted as a considerable deterrent to conversion; by disregarding them, Paul made the success of his preaching more likely (*see* I Cor. 9.21). It was a controversial decision, and Galatians and Romans are a witness to Paul's bitter struggles with more conservative Jewish Christians who felt that he had betrayed the gospel.[2] In retrospect, it can be seen that what was at issue was the future nature of the Church: was it to be a sect within Judaism, or was it to be universal in scope?

Paul differentiates himself as apostle to the Gentiles from the Jerusalem apostles with their mission to the Jews (Gal. 2.7–9). Later tradition asserts that all the apostles were engaged in preaching the gospel to Gentiles (*see* Matt. 28.19–20).

GOD In many respects, the New Testament view of God is taken over directly from the Old Testament and from Judaism. As in Judaism, God is one (Rom. 3.30), good (Mark 10.18), impartial (Rom. 2.11), just (I John 1.9), and truthful (Rom. 3.7). He is the creator of everything in heaven and on earth (Acts 17.24), and his creative activity continues in his providential ordering of the world for the sake of humanity (Matt. 5.45). The worship of the one true God is utterly incompatible with the worship of idols (I Thess. 1.9). Indeed, the New Testament's idea of God is in many ways so close to Judaism that one might well conclude that its novelty is to be found only in what it says about Jesus and not in what it says about God. But that would be a mistake because what the New Testament says about Jesus transforms its understanding of God. Four examples of this transformation are given below; many others might be added.

1 The Knowledge of God In the Old Testament and Judaism it is implicit that the natural order requires the existence of a creator. In some strands of Greek philosophy, the same point is made at a more philosophical level. The New Testament is aware of this Jewish and Greek deduction of God from the created order (Acts 17.24–29, Rom. 1.19–21), and it is also aware of the Greek idea that nature teaches us to know God's will (Acts 10.35, Rom. 1.32, 2.14–15). However, its main emphasis is that God is known not so much in the created order as in Jesus Christ. In I Cor. 1.21, Paul rejects the Greek claim that God can be known through philosophy: 'For since, in the wisdom of God, the world did not know God through wisdom, it pleased God through the folly of what we preach to save those who believe'. Here, 'folly' is an ironic reference to the content of the gospel, 'Christ crucified' (v. 23); it is paradoxically in the weakness of the crucified Christ that we come to know the power of God (v. 24). John too holds that God is known only through Christ: 'No-one has ever seen God; the only Son, who is in the bosom of the Father, he has made him known' (1.18). There is no knowledge of the Father beyond the revelation of Jesus: 'He who has seen me has seen the Father' (14.8–9, *see also* Matt. 11.27). This positive claim involves the negative presupposition that the world is a riddle, and does not point to God in a self-evident way.

2 Providence The workings of divine providence are seen not primarily in the created world (the Greek view) nor in the history of the Jewish people (the Jewish view), but in the events portrayed in New Testament narrative. Everything takes place in fulfilment of a divine plan; nothing is accidental or unforeseen. Angels are sent to announce Jesus' birth, a star guides the wise men, and a dream warns Joseph of Herod's murderous designs. Jesus' public ministry begins with the descent of the Spirit and the voice from heaven. He performs his miracles and utters his teaching in constant obedience to the will of God (John 5.19, 7.17, 14.10–11). Those who follow him have been given to him by God (6.39, 17.6). His death takes place 'in accordance with the definite plan and foreknowledge of God' (Acts 2.23). Even the details were planned in advance; for example, Judas betrays Jesus in fulfilment of Old Testament prophecy (John 17.12).[1] It is God who raises him from the dead, and God who guides the early Christian mission (Acts 11.17–18, 13.2, etc.). Paul too shares this early Christian understanding of providence: 'Thanks be to God who in Christ always leads us in triumph, and through us spreads the fragrance of the knowledge of him everywhere' (II Cor. 2.14). But he is far more aware than other New Testament writers of the reality of 'suffering' – that is, experiences which seem to contradict belief in a divine power constantly active in the world for good. But faith sees that even suffering is used by God in the fulfilment of his purpose (II Cor. 4.17).[2]

3 Election In the Old Testament and Judaism, God is the God who has chosen the Jewish people, 'the God of Israel'. He called Abraham from among the Gentiles, and promised that he would bless him and his descendants. Through Moses at Mount Sinai, he revealed his law to Israel alone. Despite sin, it is expected that this special relationship will endure.[3] The New Testament, under the influence of Paul, generally sees God as the God who once chose Israel but who has now chosen a people from among both Jews and Gentiles to constitute his church. God is impartial, so he must judge Jews and Gentiles by the same standard (Rom. 2.11). God is one, and so he must be the God not only of Jews but also of Gentiles (Rom. 3.29–30). God 'gives life to the dead and calls into existence the things that do not exist', and so even the Gentiles (who are from the Jewish point of view non-entities) can participate in salvation (Rom. 4.17). God is the sovereign Lord of his creatures, and is therefore free to bestow salvation on whomever he wills, and to withhold it from whomever he wills (Rom. 9.14–29). In this way, the scope of salvation is extended to include, potentially at least, 'all people' (Rom. 11.32), 'the whole creation' (Rom. 8.22). Salvation is as broad in scope as creation; God made the world, and it was thus the world which was the object of his love manifested in Christ (John 3.16). The Jewish view of God as the God who chose Israel to be his people has been transformed.

4 The Unity of God The great Jewish confession known as the *Shema* begins with the words, 'Hear, O Israel: The Lord our God is one Lord' (Deut. 6.4). It is fundamental to Jewish life and thought that there is one God and that God is one. The New Testament shares this conviction, but modifies it in remarkable ways. Paul alludes to the *Shema* when he writes: 'For us there is one God, the Father, from whom are all things and for whom we exist'. But he then adds, '. . . and one Lord, Jesus Christ, through whom are all things and through whom we exist' (I Cor. 8.6). Here, as is usual in Paul, the word 'God' is applied exclusively to 'the Father', but the title 'Lord' is applied not to the Father but to Jesus.[4] Before the incarnation he was already 'in the form of God' (Phil. 2.6), and he is thus the recipient of prayer (II Cor. 12.8) and worship (Rom. 10.13, I Cor. 1.2, Phil. 2.10–11). In John this is taken still further. The Word was in the beginning with God, and was God (John 1.1–2). Jesus 'makes himself equal with God' (5.18), 'makes himself God' (10.33). The Jewish belief in the one God has been transformed into the claim, 'I and the Father are one' (10.30).[5]

GOOD SAMARITAN, PARABLE OF[1]

The 'Parable of the Good Samaritan' (Luke 10.25–37) is in one sense not a parable at all. Jesus' parables generally take a situation from life in this world and use it to point to particular aspects of God's activity and the human response to it. However, the story of the Good Samaritan is not intended to tell us anything about the divine-human relationship; it is simply a vivid illustration of what it might mean to fulfil the commandment, 'You shall love your neighbour as yourself'. The story is told in response to the question, 'And who is my neighbour?' (v. 29), which seeks to limit the scope of the commandment to certain specified people, so as to make it practicable. In opposition to any such limitation, the 'neighbour' is defined as anyone one encounters who is in need. It is important that it is the Samaritan, and not the Jewish priest or Levite, who helps the wounded man. The Samaritan responds to the call of a common humanity, which overrides religious differences (normally, 'Jews have no dealings with Samaritans' (John 4.9) and vice versa). The priest and the Levite regard the performance of their religious duties as of more importance than helping their fellow human beings. Thus, the story implicitly criticizes the way in which religion can sometimes act against the interests of humanity.

GOSPEL[1]

The Greek word for 'gospel' (*euangelion*) is closely related to the verb, 'to preach good news' (*euangelizesthai*). Matthew and Mark prefer the noun, Luke, the verb; both are very common in Paul, and neither of them occurs much in any other New Testament book. The Gospel of Mark opens with the words, 'The gospel of Jesus Christ the Son of God', and it may be that this represents the first use of the term 'gospel' to refer to a written work; elsewhere in the New Testament, it always refers to the message which is preached. But Mark 1.1 is significant in indicating that the gospel in the New Testament is not a theory or a philosophy but a narrative – the story of the ministry, death and resurrection of Jesus, which is seen as God's redemptive act for the salvation of the world. Even Paul, who shows no interest in the ministry of Jesus, regards the essence of the gospel as the death, burial, resurrection and appearances of Jesus (I Cor. 15.1–8). But the gospel also has a future aspect: Jesus' 'preaching the gospel of God' involved proclaiming that 'the kingdom of God is at hand' (Mark 1.14–15).

It is Paul who has most to say about preaching the gospel. In Christ, God was reconciling the world to himself, and in addition to Jesus' death and resurrection; this meant establishing 'the ministry of reconciliation' (II Cor. 5.18–19) – that is, sending messengers to proclaim the gospel so that people might believe (*see* Rom. 10.14–15). Thus, the crucified Christ is God's saving power (I Cor. 1.24), but so likewise is the gospel in which Christ is proclaimed (Rom. 1.16–17). Although at one level the gospel consists merely of human words (and not necessarily very impressive ones (I Cor. 2.3–41), at a deeper level it is only truly understood when it is regarded as the Word of God: God proclaiming through his messengers his grace manifested in Christ and his command that people should submit to it (*see* I Thess. 1.4–5, 2.13, I Cor. 2.1–5). To believe the gospel is thus to obey the gospel (Rom. 10.16).

GRACE As with many other terms, the word 'grace' was widely used by the early Christians but attained particular prominence in the theology of Paul. What is meant by grace is that God (or Christ) in his goodness is active in the world to secure people's salvation. Grace thus refers not just to God's love in general, but to love manifested in action and power within the world. It is a dynamic concept and stresses that salvation begins with God's turning towards us rather than with our turning towards God. 'The grace of God and the free gift in the grace of that one man Jesus Christ' have entered the world to save people from the dire effects of Adam's sin (Rom. 5.15).[1] Grace is manifested in the incarnation and death of Jesus: 'You know the grace of our Lord Jesus Christ, that though he was rich, yet for your sake he became poor, so that by his poverty you might become rich' (II Cor. 8.9). But grace is also constantly active in the life of the Christian community. Thus Paul speaks of our having 'obtained access to this grace in which we stand', and of the reign of grace which now counteracts the reign of sin and death (Rom. 5.2,21). The sphere of grace established by Jesus Christ remains a permanent reality in the world. Different gifts are bestowed on different members of the community for the common good, 'in accordance with the grace given to us' (Rom. 12.6).[2] Paul's own apostleship is the result of the working of grace (Rom. 15.15, I Cor. 15.10). Even the Philippians' desire to collect money for the Christians of Jerusalem is regarded by Paul as a manifestation of the grace of God (II Cor. 8.2).

HEAVEN The New Testment writers hold a world-view according to which there are a series of heavens above the earth, of which the visible heavens are the lowest. In the highest heaven of all, the throne of God is to be found. Thus, God is referred to as 'our Father in heaven' or 'heavenly Father'. Jesus in his ascension 'passed through the heavens' and is now 'exalted above the heavens' (Heb. 4.14, 7.26).[1] Paul knows of 'a man in Christ' (he means himself) 'who fourteen years ago was caught up to the third heaven' (II Cor. 12.2); because opinions differed about the number of heavens, it is hard to know whether Paul is referring to the immediate dwelling-place of God, or to some intermediate place. The destiny of Christians is to possess 'a building from God . . ., eternal in the heavens' (II Cor. 5.1, *see also* I Pet. 1.4). In Eph. 6.12, the 'heavenly places' are occupied (somewhat surprisingly) by 'spiritual hosts of wickedness'; no doubt the lower heavens are in mind because Christ's dwelling 'in the heavenly places' is far above these powers (Eph. 1.20–21). II Peter 3.10–13 and Rev. 21.1 speak of a time when not only the earth but also the heavens will be destroyed and recreated.

By comparison with other religious literature, the New Testament is (with the exception of the Book of Revelation) remarkably reticent in its view of heaven. Its concern is not to speculate about the nature of a mysterious supernatural world, but to stress God's transcendent otherness.

HEBREWS, LETTER TO The so-called Letter to the Hebrews is in fact not a letter at all, but a learned theological treatise on the theme of the superiority of the new covenant established by Christ over the old.

1 Author In a normal Greek letter, the writer was identified right at the beginning (see the first verse of Paul's letters). There is no such opening in Hebrews – instead it launches straight into theological discourse with no introduction, and so the author remains unidentified. He only speaks directly of himself in 13.18–25, where he mentions his forthcoming visit, on which he will probably be accompanied by Timothy. This brief section contains a number of typically Pauline words and phrases, and it was probably for this reason that it was ascribed to Paul by most early Christians (though by no means all: Origen in the third century AD says that only God knows who wrote it). But Hebrews as a whole is so entirely different from the letters of Paul that no-one any longer regards it as Pauline.

The reference in 13.23 to Timothy[1] suggests that the author, like Timothy, may have been a member of the Pauline circle, writing after the death of Paul. If so, he shows a remarkable independence from the thought of his master. An alternative explanation is perhaps more probable. The effect of 13.18–25 was to convince most early Christians that Paul was the author, and this may therefore also have been the purpose of the section: the author of Hebrews wished it to be thought that his work was by Paul, and in this he was largely successful.

2 Recipients The author's preoccupation with the Old Testament led the early Christians to the conclusion that the recipients were Jewish; hence the traditional title, 'To the Hebrews'. However, this is by no means certain; because the Old Testament was Holy Scripture for Christians as well as Jews, Gentile Christians could and did show considerable familiarity with it. The argument is purely theoretical and scriptural, and bears no relation to the life of the contemporary Jewish community; this therefore suggests a Gentile writing to Gentiles. The reference to 'faith in God' as one of the first principles of the gospel (6.1) again suggests Gentiles, because for Jews faith in God would have been taken for granted.

3 Theological Themes The author is writing against a background of widespread apathy and apostasy. Christians are in danger of abandoning their 'first confidence' in Christ and 'falling away from the living God' (3.12–14). They have not progressed as they should have done (5.11–14). Some have ceased attending Christian meetings altogether (10.25). Thus, Hebrews is not intended to be a work of abstract theology, but is an 'exhortation' (13.22) intended to restore Christian confidence and hope. Instead of merely reminding readers of what they already know, the author expounds ideas which will be new and unfamiliar to them (5.11–14). His main theme is the superiority of the new covenant to the old, and he seeks to prove this by expounding Old Testament texts, especially from the Psalms.

(*i*) **Christ and the Angels** (Heb. 1–2). Ps. 8.6–8 (as quoted in Heb. 2.6–8) states: 'Thou didst make him for a little while lower than the angels, thou hast crowned him with glory and honour'. This originally referred to 'man' in general ('What is man that thou art mindful of him?'), but the author takes it as a reference to the two stages in the career of Christ: his temporary humiliation, and his exaltation.[2] Christ is no longer lower than the angels; he is superior to them. Heb. 1 discusses this superiority at length, contrasting Old Testament passages which are taken to refer to Jesus with passages referring to angels. The purpose is to present Jesus as a figure of absolute (rather than merely relative) significance. In Heb. 2 the author reflects on the earthly life and the death of Jesus, during which he was lower than the angels, and argues that it was necessary and fitting that salvation should be accomplished in this way.

(*ii*) **The Promised Rest** (Heb. 3–4). Ps. 95.7–11 (quoted in Heb. 3.7–11) warns the Israelites not to rebel against God as their forefathers in the desert had done; because of their hardness of heart, God recalls, 'I swore in my wrath, "They shall never enter my rest" ' (i.e. the promised land). The author of Hebrews takes this passage as a warning to contemporary Christians, who will lose the promised salvation if they 'harden their hearts' and fall into unbelief. However, the passage may also be taken in a more positive way: if unbelief led to exclusion from the promised 'rest', then faith will enable one to enter it.

(*iii*) **Christ as High Priest** (Heb. 5–10).[3] Ps. 110.1 ('The Lord said to my Lord, "Sit at my right hand, till I make thy enemies a stool for thy feet" ') had long been understood by Christians as a reference to the resurrection and exaltation of Jesus. The author draws attention to v. 4 of the same psalm: 'The Lord has sworn and will not change his mind, "You are a priest for ever after the order of Melchizedek" '. In a painstaking examination of this verse in Heb. 7 the author shows that it refers to Jesus, whose priesthood – exercised in his sacrificial death and in his heavenly life – was infinitely superior to the priesthood of the old covenant. In Heb. 8–9 the theme of Christ as high priest is continued, with reference to Jeremiah's prophecy of a new covenant, which was to be unlike the old one (Jer. 31.31–34, quoted in Heb. 8.8–12).[4] The author understands this in sacrificial terms. The high priest enters the Holy of Holies only on the Day of Atonement, whereas Christ is eternally present in the heavenly Holy of Holies, having offered himself as a once-for-all sacrifice (Heb. 9). His single offering of himself abolishes the ineffectual, endlessly repeated sacrifices of the old dispensation (Heb. 10).

HELL[1] Only in the Synoptic Gospels, James and Revelation is Hell directly mentioned. Paul and John speak of 'dying', 'perishing', being 'condemned' or 'lost', but do not imply an everlasting, conscious punishment. Hell is 'the eternal fire prepared for the devil and his angels' (Matt. 25.41), 'the lake of fire' into which those whose names are not found in the Book of Life are 'thrown', to be 'tormented day and night for ever and ever' (Rev. 20.10, 14–15). It is 'Gehenna', the accursed valley outside Jerusalem where in an earlier age children were sacrificed to Moloch – indeed, the Aramaic term 'Gehenna' is the word used in the Synoptic Gospels, rather than any Greek equivalent. It is a place of 'outer darkness' where people will 'weep and gnash their teeth' (Matt. 25.30).

The idea of Hell was taken over by the early Christians from popular Jewish belief, and there seems no doubt that Jesus shared it, even though the authenticity of some of the passages where it is mentioned is open to question on other grounds. Although this belief can express a hatred of one's fellow human beings, it can also express a sense of responsibility to God for the way one conducts one's life.

HERESY[1] The New Testament does not use the term 'heresy' in its later sense – that is, a belief regarded as incompatible with Christian tradition as understood by the Church, and therefore also incompatible with church membership. At this early stage, both doctrine and church organization were fluid enough to tolerate a remarkable degree of diversity. However, later books do show the beginnings of the idea of heresy. The Letter to Jude is aware of an unchanging, unanimous apostolic tradition about matters of belief and conduct, which must be preserved at all costs from those who would subvert it (vv. 3–4). Timothy is warned to guard the tradition entrusted to him (I Tim. 6.20) and to oppose those who have 'swerved from the truth' (II Tim. 2.18, see I Tim. 1.6). Here, as in later orthodoxy, heresy is regarded as novelty – the abandonment of the ancient truth taught once for all by the apostles. Similarly, the author of I John writes, 'Let what you have heard from the beginning abide in you' (2.24), thus claiming that the 'antichrists' who deny the full humanity of Jesus (2.18–23, 4.1–6) have abandoned the gospel as it was taught at first. 'False doctrine' may involve practice as well as belief: I Tim. 4.1–5 attacks those who 'forbid marriage and enjoin abstinence from foods . . .' (see also Rev. 2.6, 14–15, 20–23).

HEROD THE GREAT Recognized as 'King of the Jews' by Rome in 40 BC, Herod eventually gained possession of his kingdom in 37 BC, and reigned until his death in 4 BC. From the Roman point of view he was a faithful and trusted ally, but his non-Jewish antecedents and his brutality (even towards his own family) made him hated by many of his subjects. He was a great builder – among his outstanding achievements were the construction of the harbour at Caesarea and the rebuilding of the temple in Jerusalem.[1] Both Matthew and Luke date Jesus' birth within Herod's lifetime (Matt. 2.1, Luke 1.5). Matthew also blames him for the massacre of the male children of Bethlehem (2.16–18), a story which resembles a Jewish tradition about the Egyptians' slaughter of the Israelites' male children: Pharaoh ordered the Israelite children to be killed because of a prophecy announcing the birth of a child (Moses) who would overthrow him. Herod had ten wives and large numbers of descendants, despite putting to death 15 of his children. Of his surviving children, Archelaus, Herod Antipas, and Philip are mentioned in the New Testament; of his grandchildren, Herod Agrippa I and Herodias.[2]

HEROD ANTIPAS On the death of Herod the Great in 4 BC, the emperor Augustus divided his dominions between three of his sons. Galilee and Peraea were given to Herod (as he is called in the Synoptic Gospels and Acts – elsewhere, Antipas), who ruled from 4 BC till his exile to Gaul in AD 39.[1] Mark 6.14 calls him 'king', but Matthew and Luke give the correct title, 'tetrarch' (Matt. 14.1, Luke 3.1, etc.). He was responsible for the arrest and death of John the Baptist – according to Mark, because John had criticized his marriage to Herodias, the former wife of his half-brother (Mark 6.18). The story of the Baptist's death is well known (Mark 6.14–29). Josephus, however, tells us that the Baptist was arrested and put to death because Antipas feared that his influence over the people would lead to disorder.[2]

There are hints in the Synoptic Gospels of Herod's hostility towards Jesus: the 'Herodians' are among those who plot to put him to death (Mark 3.6), and in Luke 13.31, Jesus is warned (oddly, by Pharisees), 'Get away from here, for Herod wants to kill you'. But when (in Luke only) Jesus appears before Herod at his trial, Luke portrays him in a different light: 'When Herod saw Jesus, he was very glad, for he had long desired to see him, because he had heard about him, and he was hoping to see some sign done by him' (Luke 23.8). Two features of this narrative (Jesus' silence and his mock coronation) are duplicates of incidents elsewhere in the passion narrative.

HEROD AGRIPPA I

Acts 12 mentions a further Herod (Herod the King, 12.1, as opposed to Herod the Tetrarch, 13.1), otherwise known as Agrippa I, the father of the Agrippa who appears in Acts 25–26.[1] Herod Agrippa I was a grandson of Herod the Great and a son of Aristobulus, put to death by his father in 7 BC. He was brought up in Rome, and was a close friend of the future emperor Caligula and of Claudius, whose accession he helped to bring about. Caligula gave him the tetrarchy of Philip on the latter's death in AD 37; in AD 39 he received Galilee when Antipas was banished[2]; and in AD 41, Claudius gave him Judaea and Samaria too, thus restoring his grandfather's kingdom. In Acts 12, he is portrayed as the persecutor of the Church whose arrogance led to a gruesome death at the hands of the angel of the Lord.

HERODIAS

Mark 6.17 states that Herodias married first Philip and then his brother Herod (i.e. Antipas). This gives the impression that her first husband was Philip the Tetrarch (mentioned in Luke 3.1), one of the three sons of Herod the Great among whom his kingdom was divided – the other two being Archelaus and Herod Antipas.[1] In fact, according to Josephus her first husband was a different Herod (another son of Herod the Great). Either this Herod was also known as Philip, or Mark is mistaken. Herodias's successful scheming against John the Baptist is described in Mark 6.19–28.[2] In AD 39, she accompanied her husband into exile in Gaul, after Caligula had arbitrarily given Antipas's tetrarchy to his friend Herod Agrippa.

HIGH PRIESTHOOD

The Jewish high priests held an office which was both political and religious, presiding over the Sanhedrin and carrying out ritual functions in the temple – notably the annual entry into the Holy of Holies on the Day of Atonement. In New Testament times, they were appointed by the Romans (or by pro-Roman kings such as Herod the Great or Agrippa I), often for a very short period. Annas (AD 6–15) and Caiaphas (AD 18–36) were unusual in the length of time they held office. High priests were chosen from a small number of aristocratic families; they were generally Sadducees, but because of the power of the Pharisees often had to perform their ritual functions in the way approved by the latter.[1]

In the Letter to the Hebrews, Christ is seen as 'a great high priest' (4.14).[2] Previous Christian tradition had seen the death of Jesus as a sacrifice; Hebrews adds that he is also the high priest who offers the sacrifice. He is both priest and victim. The high priest's annual entry into the earthly Holy of Holies is contrasted with Jesus' eternal presence in the heavenly Holy of Holies, through which true access to God is at last attained (Heb. 9). The author's purpose is partly to stress Jesus' greatness: he is the ideal high priest, 'holy, blameless, unstained, separated from sinners, exalted above the heavens' (7.26). But he also uses the idea of high priesthood to stress Christ's solidarity with his people. To be a high priest, he had to be like them in every respect, tempted just as they are (2.17–18), and so able to sympathize with their weaknesses (4.15, *see also* 5.1).

HOMOSEXUALITY

In contrast to the tolerance of Greek and Roman culture towards homosexuality, Judaism and early Christianity were unequivocally opposed to it. For both Jews and Christians, the story of the destruction of Sodom in Gen. 19 was a terrible warning of the wrath of God against those who engaged in this practice. Jesus shares the traditional view of Sodom as the embodiment of vice (Matt. 10.14–15, 11.23–24). Jude 7 states that the destruction of 'Sodom and Gomorrah and the surrounding cities', which 'acted immorally and indulged in unnatural lust', is a warning to those who practice 'licentiousness' (v. 5) and who 'defile the flesh' (v. 8). II Peter 2.7–8 says that 'righteous Lot', who lived in Sodom, 'was vexed in his righteous soul day after day with their lawless deeds'. Paul in I Cor. 6.9 states that practising homosexuals, among others, are excluded from the kingdom of God; two Greek words here (misleadingly translated by the single expression, 'sexual perverts' in the Revised Standard Version of the Bible) denote the passive and the active partners respectively. In Rom. 1.26–27, Paul argues that both female and male homosexuality are 'contrary to nature', and a result of the refusal to acknowledge God.[1]

For the early Christians as for Jews, rejection of homosexuality was one of a number of ethical and religious principles demarcating the community of the righteous from the unrighteous world of the Gentiles. Their pagan critics found this exclusive attitude intolerable.

HOPE

Occasionally, 'hope' denotes the object hoped for (e.g. in Col. 1.5, 'the hope laid up for you in heaven'), but more usually it denotes the Christian's subjective attitude of confidence in the fulfilment of God's promises. The gospel proclaims not only events in the past but also events in the future (the return of Christ, the resurrection of the dead, the judgment, eternal life). 'Faith' is generally related to the past (e.g. 'If you . . . believe in your heart that God raised him [Jesus] from the dead . . .', Rom. 10.9), and 'hope' to the future.[1] The word does not occur in the gospels but is to be found mainly in the letters of Paul. In an early letter,

Paul gives a very precise account of the events which are to be hoped for (I Thess. 4.13–17): the Lord's descent from heaven, the archangel's call, the meeting with the Lord in the clouds, and so on. This is intended to comfort the Thessalonians, who are mourning the death of members of their congregation; they are not to grieve 'as others do who have no hope' (v. 13).[2] In later letters, Paul shows much more reticence about the precise content of what is hoped for, while retaining traditional beliefs such as the return of Christ and the resurrection of the dead: 'Hope that is seen is not hope. For who hopes for what he sees? But if we hope for what we do not see, we wait for it with patience' (Rom. 8.24–25). Because what is hoped for is (by definition) unseen, we cannot know its precise nature.

Here and elsewhere, Paul is interested not just in the objective reality of what is hoped for, but in the subjective reality of the person who hopes. Christian hope is a source both of joy, as the glory to come is anticipated (Rom. 5.2), and of sorrow, as it makes one more aware of the present imperfection of the created order, including oneself (Rom. 8.23).[3] 'Hope' is assailed by 'suffering' – that is, by experiences which appear to contradict the idea that God is directing the human story towards a happy ending in which 'all manner of things will be well'. And yet, even suffering can lead ultimately to an increase in hope, as one looks beyond it to the greater reality of the love of God (Rom. 5.3–5). Because like Abraham one must 'hope against hope' (i.e. hope against the evidence of everyday reality, Rom. 4.18), hope is ultimately not a human possibility but the gift of God, made possible 'by the power of the Holy Spirit' (Rom. 15.13).[4]

HUMILITY There is an ambiguity in the Greek word generally translated 'humility' which corresponds to the distinction in English between 'humility' and 'humiliation'. In II Cor. 12.21, Paul expresses his fear that on his next visit to Corinth, he will again be 'humiliated', deprived of self-esteem and esteem in the sight of others. This is something to be feared; it is not a Christian virtue, any more than the exaggerated 'humility' or 'self-abasement' of the ascetics in Col. 2.16–23.[1] As a Christian virtue, 'humility' means 'counting others better than oneself', 'looking not only to one's own interests, but also to the interests of others' (Phil. 2.3–4). This means following the example of Christ, who abandoned his heavenly prerogatives in order to serve others by taking human form and dying on the cross (2.5–8). He exemplifies the general maxim stated in Matt. 23.12, that 'everyone who humbles himself will be exalted' (*see* Phil. 2.9–11).[2] Humility is an aspect of love, which 'does not insist on its own way' (I Cor. 13.5). It is opposed to 'pride', self-assertion at the expense of the needs and rights of others: 'God opposes the proud, but gives grace to the humble' (I Peter. 5.5). It is grounded not just in the example of Christ, but in our dependence on God (5.6).

HYPOCRISY The English word 'hypocrisy' is taken directly from the Greek *hypokrisis*, meaning action which contradicts what one says and claims to believe. Thus, in Gal. 2.13, Jewish Christians are said to have been guilty of hypocrisy because according to Paul their withdrawal from Gentile members of the congregation contradicted their belief that God accepted Gentiles just as he accepted Jews. Matt. 23.3 claims that the Pharisees 'preach, but do not practise', and the phrase, 'Woe to you, scribes and Pharisees, hypocrites!' occurs seven times in this chapter. Matthew's polemic should, of course, not lead one to the historical judgment that all Pharisees were hypocrites.[1] Elsewhere, the idea of hypocrisy is used with some psychological insight. In the teaching about the mote and the beam in Matt. 7.1–5 (see also Rom. 2.1–3), hypocrisy takes the form of condemning others without perceiving one's own guilt. In Matt. 6.1–18, hypocrisy is seen in the hidden conflict between the overt intention of religious practices (to please God) and the actual intention (to impress other people).

IDOLATRY Greek and Roman religion generally involved the use of statues of the gods, and the early Christians took over the Jewish abhorrence for this practice, in accordance with the second commandment: 'You shall not make for yourself a graven image, or any likeness of anything that is in heaven above, or that is in the earth beneath, or that is in the water under the earth; you shall not bow down to them or serve them' (Exod. 20.4–5). Paul in Rom. 1.23 argues that the original sin of the human race, from which all others spring, is that 'they exchanged the glory of the immortal God for images resembling mortal man or birds or animals or reptiles'. In order to serve the 'living and true God', one must therefore 'turn from idols' (I Thess. 1.9). It was an essential part of Christian missionary preaching that 'there is no God but one' and that 'an idol has no real existence' – that is, the statue is just a statue and does not represent any real divine being (I Cor. 8.4). However, in I Cor. 8–10 Paul is opposing Corinthian Christians who argue that the non-existence of the pagan god justifies them in participating in meals in pagan temples for social reasons. Paul here moves away from the idea of the non-existence of the gods represented by the statues, and argues that the statues represent demonic beings. Warned by the fate of Israelites who practised idolatry during the wilderness wanderings (10.6–7), his readers are to 'shun the worship of idols' on the grounds that this would make them 'partners with demons' (10.14,20). Similarly, Rev. 9.20 mentions those who 'worship demons and idols', implying that the statues used in worship represent demonic beings. The Christian Church could not abolish the pagan gods at a stroke; it first had to convert them into real but anti-divine beings.[1]

INCARNATION Classical Christian theology believes that 'God became man', and that Jesus of Nazareth therefore has two 'natures' – divine and human. This 'doctrine of the incarnation' presupposes the 'doctrine of the Trinity': the Second Person of the Trinity was the eternal Son through whom the Father created the world, and it was he who descended from heaven and took human form. These doctrines were derived from the New Testament, and it was the intention of their authors to make explicit the view of God and his action which is implicit throughout the New Testament.

1 *Incarnational Statements in the New Testament* References to the incarnation are to be found primarily in Paul, John and Hebrews.

(*i*) **Pre-existence** The doctrine of the incarnation assumes that the Son of God shared the heavenly life of the Father before he took human form. Referring to this, Paul states that Christ was 'in the form of God' (Phil. 2.6), and that he was 'rich' (II Cor. 8.9).[1] He also implies that Christ was involved in creation: 'one Lord Jesus Christ, through whom are all things and through whom we exist' (I Cor. 8.6).[2] This is made more explicit in Col. 1.16: 'In him all things were created, in heaven and on earth, visible and invisible'. Similarly, Heb. 1.2–3 states that it was the Son 'through whom he [God] also created the world', and continues: 'He reflects the glory of God and bears the very stamp of his nature, upholding the universe by the word of his power'.

Both Paul and the author to the Hebrews are cautious about explicitly calling Christ 'God', although they do believe that he shares the divine nature (*see* Heb. 1.8). John goes one step further: 'the Word' (i.e. the eternal Son) was 'with God' in the beginning and 'was God' (John 1.1). Once again he is seen as the agent of creation: 'All things were made through him, and without him was not anything made' (1.3). In John 17.5, the incarnate Jesus recalls 'the glory which I had with thee before the world was made'.[3]

(*ii*) **Incarnation** Paul states that the divine Christ 'emptied himself, taking the form of a servant, being born in the likeness of men' (Phil. 2.7). Or, to put it another way, 'though he was rich, yet for your sake he became poor' (II Cor. 8.9). God 'sent forth his Son' to be 'born of woman' (Gal. 4.4) and so to take 'the likeness of sinful flesh' (Rom. 8.3). The latter phrase could mean that the flesh or humanity of Jesus was merely *like* 'sinful flesh' but not *really* 'sinful flesh'. However, the similar phrase, 'being born in the *likeness* of men' (Phil. 2.7) does not deny the real humanity of Jesus; and so 'the likeness of sinful flesh' probably implies Jesus' real participation in sinful human nature. For Paul, it is part of the self-humiliation of Christ that he takes not just human form in general but sinful humanity, even though he himself 'knew no sin' (II Cor. 5.21). Hebrews similarly stresses the solidarity between the incarnate Son and the human beings he came to save: 'Since therefore the children share in flesh and blood, he himself likewise partook of the same nature . . . For because he himself has suffered and been tempted, he is able to help those who are tempted' (2.14, 18).

John too states that 'the Word became flesh', but he regards the incarnation not so much as a humiliation for the divine Son, but as the manifestation of his glory: 'We have beheld his glory, glory as of the only Son from the Father' (1.14). Jesus' glory is not manifested only at his resurrection and exaltation (as in Paul and Hebrews) but throughout his earthly life – especially in his miracles (2.11, 11.40). In John, Jesus frequently speaks of himself as divine and as having descended from heaven. He is criticized by the Jews on the grounds that 'you, being a man, make yourself God' (10.33); in calling God his Father, he 'made himself equal with God'

(5.18). He makes statements such as 'I have come down from heaven' (6.38), and 'Before Abraham was, I am' (8.58). But the evangelist also stresses that Jesus did and said everything in obedience to the Father; 6.38 continues, 'I have come down from heaven, not to do my own will, but the will of him who sent me'.

The New Testament shows little or no interest in speculating about the nature of Christ's heavenly existence before his incarnation because its concern is with salvation and not with esoteric knowledge of heavenly mysteries. The claim that he 'came down from heaven' is intended, first, to explain and justify the early Christian belief in Jesus' absolute and ultimate significance. It asserts that Jesus does not belong to the normal course of history, in which no figure, however outstanding, has any more than a relative significance. His origin is heavenly rather than earthly. Secondly, the early Christian belief in the incarnation asserts that the God who reveals himself in Jesus is eternally the same. In Jesus, the early Christians found themselves confronted with God. God had differentiated himself from himself; he was to be known not only as the Father but also as the Son (*see* Matt. 11.27). The grounds for this self-differentiation were then found in an eternal distinction between Father and Son.[4]

Such ideas are of course difficult for the modern mind to understand, let alone to believe. But the difficulty is not a specifically modern one; in New Testament times as well, such ideas seemed hopelessly mythological to most educated people. The doctrine of the incarnation, as well as the proclamation of the crucified Christ, was 'a stumbling block to Jews and folly to Gentiles' (I Cor. 1.23). The Christian counter-claim was that it is precisely this supposed 'folly' which is actually the divine wisdom which judges the supposed wisdom of the world (*see* I Cor. 1.18–25).

2 The Synoptic Gospels and the Incarnation

At first sight it seems that the Synoptic Gospels present us with a quite different picture. In contrast to the Fourth Gospel, Jesus never here claims a divine origin in heaven. His teaching covers a wide range of subjects: the kingdom of God (often spoken of in parables), the law of Moses and the Pharisaic interpretation of it, repentance, prayer, ethical matters, and so on. In John, most of his teaching is concentrated on a single point: his divine origin. It has long been accepted by scholars that the two types of teaching are so different that they cannot both derive from Jesus, and that the Synoptic Gospels rather than John contain the teaching of the historical Jesus.

The conclusion often drawn from this is that there are two very different strands in the New Testament's portrayal of Jesus. In one, he is the divine, incarnate Son of God, who bridges the gulf between God and man. In the other, he is a man and nothing more than a man: a great teacher, a miracle-worker, the long-expected Messiah, but belonging on the human side of the gulf between God and man, however close and unique his own relationship to God may have been. If we take this view, it is then natural to conclude that the second approach brings us closer to Jesus 'as he really was', and that the first approach has confused the issue by understanding him in potentially misleading mythological language. But in fact, the distinction between the two approaches is by no means as clear-cut as this assumes. Even in the Synoptic Gospels, there are elements which appear to point in the direction of a doctrine of incarnation.

Firstly, it is important to remember that the Synoptic Gospels are not theological treatises giving a complete and self-contained account of Jesus' identity. They are essentially narratives, and their view of the significance of Jesus arises only gradually and indirectly from the story they recount. In the course of the narrative, various possible ways of understanding Jesus emerge: he is the second Moses, the Messiah, the fulfilment of prophecy, the Son of man who is to judge the world, and so on. And yet Jesus is presented as transcending each of these categories; none of them adequately resolves the mystery of his identity. The one which comes nearest to doing so is the title, 'Son of God', which occurs at key points in the narrative (e.g. at Jesus' baptism, transfiguration and death [Mark 1.11, 9.7, 15.39]). The Synoptic Gospels never explain what this title really means; but they at least leave open the possibility of the view of Paul and John, that it can only be understood in terms of divinity, pre-existence and incarnation.[5]

Secondly, the Synoptic Gospels (like the other New Testament books)[6] are remarkably unembarrassed about applying to Jesus powers and attributes which are elsewhere seen as divine. He forgives sins, although no-one 'can forgive sins but God alone', as the scribes rightly point out (Mark 2.5–7). Like God, he stills the storm (Mark 4.35–41): 'Thou dost rule the raging of the sea; when its waves rise, thou stillest them' (Ps. 89.9). Like God, he miraculously feeds his people with bread in the wilderness (Mark 6.30–44): 'He rained down upon them manna to eat. . . , he sent them food in abundance' (Ps. 78.24–25). Like God, he walks upon the water (Mark 6.45–52): 'Thy way was through the sea, thy path through the great waters; yet thy footprints were unseen'. In Matt. 28.9, the women worship the risen Jesus and are not rebuked for doing so; yet the New Testament assumes without question that only God is worthy of worship (*see* Rev. 19.10, 22.8–9). In Matt. 28.19, baptism is 'in the name of the Father and of the Son and of the Holy Spirit'.

So the Synoptic Gospels do not present us with a non-divine, purely human Jesus. The Synoptic Jesus is implicitly the divine, incarnate Son of God, and the Fourth Gospel makes this explicit – handling the tradition about Jesus in a very free manner in order to do so. It can, of course, be argued, that historical research can discover a purely human Jesus behind the veil of divinity which the early Christians cast over him,[7] but the Jesus who is recovered in this way is not the Jesus proclaimed by any of the New Testament writers.

INSPIRATION The idea of divine inspiration is not specifically Jewish or Christian. In many religious traditions it is held that God (or a god) speaks through a human agent, using the human being as a mouthpiece. It was familiar to Greek and Roman religion through such institutions as the Delphic oracle, in which the god Apollo was thought to speak through a prophetess in an ecstatic state. Inspiration could extend to books; books of 'Sibylline oracles' were widely circulated, which were thought to be the result of divine dictation. Among the New Testament writings, only the book of Revelations makes a claim to divine inspiration; the seer is told, 'Write what you see in a book . . .', while he is 'in the Spirit' (Rev. 1.10–11). Other writers base their claim to authority not on direct divine inspiration but on apostleship (Gal. 1–2), historical research (Luke 1.1–4), or eyewitness testimony (John 21.24).

Although the New Testament makes few claims about its own inspiration, it does regard the Old Testament, and notably the prophets, as having been inspired. When the author to the Hebrews quotes from Ps. 22, he attributes the words not to the psalmist (traditionally David) but to Christ (2.12, *see also* 10.5–9). A quotation from Ps. 95 begins with the words, 'Therefore as the Holy Spirit says . . .' (Heb. 3.7).[1] Matthew 4.14 speaks of events which took place 'that what was spoken through the prophet Isaiah might be fulfilled', and this suggests that the prophet is regarded as a mouthpiece for the divine word.[2] In addition to these specific quotations, there are also several general statements about the inspiration of Scripture (i.e. the Old Testament): 'No prophecy ever came by the impulse of man, but men moved by the Holy Spirit spoke from God' (II Peter 1.17, *see also* I Peter 1.10–12 and II Tim. 3.16). These statements regard the Old Testament as a divinely given norm binding on all Christians. This is a somewhat different emphasis from that of Paul, for whom Scripture is instructive and a source of encouragement (Rom. 15.4, I Cor. 10.11), but subordinate to the supreme authority of the gospel.

ISRAEL In the New Testament as in the Old, 'Israel' refers not to the land of Palestine, but to the people of God. The term applies to all Jews, not just to those who are resident in Palestine. Even in the phrase, 'the land of Israel' (Matt. 2.20–21), the reference is to the land given to the people of Israel to inhabit.

New Testament writers use 'Israel' in preference to 'the Jews' when they wish to stress the divine privileges bestowed on this community in the past, rather than the empirical reality of the community in its hostility towards the gospel.[1] Luke in particular lays stress on the fact that the Jewish people are 'Israel', the people of God. His Gospel opens with narratives about faithful Jews who 'look for the consolation of Israel' (Luke 2.25) – that is, the coming of the Messiah.[2] After Pentecost the gospel is preached at first exclusively to Israel: 'God exalted him at his right hand as Leader and Saviour, to give repentance to Israel and forgiveness of sins'. Even after the first Gentile conversions it can still be said, 'God has brought to Israel a Saviour, Jesus, as he promised' (Acts 13.23). Paul in his captivity maintains to the last that his only crime is his belief that 'the hope of Israel' is fulfilled in Jesus (28.20). In Acts it is only because of the inexplicable and implacable hostility of the Jews towards the gospel that salvation is extended to the Gentiles instead (13.46–48, 18.6, 19.8–10, 28.25–28).

Paul too wrestles with the problem of Israel – the problem that the chosen people have rejected the salvation sent to them. He develops two rather different solutions.[3] The first is to differentiate between 'Israel according to the flesh' (I Cor. 10.18) and 'the Israel of God' (Gal. 6.16). 'Israel', correctly understood, refers not to the Jewish people but to true Christians: 'Not all who are descended from Israel belong to Israel'; and so 'the word of God' – his promise of salvation to Israel – has not 'failed' as the result of Jewish unbelief (Rom. 9.6). The second solution is to accept that the Jewish people remain 'Israel', God's chosen people, and to argue that their exclusion from salvation is only a temporary measure to facilitate the salvation of the Gentiles (Rom. 11). In the end, 'all Israel will be saved' (v. 26) because they are still 'beloved for the sake of their forefathers', Abraham, Isaac and Jacob, even in their present hostility towards the gospel (v. 28).

JAMES Four men are named 'James' in the New Testament, two of whom are unimportant and will be dealt with first. Luke's two lists of disciples (Luke 6.14–16 and Acts 1.13) name a certain 'Judas son of James' as one of the twelve (*see also* John 14.22, 'Judas [not Iscariot]'). These lists and the others in Matt. 10.2–4 and Mark 3.16–19 also mention 'James the son of Alphaeus', presumably the brother of 'Levi the son of Alphaeus' (Mark 2.14), who becomes 'Matthew' in Matt. 9.9, no doubt to make him one of the twelve.[1] It is probably this James who is referred to in Mark 15.40 as 'James the Less', no doubt to contrast him with the better known James the son of Zebedee. It is strange that his mother, Mary, is here said to have been 'the mother of James the Less and of Joses' (*see also* 15.47, 16.1) because Mary the mother of Jesus also had sons called James and Joses (6.3); yet Mark does not seem to be referring to Jesus' mother in 15.40. There is evidence elsewhere in the Gospels of confusion over the names of Jesus' first followers.[2] However, only two of the men named James are of any real importance: James the son of Zebedee and James the brother of Jesus.

1 James the Son of Zebedee[3] In two of the lists of the twelve, James appears second after Simon Peter, followed by his brother John (Mark 3.16–19, Acts 1.13); in the other two his place has been taken by Andrew, whom it was natural to link with his brother Simon Peter (Matt. 10.2–4, Luke 6.14–16). James is three times linked with Simon Peter and John as members of the 'inner circle' of the twelve – at the raising of Jairus' daughter (Mark 5.37), at the transfiguration (9.2), and in Gethsemane (14.33). On three occasions, these three are joined by Andrew (1.16–20, 29, 13.3). The tradition clearly presents James as second in importance only to Peter. But he and his brother John are rebuked by Jesus on two occasions: their request for the positions of authority in the kingdom of God (10.35–41), and their desire to call down fire on the Samaritan villages (Luke 9.54). Despite his prominent position in the Synoptic Gospels, James is surprisingly not mentioned in the early chapters of Acts, where it is Peter and John who are singled out (3.1–4,11, 4.13,19, 8.14). His martyrdom at the hands of Herod Agrippa I (between AD 41 and 44) is mentioned in Acts 12.2.

2 James the Brother of Jesus[4] James is mentioned in the gospels only in Mark 6.3 (Matt. 13.55), where the inhabitants of Nazareth say: 'Is not this the carpenter, the son of Mary and brother of James and Joses and Judas and Simon, and are not his sisters here with us?' The Gospels present Jesus' family as failing to believe in him during his earthly life; Mary and his brothers try to persuade him to abandon his ministry in Mark 3.21,31–35, and John 7.5 comments, 'Even his brothers did not believe in him'. Yet I Cor. 15.7 mentions an appearance of the risen Lord to James, and I Cor. 9.5 speaks of 'the brothers of the Lord' engaging in missionary work alongside the apostles, accompanied by their wives. Acts 1.14 mentions the presence of Mary and Jesus' brothers together with the disciples after the Ascension. If it is legitimate to combine these scattered references into a single picture, it would seem that Jesus' family came to faith in him only after the resurrection.

James became the leader of the Church of Jerusalem. It is likely that he was resident there and that the twelve apostles were generally engaged in missionary work elsewhere; when Paul paid his first visit to Jerusalem after his conversion, James was there but the apostles (with the exception of Peter) were not (Gal. 1.18–19). While describing a second visit, Paul mentions that James, Peter and John were generally known as 'pillars', presumably because the leadership of the whole church was entrusted to them (Gal. 2.9). James is here named first in preference to Peter, and the authority he exercised even over Peter is demonstrated in the following narrative (Gal. 2.11–14), in which 'men from James' persuade Peter to abandon his earlier practice of eating with Gentiles. Although Paul here does not explicitly condemn James, it is clear that he is regarded as the ultimate cause of the trouble. Paul thinks that James has perverted the truth of the gospel by his negative attitude towards Gentiles, and refers sarcastically to him and the other leaders as 'those who were reputed to be something', adding, 'What they were makes no difference to me; God shows no partiality' (Gal. 2.6).[5]

Acts likewise refers to James as the leader of the Church of Jerusalem. His first appearance is in 12.17, where Peter requests that James be informed of his miraculous release from prison. In the conference about the acceptance of Gentiles into the Church in Acts 15, it is James who makes the final decision, imposing certain dietary requirements on Gentile converts. In 15.22–31 (see also 16.4) Paul himself becomes one of the 'men from James' entrusted with putting this decree into effect.[6] When Paul returns to Jerusalem for the last time, James is still in control (21.18). Here and elsewhere, he is seen as the representative of a conservative Jewish piety which remains loyal to the traditional understanding of the law. This is confirmed by Josephus, who tells of the Pharisees' indignation when James was put to death in about AD 62.

JAMES, LETTER OF

JAMES, LETTER OF Like some of the other non-Pauline letters in the New Testament, the 'Letter of James' is in fact closer to a sermon than to a letter. Only in 1.1 is it indicated that we are intended to regard this work as a letter; here, following the conventional formula for opening a letter, James sends greetings to 'the twelve tribes of the dispersion'.

1 Authorship and Date Although James describes himself simply as 'a servant of God and of the Lord Jesus Christ' (1.1), it is probable that James the brother of Jesus is meant because he was the most prominent figure with this name in the early Church. The apparent opposition to Paul's doctrine of justification by faith and not works in 2.14–26 also suggests James the brother of Jesus because he did indeed oppose Paul (Gal. 2.11–14).[1] However, it is by no means certain that the author really is James, it being common practice in the early Church to compose works under the names of the great figures of the past. There is no mention of the Jew–Gentile problem which was at the heart of James's controversy with Paul, and the author is familiar with the Old Testament in its Greek rather than its Hebrew form. The address to 'the twelve tribes of the Dispersion' (i.e. all Jews not resident in Palestine) is too broad to be credible. The 'Letter of James' was perhaps originally a sermon dating from about the last quarter of the first century.

2 Teaching The Letter of James is almost entirely composed of instructions about Christian conduct.

(*i*) **Christian themes** Of all the New Testament writings, James is the one with the fewest specifically Christian themes. The 'Lord Jesus Christ' is referred to in 1.1 and 2.1, but elsewhere 'Lord' seems to refer not to Jesus (as almost always elsewhere in the New Testament) but to God (1.5–8, 3.9, 4.6–10,15, 5.4–11). In the famous attack on 'justification by faith' in 2.14–26, 'faith' is not Paul's 'faith in Jesus Christ' but 'believing that God is one' (v. 19). Although the author shows an acquaintance with the teachings of Jesus (e.g. 5.12) and perhaps other New Testament writings, there is little in his work with which a non-Christian Jew would disagree. The Old Testament provides both the content of the ethical and religious teaching, and the examples to support it (Abraham, Rahab, Job and Elijah). Here, the strong element of continuity between Judaism and early Christianity is apparent.

(*ii*) **Hearing and Doing** The author is bitterly opposed to a form of religion which has no impact on human conduct, and this leads him to a remarkably humanistic definition of true religion: 'Religion that is pure and undefiled before God is this – to visit orphans and widows in their affliction, and to keep oneself unstained from the world' (1.27). In typically Jewish fashion, 'wisdom' is a matter more of conduct than of intellectual ability (3.13–18). The notion of a faith which does not issue in social justice is strongly opposed (2.14–26). Here, the author seems to be consciously opposing Paul. Firstly, the faith-works contrast is a distinctively Pauline idea. Secondly, the author's claim that Abraham was justified by works seems to be directed against Paul's claim that Abraham was justified by faith (Gal. 3, Rom. 4) as the author even cites Paul's favourite text, Gen. 15.6 ('Abraham believed God, and it was reckoned to him as righteousness', v. 23). Thirdly, the statement, 'A man is justified by works and not by faith alone' (v. 24) seems to be formulated in opposition to Paul's 'A man is justified by faith apart from works of law' (Rom. 3.28). However, the author has understood Paul's opposition to 'works' as an opposition to ethical action in general, whereas all Paul really opposes is the idea that one has to become a Jew and adopt the Jewish way of life in order to be a Christian.[2]

(*iii*) **Social Justice** The author's social concern is unmatched elsewhere in the New Testament.[3] He is violently hostile towards the rich: 'Behold, the wages of the labourers who have mowed your fields, which you kept back by fraud, cry out . . . You have lived on the earth in luxury and pleasure . . . You have condemned, you have killed the righteous man . . .' (5.4–6). The author is especially concerned that social divisions between rich and poor should be allowed no place in the

Church's worship (2.1–7). If the rich man is given a place of honour, and the poor man is treated with contempt, then this directly contradicts the will of God, who has 'chosen the poor in the world' to be 'heirs of the kingdom which he has promised to those who love him' (v. 6). The rich should 'weep and howl for the miseries that are coming upon you' (5.1).

JERUSALEM[1] During the reign of Herod the Great (37 BC – 4 BC), Jerusalem was transformed architecturally. The king's greatest achievement was the rebuilding of the temple, but there were others as well: the Antonia fortress next to the temple, the royal palace, a theatre and a hippodrome, the magnificent towers named after members of his family. Thus the king attempted to give outward expression to the central significance of Jerusalem for all Jews. Despite the pervasive influence of Greek culture, Jewish religious scruples were on the whole respected. During the period of the procurators, Roman military insignia which in Jewish eyes transgressed the second commandment were prohibited from entering the city. The procurator's main residence was at Caesarea, on the coast, and he normally visited Jerusalem only at the time of the feasts, when the vast influx of pilgrims made trouble likely.[2]

The New Testament frequently reflects the Jewish view of Jerusalem. Matthew's temptation narrative refers to it as 'the holy city' (4.5); the Sermon on the Mount speaks of it as 'the city of the great King' (5.35). Elsewhere, however, New Testament writers reinterpret and sometimes reject the Jewish view of Jerusalem.

1 Luke–Acts Luke adopts a generally positive view of Jerusalem. Jesus is presented as the one who will fulfil the hope for 'the redemption of Jerusalem' (2.38). Jerusalem, rather than Galilee (as in Mark), is the site of the appearances of the risen Lord, and it is also the birthplace of the Christian church and its mission.[3] Jerusalem plays a pivotal role in the simple geographical scheme which underlies Luke's two-volume work: he tells of the progress of the gospel from Galilee to Jerusalem (Luke) and from Jerusalem to Rome (Acts). A darker side is also apparent: Jerusalem is the murderer of the prophets (Luke 13.34), and the evangelist is aware of its own catastrophic destruction in AD 70 (Luke 19.41–44, 21.20–24). And yet, the time of Gentile rule over Jerusalem is limited (21.24); Jerusalem will be redeemed in due course.

2 Paul The main significance of Jerusalem for Paul is that it is the centre of Jewish Christianity, under the leadership of James. His quarrel with Jewish Christians about his acceptance of Gentiles into the Church without submission to the law led him to take a fairly negative view of Jerusalem itself. He visited it as infrequently as possible (Gal. 1–2), and contrasts 'the present Jerusalem' which is 'in slavery with her children' with 'the Jerusalem above' which is 'free' and 'our mother' (Gal. 4.25–26).[4] Gentile Christians' freedom from the Jewish way of life inevitably means that Jerusalem loses its sacred significance. However, when organizing his collection for the poor Christians of Jerusalem, Paul is more positive, arguing that Gentile Christians are indebted to the Jerusalem church (Rom. 15.27).[5]

3 John In the Gospel of John Jerusalem is the main stage for Jesus' public proclamation. His saying: 'A prophet has no honour in his own country', is applied in John 4.44 not to Nazareth (as in the Synoptic Gospels) but to Jerusalem and Judaea: Jerusalem is the proper place of his manifestation. In John 7.3–4, Jesus' brothers contrast the secrecy and obscurity of Galilee with the publicity to be obtained in Jerusalem. Yet Jerusalem is a place of rejection as well as of manifestation. In John's view the statement 'He came to his own home, and his own people received him not' (1.11) is fulfilled at Jerusalem.

JESUS

JESUS The sole subject of the New Testament is Jesus. Its writers speak of him in many and varied ways, but they hardly ever speak of anything apart from him. Of course, it is also true that the subject of the New Testament is God; and yet, God is not spoken of apart from Jesus. The New Testament does not contain general discourses about God – for example, about how we can prove his existence and his will from the created order and from the moral law – because God is always seen as the God and Father of Jesus Christ. He is also the God of the Old Testament, 'the God of Abraham, Isaac and Jacob', but the Old Testament revelation of God is understood as preparatory to, and included within, his supreme and absolute self-manifestation in Jesus. The claim of John 1.18 ('No-one has ever seen God; the only-begotten Son . . . has made him known') summarizes the view of the New Testament as a whole.

1 The Problem of 'the Historical Jesus' The great problem posed by the New Testament is that it ascribes absolute theological significance to a historical figure. Everywhere – including the Synoptic Gospels – Jesus is viewed from the standpoint of Christian faith, which sees him as unique and irreplaceable, the one eternally appointed by God as the Saviour of the human race. This uniqueness is expressed in stories of miracles: his virgin birth, his own works of power in the physical and natural realms, his resurrection and ascension. Yet it is commonly held that historical study undermines all this.[1] In this view, Jesus is understood as belonging to a specific context in first century Jewish history. He may be unique, but if so this uniqueness is relative and not absolute. More or less plausible explanations can be given of the origins of stories of miracles, which do not require any real miraculous events. The New Testament may be seen as transforming an ordinary man (although no doubt a very great one) into a divine being. The task of historical research is then perceived as the opposite: the recovery of the historical human being from the distortions of Christian dogma that have for so long hindered a real understanding of him. Thus, a split occurs between 'the historical Jesus' and the New Testament's witness to him. Whether or not one regards this position as legitimate, it has profoundly influenced the study of the New Testament for over 200 years and must be taken seriously.

Some people have responded to this situation by welcoming the separation of the message of Jesus from the message of the early Church about Jesus. Jesus, it is said, preached a message about a loving and forgiving God who was to be acknowledged as 'Father' and who established his rule in the hearts of individuals. Doctrines such as the virgin birth, the atonement and the resurrection were foreign to his own preaching, and, so the argument goes, we too must abandon the unnecessary and misleading complications introduced by the early Christians, and recapture the simple yet profound message of Jesus. Others have pointed out that this would make it impossible to ascribe any absolute significance to Jesus, for his teaching about God is by no means wholly original. In addition, some have doubted whether Jesus' own message is really so congenial; did he not apparently believe that the world would shortly come to a catastrophic end?

To those accustomed to the historical study of the New Testament, it has sometimes seemed as though attempts to defend the New Testament's claim about Jesus are fighting a desperate but futile rearguard action. Historical study, it is claimed, inevitably relativizes even the most deeply-rooted and sincerely-held claims to uniqueness and absoluteness. But in fact, the consistently historical approach has not been without problems of its own.

(i) The so-called 'quest for the historical Jesus' has made its main aim the separation of authentic material about Jesus from the reflections of the early church. Although this procedure is often helpful,[2] it can never be carried out entirely satisfactorily. In practice, it is often difficult to know where one ends and the other begins. In addition, early Christian reflections about Jesus may be profoundly true, and should not be too quickly dismissed.[3] A historical figure cannot be separated completely from the impact he made on his contemporaries.

(ii) The 'consistently historical approach' is in danger of becoming a circular argument. If it takes as its starting-point the presupposition that nothing of absolute and universal significance can occur within history, then it is not surprising if it rejects the New Testament's claim about Jesus. This approach ensures that the conclusion has been dictated by the starting-point instead of springing from a genuinely scientific consideration of the material. Many modern advocates of a historical approach to the New Testament would therefore adopt a more cautious standpoint. Historical study is essentially neutral; it cannot prove or disprove the New Testament's claim about the absolute and universal significance of Jesus, although it can help to clarify the nature of that claim. The historical approach is not the only legitimate one; theological questions may still appropriately be asked.

2 Jesus as a Historical Figure It is axiomatic in New Testament scholarship that it is impossible to write a fully-fledged biography of Jesus, because the evangelists do not provide us with much of the information generally regarded as indispensable – for example, a careful chronology of the subject's life and statements about his motives and intentions. Nevertheless, this should not lead us to the sceptical conclusion that the historical Jesus must remain completely unknown because many of the main characteristics of his life and teaching are reasonably clear.

(i) **Birth and Upbringing** The accounts of the birth of Jesus in Matthew and Luke conflict with one another,[4] and it is difficult to know how much historical information they preserve. What is certain is that Jesus was brought up at Nazareth, in Galilee in the north, that he was the eldest child of a large family, and that he became a carpenter (Mark 6.3).[5] There is no reason to doubt that he was brought up in the sphere of normal popular Jewish piety (see Luke 2.41). Although he is sometimes addressed as 'rabbi', his teaching does not suggest that he had ever received any formal training beyond an elementary education.

(*ii*) **The Impact of John the Baptist** The Synoptic Gospels are agreed that Jesus submitted to baptism by John the Baptist, and this is certain to be historically true because the early Christians would not have manufactured such a potentially embarrassing claim[6]; John's baptism was a sign of repentance in the light of the imminent arrival of God's judgment.[7] The Synoptic Gospels also claim that it was on the occasion of his baptism that Jesus became aware of his messianic vocation, through the descent of the Spirit and the divine voice.

(*iii*) **Jesus' Public Ministry** Although it has traditionally been believed that Jesus' public ministry lasted three years, this view is based on a mistaken reading of chronological information derived from the Gospel of John, and can be discounted.[8] It is possible that the ministry was much shorter – a matter of months rather than of years – but the depth of Jesus' impact makes this unlikely. Geographical information in the Gospels is scanty, but it seems that the main scene of Jesus' activity was the area of Galilee around the Sea of Galilee.[9] He is never said to have visited the two main cities of the region, Tiberias and Sepphoris. Unlike John the Baptist, baptism was no part of his message. Although individual miracle stories may be legendary, there can be no doubt that during his lifetime Jesus achieved fame as a healer and exorcist.[10] It is equally certain that the choice of twelve disciples is genuinely historical because the early Church would never have included Judas Iscariot in the twelve if the historical facts had not required it. According to the Gospels, they shared in Jesus' activity and were the main recipients of his teaching, and there is no reason to doubt this presentation.

(*iv*) **The Kingdom of God**[11] At the heart of Jesus' teaching was his proclamation of the kingdom of God. God's 'kingdom' or 'reign' refers to his destruction of the evils which at present defile his creation, and his establishment of his own direct rule over his world. Jesus saw the kingdom already dawning in his own ministry: 'If it is by the finger of God that I cast out demons, then the kingdom of God has come upon you' (Luke 11.20). Yet the full realization of the kingdom remains future, and so Jesus teaches his disciples to pray, 'Thy kingdom come' (Luke 11.2). He seems to have refrained from the detailed accounts of the time and manner of the kingdom's coming that some of his contemporaries engaged in (Luke 17.20–21).

(*v*) **The Pharisees and the Sinners**[12] Jesus saw the presence of the kingdom of God in the response of 'tax collectors and sinners' to his message. He was notorious among the community's religious leaders for his positive attitude towards these social outcasts, and a number of his parables attempt to vindicate his behaviour in this respect. He was as critical of his opponents as they were of him. Above all, he was critical of the attitude towards God which held that the complex traditional interpretation of the law was the definitive statement of his will. Jesus' sense of the immediacy of God led him to disregard traditional views on religious duties such as fasting and observing the Sabbath.[13]

(*vi*) **The Arrest, Trial and Death of Jesus**[14] According to Josephus, John the Baptist was put to death by Herod Antipas because his preaching of the imminent judgment of God and the overthrow of the old order was regarded as potentially politically destabilizing. We know of other comparable figures who met with a similar fate. Jesus too preached about the imminent coming of the kingdom of God, and such a message would be particularly unwelcome in the volatile mood of Jerusalem at Passover time. The expulsion of the traders from the temple – whatever its purpose – would seem like a highly provocative gesture.[15] It was probably the political concern for stability, rather than any religious accusations, that led the Jewish leaders to arrest Jesus and to hand him over to the Romans. Because it was in the interests of both the Jewish leaders and of the Romans to preserve political stability, the view that the Jews virtually forced a reluctant Pilate to crucify Jesus has probably been exaggerated for polemical reasons.

JEWS On a few occasions in the New Testament, being a Jew is something to be proud of: 'What advantage has the Jew? . . . Much in every way!', for 'the Jews are entrusted with the oracles of God' (Rom. 3.1–2). Thus, the message of salvation is offered 'to the Jew first and also to the Greek' (1.16). Paul's opponents at Corinth, and Paul himself, regarded the fact that they were Jews ('Hebrews') as something to boast of (II Cor. 11.22). In Rom. 2.28–29 being a Jew is still regarded as a privilege but it is reinterpreted: 'He is not a real Jew who is one outwardly . . . He is a Jew who is one inwardly' (2.28–29). Even Gentiles who obey God can be 'Jews' in this sense.

Generally, however, the New Testament writers refer to 'Israel' when they have in mind the privileges of the chosen people, and 'the Jews' when they have in mind their present rejection of the gospel.[1] In Acts, it is usually Jews who are responsible for the opposition that Paul encounters in city after city, often stirring up the Gentiles against him. On one occasion, Paul bitterly attacks 'the Jews, who killed both the Lord Jesus and the prophets, and drove us out, and displease God and oppose all men by hindering us from speaking to the Gentiles that they may be saved' (I Thess. 2.15–16). In John, it is 'the Jews' as a whole who reject Jesus' claim (6.41) and who seek to kill him (7.1); they are the representatives of the hostile world which 'knew him not' (1.10). In Matthew, too, it is the whole Jewish people who are responsible for the death of Jesus. Pilate washes his hands as a sign of his innocence, and 'all the people' cry out, 'His blood be on us and on our children!' (Matt. 27.24–25).

Is the New Testament anti-Semitic? Anti-Semitism as practised by the Nazis was based solely on race, and there is no trace of this in the New Testament. New Testament writers are opposed to Jews on purely religious grounds, in the same way that both they and the Jews themselves were opposed to paganism. However, there is sometimes a depth of bitterness in statements about Jews which is missing from the attacks on paganism, and which clearly derives from the general Jewish rejection of the Christian gospel. In particular, the idea that the Jews were collectively responsible for the crucifixion was to have fateful consequences.[2]

JOHN[1] In the Synoptic Gospels, the apostle John is seen as a member of the 'inner circle' of the twelve, alongside his brother, James, and Peter (Mark 5.37, 9.2, 14.33; they are joined by Andrew in 1.16–20,29, 13.3). Only in Mark 9.38 does he make an independent appearance, informing Jesus that 'we saw a man casting out demons in your name, and we forbade him, because he was not following us'. Jesus' reply is summed up in the saying, 'He that is not against us is for us' (v. 40), and the incident is obviously intended to oppose the narrow exclusiveness into which Christians could so easily fall. Matthew and Luke omit this story, and Matt. 12.30 reverses the meaning of Jesus' saying. John and James are mentioned together on two occasions: their request (or, according to Matthew, their mother's) to be given the highest positions in the kingdom of God (Mark 10.35–41), and their desire to call down fire from heaven upon the Samaritan villages (Luke 9.52–56). These incidents, together with the mysterious nickname 'Boanerges' ('that is, sons of thunder') which Jesus gave them (Mark 3.17), have led some to suppose that the two brothers were temperamentally ambitious, domineering and impetuous. Yet the early Christians were not interested in the psychology of the disciples, and in these narratives John and James merely act as spokesmen for tendencies that need to be opposed: the tendency towards exclusiveness, the quest for status and the desire for vengeance on unbelievers. In any case, whatever the Aramaic phrase underlying 'Boanerges' may have meant, it does not seem to have been 'sons of thunder'.

John, rather than James, is linked with Peter on several occasions in the early chapters of Acts: the healing of a lame man in the temple (chapter 3), their arrest and trial before the Sanhedrin and subsequent release (chapter 4), and their journey to Samaria to impart the gift of the Holy Spirit to the converts there (chapter 8).[2] But it is Peter who plays the leading role, and John is given no independent significance. However, his prominent position in the Jerusalem church is confirmed by Paul in Gal. 2.9, where he is one of the three 'pillars', together with Peter (Cephas) and James (Jesus' brother).

The authorship of five New Testament books has traditionally been ascribed to John: Revelation, the Gospel of John, and the three Letters of John.[3] However, only one of these writings (Revelation) claims to have been written by 'John' (Rev. 1.9, 22.8), and it is doubtful whether he is to be identified with the apostle John.

JOHN, GOSPEL ACCORDING TO
The Fourth Gospel was perhaps the most influential of all the books of the New Testament in the early centuries of the history of the Church. The doctrines of the Incarnation and the Trinity, which were among the main areas of theological controversy during this period, were derived mainly from the Gospel of John.[1] Since the early nineteenth century the focus of attention has shifted more to the Synoptic Gospels because it has been recognized that they bring us closer to the historical Jesus than John does.

1 Authorship Tradition dating back to the second century ascribes the authorship of the Fourth Gospel to the apostle John (hence its traditional title). This, however, has been disputed by modern scholarship.

(i) John and the Beloved Disciple After describing an encounter between Jesus, Peter and the unnamed 'disciple whom Jesus loved', John 21 tells us: 'This is the disciple who is bearing witness to these things, and who has written these things, and we know that his testimony is true' (v. 24). John himself is only once indirectly alluded to in the Fourth Gospel: in 21.2, 'the sons of Zebedee' are among the six disciples for whom the risen Lord cooks breakfast on the beach after a night's fishing. There is nothing in the Gospel which directly supports the unanimous second century identification of 'the disciple whom Jesus loved' with the apostle John; but it is still possible to guess how this identification might have arisen. Second century Christians were interested in the question of authorship because it had a considerable bearing on the authority of the work in question, and so there would naturally have been a desire to identify the unnamed figure who is said to have written the Fourth Gospel. Because the author is referred to as 'the disciple whom Jesus loved', he might be expected to belong to the 'inner circle' of Jesus' disciples, consisting of Peter, James and John, mentioned in the Synoptic Gospels. Peter is repeatedly differentiated from the beloved disciple and James died early (Acts 12.2), thus leaving John as the author. Yet if one concludes that it is mistaken to try to harmonize the Fourth Gospel with the Synoptics, then this identification becomes questionable.

(*ii*) **The Fourth Gospel and the Beloved Disciple** The assertion in 21.24 that the beloved disciple is the author of the Gospel is confusing, because the statement 'We know that his testimony is true' differentiates the author (and the community for which he is writing) from the beloved disciple. There are a large number of works dating from the second century onwards which claim to have had apostles as their authors. For example, the so-called Gospel of Thomas opens, 'These are the secret words which Jesus the Living spoke and which Didymus Judas Thomas wrote'.[2] Thomas is seen as the disciple with the closest relationship to Jesus, and the community in which this Gospel was written thus claims that it alone possesses the authentic tradition about Jesus. It is possible that the same motivation underlies the Fourth Gospel.

It is striking that wherever the beloved disciple is mentioned he is seen as superior to Peter. At the Last Supper, he rather than Peter is in the place of honour (13.23–25). Whereas Peter denies Jesus, the beloved disciple is faithful to the end and is entrusted with the care of Jesus' mother (19.25–27). When Peter and the beloved disciple run to the empty tomb, it is the latter who is the first to believe in the resurrection (20.1–10). It is the beloved disciple and not Peter who recognizes the risen Jesus at the lakeside (21.7), and even when Peter is commanded, 'Feed my lambs', there is still a hint of a special relationship between Jesus and the beloved disciple from which Peter is excluded (21.15–23). In the Synoptic Gospels, Peter is seen as the chief of the apostles; in the Fourth Gospel, the beloved disciple has supplanted him. The most likely explanation is that the community in which the Gospel was written are claiming access to a special insight of the person of Jesus denied to other Christians.

(*iii*) **The Evolution of the Fourth Gospel** In the case of the Synoptic Gospels, it is misleading to regard them as the work solely of individual authors. The evangelists mark the end of a long process of development in the traditions about Jesus, which took both oral and written forms. Although the Fourth Gospel has traditionally been regarded as the work of a single author, the same is probably true here as well: the Gospel has evolved, and evidence of this is to be found at a number of points. For example, after the healing of an official's son the comment is made, 'This was now the second sign that Jesus did when he had come from Judaea to Galilee' (4.54).[3] The first sign is the changing of water into wine at

Cana, which immediately followed Jesus' arrival in Galilee from Judaea (2.11), and 4.54 suggests that in an earlier form of the Gospel the two miracles followed one another closely. In the final form of the Gospel, however, they are separated by extra material involving activity in Judaea and a journey to Galilee (2.13–4.45), during which further 'signs' are mentioned (2.23, *see* 4.45). Another example occurs in 14.31, where the words, 'Rise, let us go hence' are obviously intended to mark the transition from the Last Supper discourses to the account of Jesus' arrest. In the present form of the Gospel, however, three extra chapters of discourse and prayer have been added before Jesus and his disciples leave the upper room (*see* 18.1).

2 John and the Synoptic Gospels The Fourth Gospel has a certain amount of material in common with the Synoptics. Nevertheless, the difference in present-ation between John and the Synoptics is obvious even to the most casual reader. In the Synoptics, Jesus visits Jerusalem only at the end of his ministry, whereas in John he is there repeatedly (John 2–3, 5, 7–10, 12–19). In John, his preaching both in Jerusalem and in Galilee (John 6) is about one thing only: his own unique relationship with the Father. He claims to have descended from heaven: 'I have come down from heaven not to do my own will but the will of him who sent me' (6.38). This sets him apart from his hearers: 'You are from below, I am from above; you are of this world, I am not of this world' (8.23). His words and works are the words and works of the Father (7.16, 5.19), and in a sense he is equal to the Father (5.18) and makes himself God (10.33): 'I and the Father are one' (10.30). Hence, the Jews constantly try to stone him for blasphemy (5.18, 8.59, 10.31). The proclamation of Jesus in the Fourth Gospel presents us with a stark choice: either Jesus is a blasphemer, perhaps possessed by a demon (7.20, 8.48, 52), or his claim is true and he is indeed the Son of God, God come down to earth in human form.

In the Synoptics, Jesus makes no such claims. He proclaims the kingdom of God, and, although this may be related to his own person, there is no hint that he is aware of a previous existence in heaven followed by a descent to earth. Indeed, Jesus has very little to say specifically about himself; there is an indirectness in his teaching which is entirely lacking in John. He speaks in parables, gives ethical instruction, and engages in controversy, but never makes the exalted claims we find in John. It is sometimes argued that because John concentrates on Jesus' Jerusalem ministry and the Synoptics on Galilee, the difference is explicable: Jesus spoke differently in the two contexts. Yet this argument collapses when one observes that in John Jesus makes the same claims in Galilee (John 6) as in Jerusalem. The only real explanation is that the evangelist ascribes his own theological ideas to Jesus.

The fact that John is in one sense less reliable historically than the Synoptic Gospels does nothing to diminish its value or interest. It is sometimes said that the function of John is to make explicit what is only implicit in the Synoptic Gospels, and there is some truth in this claim.[4] For example, the Synoptic Gospels portray Jesus' activity as confined almost entirely to the Jews; he is 'sent only to the lost sheep of the house of Israel' (Matt. 15.24). Yet the early Church eventually came to believe that his activity was for the salvation of the world, and not just Israel. When the Fourth Evangelist places in Jesus' mouth the words, 'I did not come to judge the world but to save the world' (12.47), he is making explicit the significance of Jesus as the early Church had come to perceive it. Precisely because it is not historical in a literal sense, the Fourth Gospel articulates the Christian consciousness of the significance of Jesus with extraordinary clarity. Whether its claim is true or not is a matter for faith, not historical research.

3 Theological Themes Paul and the Fourth Evangelist (who is still generally referred to as 'John', for convenience) are often rightly seen as the most considerable theologians represented in the New Testament. John's remarkably coherent theological structure is built on a few simple yet profound ideas, which occur again and again in a variety of forms.

(*i*) **Dualism** John's thought is based on opposites: light and darkness, truth and falsehood, above and below, life and death, knowledge and ignorance, spirit and flesh, heaven and earth.[5] There are two realms, and they are separated from each other. One is heaven, the realm of God; here he has dwelt with his Son from all eternity, and here light, truth and life are to be found. The other is the world, the realm of the human race. The world was made by the Father through the Son, and yet it has fallen away from him and succumbed to the power of Satan, 'the ruler of this world' (12.31, 14.30, 16.11), who personifies the world's darkness, falsehood and death. The problem is, therefore, that the human race is now cut off from the light, truth and life which are to be found only in the heavenly world. For this reason, the Son of God descends from heaven to earth, takes human form, and brings light, truth and life to those who believe in him. Indeed, he himself *is* 'the light of the world' (8.12), 'the way, the truth and the life' (14.6).

(*ii*) **The Knowledge of God**[6] John's portrayal of Jesus is dominated by the theme of descent and ascent: 'I came from the Father and have come into the world; again, I am leaving the world and going to the Father' (16.28). Because he comes from heaven, he alone knows and reveals the Father: 'No-one has ever seen God; the only Son, who is in the bosom of the Father, he has made him known' (1.18, *see also* 3.11–13, 6.46). If God is to be known, he can be known only in Jesus; in response to Philip's request, 'Show us the Father and we shall be satisfied', Jesus says, 'He who has seen me has seen the Father' (John 14.8–9).

The evangelist is apparently reinterpreting a widespread myth (found in Plato and elsewhere) about the origins of the soul. In the myth, the soul originated in the heavenly world, where it possessed knowledge of the heavenly realities, but fell into the material world and became imprisoned in the material body. Yet because of the soul's heavenly origin, it is still possible to free oneself from the encumbrances of the material world and ascend to the world to which one truly belongs. Here, the knowledge of God is inherent in human nature. It is just this which is denied in John's application of the descent–ascent pattern exclusively to Jesus. He alone originally dwelt in heaven and knew God; he alone descended from there, and – because he belonged by nature to the world above – was able to return there. There is nothing in human nature which enables people to know God, and it is only Jesus who can enable them to do so, and to ascend with him: 'I am the way . . .' (14.6, *see* 13.36, 17.24).

(*iii*) **The Presence of the Age to Come** The earliest Christian thought was dominated by the idea of the return of Christ in the near future. The Son of man would descend from heaven, granting eternal life to those who had believed in him and judging and condemning the rest. According to the Fourth Gospel, all this has already happened. 'The Son of man' has already 'descended from heaven' (3.13). Eternal life is available now: 'Truly, truly I say to you, he who hears my word and believes him who sent me, *has* eternal life' (5.24). Judgment also takes place now: 'the judgment' consists in the fact that 'the light has come into the world, and men loved darkness rather than light, because their deeds were evil' (3.19). People pass judgment on themselves by refusing to come to the light, which would expose their evil deeds (3.20), and they are thus condemned to live in darkness.

Despite the fact that the events expected to accompany Jesus' second coming are applied by the evangelist to the past, Jesus is still able to say, 'I will come again' (14.3), 'I will not leave you desolate, I will come to you' (14.18). However, this is not the public manifestation of the Son of man, returning with great power and glory, expected by many early Christians; it is a manifestation not to the world but to the disciples (14.19). The Spirit will come and take the place of the earthly Jesus, who is returning to his Father (14.16–17), and indeed the coming of the Spirit *is* the return of Jesus to his disciples, in a new form. Thus, whether it is said that the Spirit 'will be in you' (14.17) or that Jesus and the Father will dwell in the one who keeps Jesus' word (14.23), the meaning is the same. The coming of the Spirit is identified with the return of Jesus.[7]

JOHN, FIRST LETTER OF The three letters of John share much of the vocabulary and theology of the Fourth Gospel, although there are also significant differences between them. If the Fourth Gospel was produced in and for a particular, somewhat distinctive Christian community, then the letters of John seem to belong to a slightly later phase in the history of that community. The three letters are probably by the same author, identified only as 'the elder' (II John 1.1, III John 1.1). Traditionally, he has been identified with the apostle John, who was believed to be the author of the Gospel, but the author of the letters never claims to have written the Gospel, and there is no real reason to suppose that he did so.[1]

1 Situation and Purpose The first letter is written in response to a crisis caused by a split in the Church. The author describes the members of the opposing group as antichrists who 'went out from us' but 'were not of us' (2.18–19). He claims that, because his readers have been anointed by the Holy Spirit, they already understand the truth and are not deceived by their opponents' false teaching; there was no real need to write to convince them (2.20–27). Yet the letter as a whole seems to tell a different story. Answers are repeatedly given to the implied question: How do we know that we are right and they are wrong? This question must underlie statements such as, 'By this we may be sure that we know him . . .' (2.3), 'By this it may be seen who are the children of God, and who are the children of the devil . . .' (3.10), and 'By this we shall know that we are of the truth . . .' (3.19). The letter is written to anxious and confused people who want to be sure that they have done the right thing in rejecting the views of the opposing group.

2 The Theology of the Author's Opponents[2] After complaining that 'false prophets have gone out into the world', the author gives a test for identifying them: 'Every spirit which confesses that Jesus Christ has come in the flesh is of God, and every spirit which does not confess Jesus is not of God' (4.1–3). The opponents' view must have contained some kind of denial of the humanity of the Son of God. Further evidence of their position occurs in the claim that Jesus Christ came 'not with the water only, but with the water and the blood' (5.6). We know from other sources of an early Christian heresy that taught that the divine Christ descended on to the man Jesus at his baptism, but reascended to the Father *before* Jesus' crucifixion (which was why Jesus on the cross said, 'My God, my God, why hast thou forsaken me?'). This, or something like it, may be the view that is opposed in I John 5.6. The insistence that Jesus Christ 'came with the blood' would mean that because the Son of God truly became man, then he truly suffered; this opposes the claim that the divine Christ or Son cannot be subject to suffering and that the union between him and the man Jesus must therefore have been only temporary.

Other aspects of the opponents' theology may be refuted in the negative statements in chapter 1: 'God is light, and in him is no darkness at all. If we say that we have fellowship with him while we walk in darkness, we lie and do not live according to the truth . . . If we say we have no sin, we deceive ourselves, and the truth is not in us' (1.5–6,8). Early Christian heretics, who differentiated radically between the divine and human elements in Jesus Christ, also tended to separate the two constituent elements they found in themselves: the divine soul and the material body in which it had become imprisoned. Because one found oneself imprisoned in an alien world, one's actions did not matter, and one could not be held accountable for them. One might therefore claim to 'have no sin', ascribing one's position in the 'darkness' not to one's own disobedience but to God's mysterious decree. Some such view appears to have been held by the author's opponents.

3 The Author's Response

The author is writing to reassure his readers that their position is the true one. They are to let what they heard in the beginning abide in them (2.24) and not be deceived (2.26). In the face of doubts and anxieties, the author proposes three tests by which the readers may be sure that they are of the truth, and that their opponents are not: the tests of faith in Jesus Christ, love for the brethren, and obedience to God's commandments.[3]

(i) **Faith** The heretics' separation between Jesus and Christ – the human being and the divine Son of God – is a denial of the basic Christian confession, that Jesus *is* the Christ (2.22). On the other hand, 'Whoever confesses that Jesus is the Son of God, God abides in him, and he in God' (4.15). Knowledge of the Father is dependent on knowledge of the Son, and so 'no-one who denies the Son has the Father', whereas 'he who confesses the Son has the Father also' (2.23). The readers should be confident that 'the Son of God has come and has given us understanding, to know him who is true' (5.20).

(ii) **Love** The heretics have 'gone out from us' (2.19); they have separated themselves from the author and his congregations, and no longer associate with them. Their false beliefs have led them to abandon Christian love. This love is a sign of whether or not one is 'in the truth': 'Love is of God, and he who loves is born of God and knows God. He who does not love does not know God; for God is love' (4.7–8). The famous statement, 'God is love' (repeated in 4.16) is grounded in a specific act of God: 'In this the love of God was made manifest among us, that God sent his only Son into the world, so that we might live through him' (4.9).

75

This act of God is the basis for Christian love: 'If God so loved us, we also ought to love one another' (4.11).

(*iii*) **Obedience** The author rejects the view that because this world is not our true home, our actions within it do not matter. The heretics believe that they 'have no sin' (1.8, *see* 1.10) in the sense that God does not hold them responsible for their actions. The author agrees that 'no-one born of God commits sin' (3.9) – but he means that those born of God 'do right' (3.10), 'keep his commandments and do what pleases him' (3.22). The reason why the Son of God came was 'to destroy the works of the devil', the author of sin (3.8), and not to relieve us of personal responsibility for our conduct. Because of this responsibility we have to face a judgment, but because 'perfect love casts out fear', this is not something to be afraid of (4.17–18).

JOHN, SECOND LETTER OF[1] This short note is addressed by 'the elder' (most probably the author of I John) to 'the elect lady and her children' (v. 1), and the greeting in v. 13 from 'the children of your elect sister' suggests that the two 'ladies' are in fact churches, and that their children are the congregations (*see* I Peter 5.13, where 'she who is at Babylon, who is likewise chosen' probably refers to the church at Rome). The author requests 'that we love one another' – the commandment 'we have had from the beginning (vv. 5–6). Here, the reference is probably to the maintenance of fellowship between his own congregation and the congregation he is addressing. The request is all the more urgent because 'many deceivers have gone out into the world, men who will not acknowledge the coming of Jesus Christ in the flesh' (v. 7). The author is writing to warn his readers of such people (vv. 8–9), and to exhort them not to welcome them into their homes or give them any greeting (vv. 10–11).

II John gives us some vivid insights into the situation described in more theoretical terms in I John. The author feels himself responsible not just for his own congregation but for other congregations in the area. Among the heretics are itinerant teachers who rely on the hospitality of the congregations which they visit; such hospitality must no longer be given. Despite the claim of I John 2.19 that 'they went out from us', the implication of II John 10–11 is that the 'orthodox' separated themselves from the 'heretics', and not the other way round.

JOHN, THIRD LETTER OF In this letter 'the elder' is addressing an individual, Gaius, having heard good reports of his faith from members of his own congregation to whom Gaius had extended hospitality (vv. 1–6). He exhorts him to continue this practice of welcoming itinerant Christian teachers, so as to be 'fellow workers in the truth' with them (vv. 6–8). The real reason for writing emerges in the following verses. A certain Diotrephes has set himself up over the congregation of which Gaius was also a member[1]; he denies the elder's authority over it and does not allow visitors from his own congregation within his own, even excommunicating members of his congregation who disagree with him (vv. 9–10). Gaius is no doubt under pressure to conform, and the elder writes to exhort him not to do so. He is to welcome Demetrius, the bearer of the letter (v. 12), as he had previously welcomed brethren from other congregations.

In III John the situation in II John is reversed. There, 'the elder' tried to persuade his readers not to extend hospitality to heretical teachers; here, he finds himself on the receiving end of his treatment. There is no suggestion that Diotrephes was himself one of the 'deceivers' who denied 'the coming of Jesus Christ in the flesh' (II John 7), and his hostility towards the elder and those who agree with him suggests that he regarded the elder himself as heretical. Only this can account for his 'prating against me with evil words', and his expulsion from the church of those who wished to welcome the elder's messengers (v. 10). But the precise nature of the dispute remains unknown.

JOHN THE BAPTIST

JOHN THE BAPTIST It is important to differentiate between John the Baptist as a historical figure and his significance for early Christian faith. Historically, it is very doubtful if the Baptist ever recognized Jesus as the promised Messiah, but from the standpoint of Christian faith he becomes the first great witness to the Messiahship of Jesus.

1 John the Baptist as a Historical Figure[1] According to the Jewish historian Josephus, writing at the end of the first century AD, John was 'a good man' who 'exhorted the Jews to lead righteous lives, to practise justice towards their fellows and piety towards God, and so doing to join in baptism'. Baptism did not secure forgiveness unless 'the soul was already thoroughly cleansed by good behaviour'. Herod Antipas became alarmed when he saw the crowds attracted by John: 'Eloquence that had so great an effect on mankind might lead to some form of sedition, for it looked as if they would be guided by John in everything that they did'. He therefore arrested John, imprisoned him in the fortress of Machaerus, near the Dead Sea, and had him executed. At about this time, Herod divorced his wife, the daughter of King Aretas, and married Herodias, the wife of his half-brother, another Herod. Herod was severely defeated in the ensuing battle with Aretas, and some saw this as divine judgment on him for his treatment of the Baptist.

The Synoptic Gospels complement this picture. They indicate that the Baptist was not just a preacher of righteousness, but that he proclaimed the imminent judgment of God (*see* Matt. 3.7,10). The agent of the divine judgment is coming soon, who is to 'baptize you with the Holy Spirit and with fire' (Matt. 3.11).[2] Here, 'Holy Spirit' is probably a Christian interpretation; the Greek *pneuma* can mean 'wind' as well as 'Spirit', and the imagery of the following verse requires 'wind' as well as 'fire': 'His winnowing fork is in his hand, and he will clear his threshing floor and gather his wheat into his granary, but the chaff he will burn with unquenchable fire'. John the Baptist was seen, and perhaps saw himself, as 'Elijah', the prophet whose return was expected to prepare people for 'the great and terrible day of the Lord' (Mal. 4.5–6).

2 The Christian Interpretation of John the Baptist The importance of John the Baptist was recognized by all of the early Christians because his ministry was closely related to the beginning of Jesus' own. Although the chief priests, scribes and elders felt unable to answer Jesus' question, 'Was the baptism of John from heaven or from men?' (Mark 11.30), the early Christians answered unhesitatingly, from heaven. Yet there is also a recognition of a wide difference

77

between the ministries of John and Jesus. John is acknowledged as 'a prophet, and more than a prophet', and 'among those born of women none is greater'. Yet such is the contrast between his time and the present time of fulfilment that it can also be said: 'He who is least in the kingdom of God is greater than he' (Luke 7.26–28). He marks the boundary between the two ages: 'The law and the prophets were until John' (Luke 16.16). A difference between the two ages may also have been seen in the contrast between the austerity of John, who 'came eating no bread and drinking no wine', and Jesus, who 'has come eating and drinking' (Luke 7.33–34, *see* Mark 2.18–19). Because of this distinction, it is a matter of theological as well as historical importance for Mark that Jesus' ministry begins 'after John was arrested' (Mark 1.14).[3]

Did John the Baptist explicitly recognize Jesus as the Messiah? The Synoptic Gospels are ambiguous here, but it is likely that he did not. Despite his saying about the coming of 'him who is mightier than I, the thong of whose sandals I am not worthy to stoop down and untie' (Mark 1.7), it is not said that John saw this as fulfilled in Jesus. On the contrary, John in prison sends messengers to Jesus to ask, 'Are you he who is to come, or shall we look for another?' (Matt. 11.3), and Jesus' response contains a note of implied criticism: 'Blessed is he who takes no offence at me' (11.6). This story reflects the early Christian consciousness that neither the Baptist nor his followers believed in Jesus.

It is the Fourth Gospel which reinterprets the figure of John in the most radical way. John is seen as having no significance at all except as the first witness to Jesus, whom he acknowledges as 'the Lamb of God who takes away the sin of the world' (1.29), and as 'the Son of God' (1.34). His baptism is no longer 'a baptism of repentance for the forgiveness of sins' (Mark 1.4) because its purpose is solely the manifestation of Jesus: 'For this I came baptizing with water, that he might be revealed to Israel' (1.31). Although John did not initially recognize him (1.31,33), the descent of the Spirit onto Jesus was a private vision granted to John to enable him to identify him as the Messiah (1.32–33). He therefore persuades his own disciples to follow Jesus instead (1.35–37) on the grounds that 'he must increase, but I must decrease' (3.30). Unlike the Synoptics, the Fourth Gospel includes no teaching of John the Baptist that does not directly relate to Jesus.

JOSEPH[1] Despite the virgin birth story in Matthew and Luke, Joseph is generally presented in the Gospels as the legal father of Jesus. Matthew and Luke both present genealogies of Jesus in which his descent is traced through Joseph. Although they stress that Joseph was not Jesus' real father (Matt. 1.16, Luke 3.23), he must be understood as his adoptive father, for otherwise the genealogies would not apply to Jesus at all. The story about the child Jesus in the temple refers to 'his parents' (Luke 2.14,43), and Mary speaks of 'your father and I' (2.48; *see also* 2.27,33). Matthew 13.55 replaces Mark's 'Is not this the carpenter?' (Mark 6.3) with 'Is not this the son of the carpenter?' (Matt. 13.55). Jesus is described as 'the son of Joseph' in John 1.46 and 6.42.[2]

Joseph is more prominent in Matthew's nativity narrative than in Luke's. In Matthew the angelic annunciation is granted to him rather than to Mary, and he receives further messages from angels warning him to flee from Herod and to return to the land of Israel after Herod's death. He is never mentioned in connection with Jesus' ministry, and so the tradition of his early death may well be correct. However, the tradition that he was already an old man when he married Mary is motivated by belief in the perpetual virginity of Mary. The Gospels imply that the brothers and sisters of Jesus were the offspring of Joseph and Mary, and the belief that they were Joseph's children by a former marriage, or that they were cousins of Jesus, is not supported by the New Testament.[3]

JOSEPH OF ARIMATHEA[1] In all four Gospels, Joseph of Arimathea is responsible for the burial of Jesus, which he undertakes on his own initiative. He was 'a respected member of the council' (Mark 15.43),[2] 'a good and righteous man who had not consented to their purpose and deed' (Luke 24.51), and part of the interest of the narrative is the utterly unexpected way in which a member of the body that had condemned Jesus defies his colleagues and the Roman procurator and implicitly challenges the justice of their action. The earliest version of this story simply says that he 'was himself looking for the kingdom of God' (Mark 15.43), and this suggests that his motive was concern over a miscarriage of justice rather than specific devotion to Jesus.

Various details are added in the later Gospels. Matthew makes Joseph 'a disciple of Jesus', and adds that he was rich, that the tomb was his own, and that it was new (27.57–60; *see* Isa. 53.9, '. . . and with a rich man in his death'). Luke similarly emphasizes that 'no-one had ever yet been laid' in the tomb (23.53), this point is obviously important in the empty tomb story that follows. John makes Joseph 'a disciple of Jesus, but secretly, for fear of the Jews' (19.38) – not very aptly because Joseph was performing a public act of defiance. The tomb (again, a new tomb) is located in a garden 'in the place where Jesus was crucified', and Joseph (assisted by Nicodemus) buries him there in a hurry because the Jewish day of Preparation was about to begin (19.41–42). Nicodemus provides an enormous quantity of valuable spices (19.39–40), and so nothing is said in John's empty tomb story about the women's spices (in contrast to Mark and Luke).[3]

One purpose of the burial story is to rule out two sceptical responses to the claim that Jesus rose from the dead. The suggestion that he had never really died at all is excluded by the reference to Pilate's careful inquiry about his death, and the suggestion that the women visited the wrong tomb on Easter morning is excluded by the reference to their presence at Jesus' burial.

JUDAS THE GALILEAN In Acts 5.34–39 Gamaliel the Pharisee urges that persecution of the Church should cease on the grounds that 'if this plan or this undertaking is of men, it will fail, but if it is of God you will not be able to overthrow them'.[1] Two examples are given to prove this point: Theudas, and 'after him, Judas the Galilean', who 'arose in the days of the census and drew away some of the people after him; he also perished, and all who followed him were scattered'. In fact, Theudas's revolt took place in about AD 45, and Judas's in AD 6.[2] Judas saw a contradiction between the sole sovereignty of God over Israel and the Roman census (preparatory to taxation), which seemed to proclaim Israel's slavery to the Gentiles. He proclaimed that God would help those who in faith took up arms against the Gentile oppressors. Although he was defeated, the issue he raised

79

was not resolved. It is present in the question put to Jesus, 'Is it lawful to pay taxes to Caesar or not?' (Mark 12.14),[3] and it eventually led to the great Zealot uprising of AD 66–70.

JUDAS ISCARIOT In the Gospels (together with Acts 1), the decline and fall of Judas Iscariot takes place in four stages. There is a tendency for later Gospels (Matthew, Luke and especially John) to add details which are not present in Mark.

(*i*) The Synoptic Gospels mention an initial meeting between Judas and the chief priests, and state that the motive for the betrayal was greed (Mark 14.10–11, Matt. 26.14–16, Luke 22.3–6). Matthew alone specifies the exact sum of money decided upon, thirty pieces of silver – a figure which he has derived from an obscure prophecy, which he wrongly attributes to Jeremiah (27.9–10).[1] Whether greed was Judas's only motive is unknown, but fear may have been another and disillusionment with Jesus a third.

(*ii*) At the Last Supper, Jesus predicts that one of his own disciples is to betray him (Mark 14.17–21). In Matthew, Judas is explicitly identified: he asks, 'Is it I, Master?', and Jesus replies, 'You have said so' (26.25). In John 13.21–30, Jesus identifies him by giving him a morsel of food; only here is his exit into the night mentioned.[2]

(*iii*) Judas guides the chief priests' soldiers to Jesus, and enables them to arrest him. In Mark 14.44–46 he identifies Jesus with a kiss; Jesus remains silent, and is arrested. In Matt. 26.50 Jesus utters the words, 'Friend, why are you here?', and in Luke 22.48 he will not allow Judas to kiss him: 'Judas, would you betray the Son of man with a kiss?' Matthew and Luke cannot quite accept the extreme passivity of Jesus as presented by Mark. In John 18.3–6, there is no need for the kiss because Jesus identifies himself with the words, 'I am he', at which the soldiers all fall to the ground.[3]

(*iv*) Judas's repentance and suicide is graphically described in Matt. 27.1–10. Here, Judas hangs himself, and the chief priests buy a field with the money he has flung back at them. However, in Acts 1.18–19, it is Judas himself who buys the field, and his death (in the field?) is an accident: 'Falling headlong he burst open in the middle and all his bowels gushed out'. The Acts version is perhaps the earlier.

JUDE, LETTER OF[1] The brief letter of Jude is closely related to II Peter 2, where similar arguments and vocabulary are employed. One writing clearly uses the other as a source, and it is perhaps more likely that II Peter has used Jude than the other way round. It is easier to see why Jude should have been expanded than why II Peter should have been abbreviated. The references to apocryphal books in Jude 9.15 are absent from II Peter, and it is more natural to suppose that these have been omitted by an author who was unsure of their authority than that they have been inserted by the later author.

The author claims to be 'Jude, a servant of Jesus Christ and brother of James' (v. 1). We know from Mark 6.3 of a Judas (or Jude – the names are almost identical in

Greek) who was a brother of James, and also of Jesus himself. But whether or not this figure is supposed to have been the author, the letter clearly derives from the post-apostolic age. It looks back to the apostles as figures of the past (vv. 17–18) and appeals for the preservation of the original message which they preached (v. 3). The letter is concerned with a single problem: the fact that there are people within the Church who seem to the author to be denying 'the faith which was once for all delivered to the saints' (v. 3) by their behaviour and beliefs. They 'pervert the grace of our God into licentiousness' (v. 4); they 'defile the flesh, reject authority, and revile the glorious ones' (v. 8); they 'boldly carouse' at Christian communal meals (v. 12); and they are 'grumblers, malcontents, following their own passions, loud-mouthed boasters, flattering people to gain advantage' (v. 16). They repeat the errors of the ungodly in the Old Testament: the wilderness generation, the fallen angels, the inhabitants of Sodom and Gomorrah, Cain, Balaam and Korah (vv. 5–7,11).

Theologically, the letter makes two main points. The first is that right belief and conduct is not something which is determined anew by each generation of Christians, but something which is given 'once for all' (v. 3). The second is that there is inevitably a contrast between the Church as it should be and the Church as it is – infiltrated by those who pervert the integrity of its gospel.[2]

JUDGMENT[1] It is assumed almost everywhere in the New Testament that 'it is appointed for men to die once, and after that comes judgment' (Heb. 9.27). The philosophy which teaches, 'Let us eat and drink, for tomorrow we die' (I Cor. 15.32) is excluded because people are seen as accountable to God for their conduct. Thus, 'the Gentiles' (i.e. non-Christians) who live in 'licentiousness, passions, drunkenness, revels, carousing and lawless idolatry', will have to 'give account to him who is ready to judge the living and the dead' (I Peter 4.3,5). But Christians, too, face the judgment, and must continually remind themselves of this fact: 'If you invoke as Father him who judges each one impartially according to his deeds, conduct yourselves with fear throughout the time of your exile' (I Peter 1.17). Despite Paul's stress on divine grace, he too teaches that Christians face judgment together with everyone else[2]: 'We must all appear before the judgment seat of Christ, so that each one may receive good or evil, according to what he has done in the body' (II Cor. 5.10).

In John, the picture is significantly different. The judgment occurs in the crucifixion of Jesus: 'Now is the judgment of this world, now shall the ruler of this world be cast out' (12.31; the following verses show that the crucifixion is here referred to). People pass judgment on themselves through their failure to believe in Jesus: 'This is the judgment, that the light has come into the world, and men loved darkness rather than light, because their deeds were evil' (3.19). Judgment is the effect but not the purpose of the coming of the Son of God into the world: 'God sent the Son into the world not to condemn the world, but that the world might be saved through him' (3.17).[3]

It is at first sight paradoxical that a message which proclaims good news nevertheless holds the threat of judgment over people. The explanation is that throughout the New Testament, the grace of God sets people under the responsibility 'to live no longer for themselves but for him who for their sake died and was raised' (II Cor. 5.15). In holding together the grace and the judgment of God, the New Testament also holds together human frailty (which requires grace) and human responsibility (which is subject to judgment). There is no precise explanation to be found of how the two relate to one another, but the New Testament writers generally avoid two extreme positions. One is a stress on the grace of God which excludes responsibility and creates presumption; the other is a stress on the judgment of God which excludes grace and creates fear. It is true that — in opposition to presumption – 'fear' is sometimes commended as an appropriate attitude, but at a deeper level, 'There is no fear in love, but perfect love casts out fear' (I John 4.18). The motive for Christian conduct is not fear but the love of God manifested in the incarnation: 'We love because he first loved us' (I John 4.19).[4]

JUSTIFICATION The term 'justification' is found almost exclusively in the writings of Paul and is linked not only with the verb 'to justify' but also with the noun 'righteousness' and the adjective 'righteous'; the Greek words all belong to the same group. Paul generally uses this terminology in the context of his controversy with Judaism (Romans) and Jewish Christianity (Galatians). Phil. 3 and II Cor. 3 also make use of this language to some extent.

Paul emphasizes that justification occurs through faith in Christ and not through works of the law. Faith involves a person's complete response to the gospel message, and includes not only acceptance of it as true but the reorientation of one's life that it requires. In Paul's view, faith is a way to God open to Jew and Gentile alike. 'Works' means not obedience to God's will in general, but the obedience of the Jew to the law of Moses, participation in the way of life of the Jewish community. Justification by faith and not works therefore means that participation in the life of the Jewish community is no longer rewarded as essential for salvation.[1]

To be justified means to become righteous, and in this context 'righteous' refers not just to right conduct but to a right relationship with God. The presupposition here is that in their natural state human beings are not in a right relationship with God. 'All have sinned and fall short of the glory of God' (Rom. 3.23), and this means not just that everyone has from time to time transgressed God's law, but that all stand before God as guilty, liable to his wrath and condemnation (Rom. 3.9–20).[2] The curse the law pronounces on the disobedient applies to everyone, supposedly obedient Jews as well as disobedient Gentiles (Gal. 3.10). In the light of God's judgment, relative differences between human beings disappear.

This is the background against which Paul sets the preaching of the gospel. The gospel proclaims that God has acted for the salvation of the world in the life, death and resurrection of Jesus Christ. It proclaims that on the basis of these events, an amnesty is possible for God's enemies; the guilty may be acquitted.[3] Those who believe the gospel and submit to baptism are transferred from the category of the unrighteous to the category of the righteous. Those who are justified by faith 'have peace with God through our Lord Jesus Christ' (Rom. 5.1).[4] Being justified, or receiving the gift of righteousness, refers to the whole transformation which in Paul's view becoming a Christian entails.

KINGDOM OF GOD/HEAVEN

KINGDOM OF GOD/HEAVEN The phrase 'kingdom of God' or 'kingdom of heaven' is, with a few exceptions, confined to the Synoptic Gospels and to the teaching of Jesus. Matthew usually substitutes 'kingdom of heaven' for 'kingdom of God', and 'heaven' is here synonymous with 'God'. 'Kingdom of heaven' suggests a place (heaven) ruled over by a king (God), but that is not what the phrase means: the kingdom of God or of heaven refers to God establishing his rule over the world. The prayer, 'Thy kingdom come' is therefore a request that God should exercise the sovereignty that is his by right and rid the world of all the evils which at present defile it: sin, oppression, evil powers and death.

The hope that God's kingdom would shortly be established is not unique to Jesus.[1] In the Book of Daniel (mid-second century BC) a contrast is drawn between the series of pagan empires which hold dominion over the present age and the establishment of God's dominion. In Dan. 2 the successive empires are portrayed in the form of a statue that is to be overthrown: 'The God of heaven will set up a kingdom which shall never be destroyed, nor shall its sovereignty be left to another people. It shall break in pieces all these kingdoms and bring them to an end, and it shall stand for ever' (v. 44).[2] During the three centuries before the birth of Jesus such hopes were widely held by Jews conscious of the tension between their unique relationship with the one God and their actual experience of political servitude and oppression.

The kingdom of God was at the heart of the preaching of Jesus, and his message is therefore bound up with the circumstances of his own day. Yet there are striking differences between his preaching of the kingdom of God and the common ideas exemplified by Daniel.

(*i*) The idea that Israel will rule the world is not taught by Jesus. For popular Jewish thought, the reign of God was identified with the reign of his people Israel, and this outlook could claim support in Old Testament prophecy. Yet when Jesus teaches that, for example, the kingdom of God is 'like a grain of mustard seed' (Mark 4.30–31), or 'like treasure hidden in a field' (Matt. 13.44), Jewish hopes for world domination are entirely absent. Nor is there any particular hostility towards the Romans, whom some of Jesus' contemporaries identified with the fourth and final world-empire mentioned by Daniel, which was destined to be violently destroyed. For Jesus, the kingdom of God is apparently concerned with the whole created order, and not just with the status of Israel.[3]

(*ii*) Unlike some of his contemporaries, Jesus refuses to indulge in speculations about precisely when and how the kingdom of God will come. When the Pharisees ask when the kingdom of God will come, he replies: 'The kingdom of God is not coming with signs to be observed; nor will they say, "Lo, here it is!" or "There!", for behold, the kingdom of God is in the midst of you' (Luke 17.20–21). His proclamation of the kingdom by means of parables has a certain indirectness; he refuses to describe the kingdom of God directly and will only say what it is like. The occasional detailed predictions ascribed to Jesus (e.g. Mark 13) are foreign to him, and are probably largely the work of the early Church. Jesus is entirely confident that the kingdom of God will come, but the precise manner of its coming is left in God's hands.

(*iii*) In one sense, the kingdom is still future in that the evils which defile God's creation still remain. The disciples must therefore pray, 'Thy kingdom come'. In another sense, however, God is already beginning to establish his kingdom in and through the ministry of Jesus. Jesus sees this in his own exorcisms: 'If it is by the finger of God that I cast out demons, then the kingdom of God has come upon you' (Luke 11.20).[4] The time of Jesus' ministry is thus a time of fulfilment: 'Blessed are the eyes which see what you see! I tell you that many prophets and kings desired to see what you see, and did not see it, and to hear what you hear, and did not hear it' (Luke 10.23–24). The great feast that was expected to occur at the end of time is already present, and fasting is therefore inappropriate: 'Can the wedding guests fast while the bridegroom is with them?' (Mark 2.19).[5]

LABOURERS IN THE VINEYARD, PARABLE OF[1] This parable occurs only in Matt. 20.1–16. Its point is the eccentric generosity of the owner of the vineyard, who gives the labourers who have worked only part of the day the same wages as those who have worked for the whole day. The full-time workers complain, and although the owner replies, 'Am I not allowed to do what I choose with what belongs to me?' (v. 15), he gives no explanation for his capricious behaviour, which defies all the normal conventions about the relationship between employer and employed. The parable concerns 'the kingdom of heaven' (v. 1): God's reign requires willing subjects just as the owner of the vineyard requires labourers. Some achieve much and others little, but in the unpredictable goodness of God there is no very precise correspondence between what is done and the wages given. The parable thus qualifies the stress on 'reward' found elsewhere in the Gospel of Matthew (e.g. 5.11–12, 6.3–4).

LAW OF MOSES In Judaism the God who is worshipped and obeyed is supremely revealed in the Law of Moses. The Jew believes that he possesses 'the embodiment of knowledge and truth' in the law (Rom. 2.20). Christians, however, found the revelation of God supremely in Jesus the Messiah, and so the question naturally arose of the relation of the old revelation to the new. For some conservative Jewish Christians it seemed as though there could be no possible conflict, but some of Jesus' own sayings were at least ambiguous on this point. The problem became still more intense when people came to believe that Jesus was a universal figure whose significance could not be confined to the community of Israel that observed the law.

1 Jesus Jesus' attitude towards the law is very hard to define for both conservative and radical sayings are attributed to him by the Synoptic Gospels. To take the conservative sayings first, Jesus states, 'Think not that I have come to abolish the law and the prophets' (Matt. 5.17), and 'it is easier for heaven and earth to pass away than for one dot of the law to become void' (Luke 16.17, *see also* Matt. 5.18–20). Although he contrasts 'the weightier matters of the law, justice and mercy and faith' with the Pharisees' scrupulous practice of extending the law of tithing to 'mint and dill and cummin', he still tells them not to neglect the latter (Matt. 23.23). Because 'the scribes and the Pharisees sit on Moses' seat', the disciples are to 'practise and observe whatever they tell you' (Matt. 23.2–3).

However, much more radical sayings are also to be found. Jesus works on the sabbath (Mark 2.23–3.6), teaching that 'the sabbath was made for man, not man for the sabbath' (Mark 2.27); the sabbath is a divine gift, and not a tyrannical law. He does not practise fasting (Mark 2.18–19), and he is not concerned with the purity rules (Mark 7.1–23). Nor is his criticism confined to the traditional interpretation of the law; it extends to the law itself. The law permitting divorce is set aside on the grounds that it does not reflect the original will of God (Mark 10.1–9).[1] When in Matt. 5 Jesus repeatedly contrasts what the law said 'to the men of old' with what 'I say to you', he is setting his own authority over that of the law in a remarkable way.

There seem to be two possible ways of explaining this apparent contradiction between conservative and radical sayings, and both of them probably contain an element of truth. The first is to point out that Jewish Christianity seems to have been more conservative about the law than Jesus himself; the conservative sayings may represent a Jewish Christian attempt to tone down Jesus' unacceptably radical teaching and practice. The second begins from the contrast in Mark 10.1–9 between what Moses commanded 'for your hardness of heart' and the true will of God. The whole Law of Moses is necessary for the maintenance of (Jewish) society, and has a relative legitimacy in this sphere; but it is not to be immediately identified with God's will (*see also* Matt. 17.24–27).

2 Paul The law was a problem for Paul because he saw himself as Apostle to the Gentiles, entrusted with the task of establishing mainly Gentile congregations which did not observe the Jewish law. Circumcision was forbidden (Gal. 5.2), and the Jewish feasts (Gal. 4.8–10) and food laws (I Cor. 10.25–27) were ignored.[2] Paul sometimes claims that the law is observed in his congregations, at least in its essence: 'The whole law is fulfilled in one word, "You shall love your neighbour as yourself" ' (Gal. 5.14, *see* Rom. 13.9–10). But more usually he concedes that the law is the possession of the Jewish community. In accordance with his principle of separation between the Jewish community and his Gentile congregations, he argues that the law has a disastrous effect on the community that tries to observe it. The law pronounces a curse on the disobedient, and because no-one fully obeys it, the curse applies to all (Gal. 3.10–12). It 'brings wrath' (Rom. 4.15), 'increases the trespass' (5.20), and arouses 'sinful passions' (7.5). To be under the law is to be under the dominion of sin (6.14), and salvation must therefore involve freedom from the law and its terrible effects (7.1–6).[3] In Rom. 7, the divine origin of the law is affirmed, but in Gal. 3.19–4.10 the law is ascribed to the inferior angelic beings to whom the rule of the world has temporarily been entrusted.

3 Hebrews[4] Much of the Law of Moses concerns the duties of priests in their work of offering sacrifices, and for both Jews and Christians the destruction of the temple in AD 70 made these laws irrelevant. Yet because the divine origin of the whole law was generally accepted, they could not entirely be ignored. The Letter to the Hebrews resolves this problem by arguing that the laws concerning sacrifices are 'a shadow of the good things to come instead of the true form of these realities' (10.1); that is, the sacrificial system prefigures the one, great sacrifice of Christ. Because it is *only* a prefigurement, it is 'weak and useless', 'obsolete and growing old' (7.18, 8.13) in itself. The sacrifices it prescribes to take away sins are unable to do so (7.19, 10.1–4, 11). Although the emphasis is on the contrast between the old covenant and the law, the author also regards the law's prefiguration of Christ in a positive light.

4 James[5] The Letter of James refers to the law as 'the perfect law', 'the law of liberty' and 'the royal law' (1.25, 2.8, 12). In the exhortation, 'Be doers of the word, and not hearers only' (1.22), 'word' (i.e. 'gospel') is virtually synonymous with 'law' (1.25). The law is summed up in the commandment, 'You shall love your neighbour as yourself' (2.8), and although the author refers to 'keeping the whole law' (2.10), it seems to be mainly the Ten Commandments that he has in mind (2.11). Thus, the Law of Moses has been reduced to its essential ethical content; distinctively Jewish features have been set aside. The law becomes indistinguishable from the contents of Christian ethics, and the transition from the law of the Jewish community to the law of the Christian community is complete.

LAZARUS

Two men named Lazarus are mentioned in the New Testament, and there seems to be a close relationship between them. In the parable of the Rich Man and Lazarus in Luke 16.19–31 the relationship between rich and poor in this life is reversed in the next: Abraham says to the rich man, 'Son, remember that you in your lifetime received your good things, and Lazarus in like manner evil things; but now he is comforted here, and you are in anguish' (v. 25). The emphasis in the parable lies on the second half, which asks how people can be persuaded to live a life of righteousness and so escape the fires of hell (vv. 27–31).[1] Abraham insists that Moses and the prophets provide sufficient warning, and asserts that if they do not heed this warning, they will not be convinced by Lazarus rising from the dead (v. 31, *see* vv. 27–28).

In John 11 Abraham's prophecy is fulfilled: Lazarus is indeed raised from the dead, and yet most people still do not believe. A figure in a parable has become the subject of a miracle. The evangelist stresses that it is precisely because of the resurrection of Lazarus that the chief priests and Pharisees begin to plan the action in which unbelief reaches its climax, the crucifixion of Jesus (11.45–54, 12.9–11).

Lazarus is presented as the brother of Mary and Martha (11.1). In Luke 10.38–42 these two sisters are again mentioned in an unnamed village (which can hardly be Bethany, which is too close to Jerusalem for this point in the narrative).[2] John has linked them with Bethany by incorporating them into the story of the anointing of Jesus by an unnamed woman, 'in the house of Simon the Leper' at Bethany (Mark 14.3–9, *see* John 12.1–8).

LORD[1]

The title 'Lord' (*kyrios*) was frequently applied to the deities of the Graeco–Roman world. In I Cor. 8.5 Paul acknowledges that 'there are many "gods" and many "lords" ' – that is, many deities who are acknowledged as Lord. For Christians, Jesus alone was Lord (I Cor. 8.6), but it may be that the use of this title in the surrounding paganism accounts for its popularity among Gentile Christians. As the title 'Christ' (or 'Messiah') derives from a non-Christian Jewish context, so the title 'Lord' derives (at least in part) from a Gentile context. In Paul's Gentile churches, the confession, 'Jesus is Lord' (Rom. 10.9, I Cor. 12.3, Phil. 2.11) supersedes the earlier Jewish Christian confession, 'Jesus is the Christ' (Mark 8.29, John 1.41, Acts 9.22). Early Christian preachers used terminology that was already familiar to their hearers, while generally giving it a quite new content.

However, 'Lord' also has an important Jewish Christian background. In I Cor. 16.22, Paul uses the Aramaic phrase, 'Maranatha!', meaning, 'Our Lord, come!', and this shows that even in the Aramaic-speaking Jewish churches, Jesus was referred to as 'our Lord'. The origin of this usage is probably to be found in a verse from the Psalms which was understood as a reference to Jesus' resurrection and exaltation: 'The Lord says to my Lord, "Sit at my right hand, till I make your enemies your footstool" ' (Ps. 110.1). This verse is used in Mark 12.35–37 to prove that the Christ is to be acknowledged as Lord, and in Peter's Pentecost speech it is specifically applied to the exalted Jesus (Acts 2.34–36 *see also* Rom. 8.34, I Cor. 15.25, Eph. 1.20–22, Heb. 1.13). Ps. 110.1 provided justification for applying the title 'Lord' to someone other than God himself.

In the Septuagint (the Greek translation of the Old Testament), 'Lord' (*Kyrios*) renders the Hebrew 'Yahweh', the divine name which had become too sacred to be pronounced. Some parts of the New Testament retain this usage; but elsewhere it is remarkable how Old Testament passages referring to 'the Lord' are applied to Jesus.[2] Paul twice quotes from Isa. 40.13 ('Who has known the mind of the Lord. . . ?'), and applies this to God in Rom. 11.33–34, but to Christ in I Cor. 2.16. Similarly, Isa. 45.23 ('As I live, says the Lord, every knee shall bow to me, and every tongue shall give praise to God') is applied to 'the judgment seat of God' in Rom. 14.10–11, but is reinterpreted in Phil. 2.10–11: '. . . that at the name of Jesus every knee should bow . . . and every tongue confess that Jesus Christ is Lord, to the glory of God the Father'. In Heb. 1.10–12, the 'Lord' addressed in Ps. 102 as the creator of heaven and earth is identified with Jesus.

But the most remarkable reinterpretation of an Old Testament passage referring to 'the Lord' occurs in I Cor. 8.6: 'For us there is one God, the Father, from whom are all things and for whom we exist, and one Lord Jesus Christ, through whom are all things and through whom we exist'. This verse alludes to the basic Jewish confession of the oneness of God known as the *Shema*: 'Hear, O Israel: the Lord our God is one Lord . . .' (Deut. 6.4). In I Cor. 8.6, however, a distinction is drawn between the 'one God' and the 'one Lord', in a way that would be quite unacceptable in Judaism.

LORD'S PRAYER[1]

The Lord's Prayer is found in two versions (Matt. 6.9–13, Luke 11.2–4). It is Matthew's version that is used in Christian worship (sometimes with the addition of a doxology ['Thine is the kingdom . . .'] derived from I Chron. 29.11). Luke's shorter form is much less well-known: 'Father, hallowed be thy name. Thy kingdom come. Give us each day our daily bread; and forgive us our sins, for we ourselves forgive everyone who is indebted to us; and lead us not into temptation'. This shorter form is likely to be closer to the original taught by Jesus; the expansions and additions in Matthew's version aim to make the prayer more suitable for liturgical use. In Matthew, Jesus' simple 'Father' (in Aramaic, *Abba*) is replaced by the more sonorous 'Our Father which art in heaven'. Matthew's version adds 'Thy will be done, on earth as it is in heaven' to the petition, 'Thy kingdom come'. The purpose of the addition is perhaps to clarify the meaning of 'Thy kingdom come': to pray for the coming of God's kingdom is to pray for the fulfilment of his purposes on earth. Similarly, 'Lead us not into temptation' is augmented by 'But deliver us from evil'. 'Lead us not into temptation' might suggest that God himself tempts people (a false deduction specifically opposed in James 1.13–14). 'But deliver us from evil' (or, 'from the Evil One') is intended to clarify the meaning of the petition.

LORD'S SUPPER

The term, 'Lord's Supper' occurs in I Cor. 11.20. 'Holy Communion' derives from I Cor. 10.16, which speaks of 'communion' (or 'participation') in the body and blood of Christ. Jesus' thanksgiving for the bread (I Cor. 11.24) and for the cup (Mark 14.23) accounts for the term 'Eucharist' ('thanksgiving').

1 The Institution of the Lord's Supper[1] There are four versions of the traditional narrative, in I Cor. 11, Mark, Matthew, and Luke; there is also some related material in John 6. The two oldest accounts are I Cor. 11.23–26 and Mark 14.22–25, which differ from one another in several respects. Paul has the command to repeat Jesus' actions in connection both with the bread and with the cup: 'Do this . . . in remembrance of me'. Mark's narrative on its own does not suggest that the action is to be repeated. Mark's 'Take; this is my body' becomes 'This is my body which is for you' in Paul. Paul, unlike Mark, states that the cup was given 'after supper'; this links it with the Jewish 'cup of blessing' (I Cor. 10.16), which was drunk at the close of a meal. In Mark, Jesus says, 'This is my blood of the covenant which is poured out for many', whereas in Paul he says, 'This cup is the new covenant in my blood'. Mark's simpler form balances 'This is my body'. For Mark, but not for Paul, the supper is the Passover meal (14.12–16).

Matthew's version (26.26–29) follows Mark's closely, except that he adds

'. . . for the forgiveness of sins' to Mark's 'This is my blood of the covenant which is poured out for many'. But Luke's version (21.17–20) is puzzling. Many manuscripts have a short form of the text, in which the cup is distributed first, with no reference to Jesus' blood, followed by the bread, accompanied by the words, 'This is my body'. Other manuscripts add at this point further words about the bread and a second distribution of the cup, derived from I Cor. 11. It is likely that the shorter form was what Luke wrote, and that the longer form was an attempt by a scribe to reconcile Luke's narrative with Paul, Mark and Matthew. Finally, although John has no equivalent account in his Last Supper narrative, John 6.51–58 is apparently related to the other narratives: 'Truly, truly I say to you, unless you eat the flesh of the Son of man and drink his blood, you have no life in you' (v. 53).

The variety of the different versions suggests that a lengthy process of development and reinterpretation has taken place. It is therefore impossible to be sure exactly what Jesus did and said 'on the night when he was betrayed'. Some aspects of the narratives are difficult to understand in a Jewish context – notably the idea of drinking blood (which is, however, absent from Paul's version). But Jewish features are also present: for example, the thanksgivings over bread and wine, and the ideas of a new covenant and a sacrifice for sins. The narratives cannot simply be seen as originating in Greek-speaking Christianity, however much this context may have influenced their development. It is quite possible that Jesus distributed the bread and the wine which accompanied the Passover meal in the context of teaching about his forthcoming death, understood as a sacrifice which would establish a new covenant.

2 The Interpretation and Practice of the Lord's Supper I Cor. 10.14–22 and 11.17–34 are the only passages in the New Testament which explicitly state that the Last Supper was repeatedly re-enacted in the early church. The first of them indicates that Paul sees a link between the Christian Lord's Supper and pagan meals in honour of particular gods. Some Christians at Corinth wish to take part in these pagan ceremonies, on the grounds that, because the gods concerned do not exist, meals in their honour do no harm (I Cor. 8). Paul identifies these gods with demons and draws a parallel between the cup and table of the Lord and the cup and table of demons.[2] Because both of these establish 'participation' or 'fellowship' with the Lord or with the demons, taking part in one of them is incompatible with taking part in the other (10.14–22). As the 'many lords' (8.5) of the pagans have their cultic meals, so does the 'one Lord' (8.6) acknowledged by Christians. In the Christian meal, the cup and the bread convey a shared fellowship with the Lord who shed his blood and gave up his body as a sacrifice for many. The Jewish sacrificial language of the older tradition (quoted in 11.23–25) has been combined with the idea of 'fellowship' or 'communion' with a divine being, taken over from the pagan environment.

I Cor. (11.17–34) criticizes the Corinthians for their conduct at the Lord's Supper: 'In eating, each one goes ahead with his own meal, and one is hungry and another is drunk' (v. 21). The Lord's Supper is being celebrated as a genuine meal, at which everyone provides their own food, but the result is that the poorer members of the congregation are humiliated by the extravagance of the rich. This individualism is a travesty of the Lord's Supper, which is a corporate celebration in which the whole congregation must participate. The solution is not (as one might expect) that food and drink should be shared, but that the Lord's Supper should cease to be a true meal. People should satisfy their hunger and thirst in their own homes (vv. 22,34).

LOVE When asked, 'Which commandment is the first of all?', Jesus quotes first the commandment to love God, and second the commandment to love one's neighbour (Mark 12.28–31). In Matthew's version of this incident, the two commandments are linked with the words, 'A second is like it . . .', which may suggest that one cannot love God without also loving one's neighbour, or one's neighbour without also loving God (Matt. 22.39). Jesus also extends the meaning of the commandment on his own authority: 'You have heard that it was said, "You shall love your neighbour and hate your enemy". But I say to you, Love your enemies and pray for those who persecute you . . .' (Matt. 5.43–44). The words quoted are a paraphrase of Lev. 19.17–18, where the commandment, 'You shall love your neighbour as yourself ', is related to 'You shall not hate *your brother* in your heart'; 'your brother' means 'the sons of your own people'. Here, hatred for others is quite in order. In the parable of the Good Samaritan (Luke 10.29–37) Jesus explains how 'neighbour' is to be understood: it does not refer to 'the sons of your own people', but to anyone in need.[1]

Outside the Synoptic Gospels, 'love' is discussed mainly in the context of life within the Christian congregation, rather than life within the world. It is not denied that love for those outside the congregation is appropriate, but that is not where the emphasis lies: 'So then, as we have opportunity, let us do good to all men, and especially those who are of the household of faith' (Gal. 6.10). The famous hymn to love in I Cor. 13 is addressed specifically to the tensions within the congregation discussed in I Cor. 12; love is the antidote to the jealousy, arrogance and divisions which characterize the body of Christ at Corinth.[2] In John 13.34, Jesus' 'new commandment' is 'that you love *one another*' – that is, fellow Christians. This love is motivated by Jesus' prior love: '. . . even as I have loved you, that you also love one another'. This link between the disciples' love for one another and Jesus' love for them is worked out with great eloquence in I John: 'In this is love, not that we loved God but that he loved us and sent his Son to be the expiation of our sins. Beloved, if God so loved us, we also ought to love one another' (4.10–11).[3]

In one sense, this concentration on love among Christians represents a narrowing of the sphere of love in comparison with Jesus' own teaching. It could even be argued that this is a return to the old, limited concept of the 'neighbour' which Jesus opposed, but that would be an exaggerated view. Firstly, the stress on love among members of the congregation shows that love is always concrete, and concerns real people rather than a vague universal benevolence. Secondly, it is the world, and not only the Church, that is the object of the love of God manifested in his Son (John 3.16, I John 2.2). The deepest truth about the world is therefore not that it does not know God, but that God loved it (*see* Rom. 11.28–32).

LUKE, GOSPEL ACCORDING TO[1] The traditional arrangement of the books of the New Testament separates the two volumes of a single work. The

Acts of the Apostles begins with the words, 'In the first book, O Theophilus, I have dealt with all that Jesus began to do and teach . . .', and the Gospel of Luke is clearly that 'first book'. It too is dedicated to the 'most excellent Theophilus' (1.3), who seems to have been an aristocratic convert to Christianity. Unlike the other evangelists, Luke emphasizes his qualifications as a historian; the elegantly-written preface (1.1–3) sets his work in the category of Graeco-Roman historical writing. He stresses the many authentic sources at his disposal, his own laborious research, and the resulting orderliness and reliability of his narrative. In the Roman world, literary artistry was often expected of the historian (and not just a pedantic recounting of the facts), and Luke excels in this. As a historian, he has his shortcomings. He erroneously places the census which took place 'when Quirinius was governor of Syria' (2.2) in 'the days of Herod king of Judea' (1.5). He states that Annas and Caiaphas were both high priests at the same time (3.2).[2] In Acts too, there are errors of fact, minor contradictions, and a very different view of early Christian history from the one provided by Paul.[3] In the Gospel, there is little evidence of any serious historical research; much of the time, the author is simply rewriting the Gospel of Mark, most of which he incorporates into his own work (without acknowledgment).[4] This does not diminish the value of Luke or Acts for the study of Christian origins, but it does suggest that they should be read critically.

1 The Construction of Luke The Gospel of Luke is constructed out of eight large blocks of material, most of which is derived either from Mark or from the lost work also used by Matthew (generally known as 'Q', from the German, *Quelle*, 'source', and consisting mostly of teaching). However, some material is to be found only in Luke.

(*i*) **Luke 1–2** consists of nativity stories concerning the birth of John the Baptist and of Jesus. The evangelist has skilfully imitated the style of Old Testament narratives, and vividly depicts the joy of faithful Jews that now at last the ancient promise of redemption is being fulfilled.[5] This section has little in common with Matthew's nativity narrative, other than the bare facts of the virgin conception and the birth of Jesus in Bethlehem.[6]

(*ii*) **Luke 3.1–4.13** comprises material about the ministry of John the Baptist and the temptations of Jesus, which is also to be found in Matthew.[7] Because the two Gospels appear to be independent of one another, this material seems to derive from a lost source, 'Q'.[8]

(*iii*) **Luke 4.14–6.19** is the first section derived from Mark, and follows closely the order of events in Mark 1.14–3.19: initial healing activity, mainly at Capernaum, controversies with the Pharisees, and the calling of the twelve. Luke has made two major alterations to Mark: he prefaces Jesus' ministry with a lengthy account of his rejection in Nazareth (4.16–30, an expansion of Mark 6.1–6), and he links the call of the first disciples with a miraculous catch of fish (5.1–11, *see* Mark 1.16–20, John 21).[9]

(*iv*) **Luke 6.20–7.50** is a second block of material mostly shared with Matthew and deriving mainly from 'Q'. It includes the 'Sermon on the Plain' (the basis for Matthew's better-known 'Sermon on the Mount'), the story of the centurion's servant, and teaching about the relationship between John the Baptist and Jesus.[10] The stories of the resurrection of a young man at Nain and the anointing of Jesus' feet occur only in Luke (although there is a different version of the latter in Mark 14.3–9).

(v) **Luke 8.1–9.50** is the second section derived from Mark. Again, Luke follows closely Mark's order; but he omits one long passage, moving straight from the feeding of the five thousand (Mark 6.30–44) to Peter's confession at Caesarea Philippi (Mark 8.27–33).[11] The reason for this omission is unknown, but it is possible that Luke used a version of Mark that lacked the intervening material.

(vi) **Luke 9.51–18.14** consists mainly of teaching material, against the background of Jesus' journey from Galilee to Jerusalem. Much of this material occurs also in Matthew and derives from 'Q', but some of it is unique to Luke, including a number of parables (e.g. the Rich Fool, the Good Samaritan, the Prodigal Son, the Unjust Steward, Dives and Lazarus, the Unjust Judge, the Pharisee and the Tax Collector).[12] This block of teaching is apparently arranged in a very haphazard manner and lacks the orderliness of Matthew's discourses.

(vii) **Luke 18.15–21.38** is the third section from Mark, and includes incidents from the journey to Jerusalem, the triumphal entry, controversies in the temple, and the discourse about the events leading up to the Second Coming. Luke has added some material which is unique to him (the conversion of Zacchaeus, Jesus weeping over Jerusalem), and the parable of the Talents (from 'Q').[13] He has also substantially rewritten Mark's discourse about the last things.

(viii) **Luke 22–24** gives Luke's account of Jesus' passion and resurrection. Although he uses Mark here, he does so with considerable freedom and evidently possesses independent tradition that he incorporates into Mark's framework. He alone tells of Jesus' trial before Herod Antipas, the grief of the women of Jerusalem, the appearance of the risen Jesus on the way to Emmaus, and the Ascension.[14]

2 Special Emphases Despite the fact that so much of his material is shared with Mark and Matthew, Luke presents a view of Jesus which is quite distinctive. This comes out both in the material found only in Luke, and in editorial comments and alterations in material shared with another evangelist.

(i) **Sinners and Pharisees** Jesus' solidarity with the 'tax collectors and sinners' against the Pharisees is mentioned in both Mark and Matthew, but is far more strongly emphasized in Luke. In 7.36–50 the love shown to Jesus by 'a woman of the city, who was a sinner' is contrasted with the coldness of Simon the Pharisee. In Luke 15 the parables of the Lost Sheep, the Lost Coin, and the Prodigal Son (the last two of which are unique to Luke) are told in response to the Pharisees' complaint that 'this man receives sinners and eats with them'. The parables stress that God seeks and welcomes home sinners, and Jesus is therefore his representative. In the parable of the Prodigal Son, the figure of the elder brother represents a criticism of the Pharisees' own attitude, and this criticism recurs in the parable of the Pharisee and the Tax Collector in 18.9–14 (again found only in Luke). Finally, the story of Zacchaeus in 19.1–10 (which is inserted into a context in which Luke is following Mark) illustrates Jesus' attitude as portrayed in 15.1–2. Luke clearly sees an important aspect of the gospel in this attack on self-righteousness and defence of the outcasts. Does he have in mind the scorn felt by the non-Christian associates of the 'most excellent Theophilus' towards a Christianity which appealed mainly to the lower classes (*see* I Cor. 1.26–29)?

(*ii*) **Prayer** Luke has a number of references to Jesus praying, in contexts where there is no such reference in the other Gospels. Jesus prays after his baptism (3.21), after the healing of a leper (5.17), before choosing the twelve disciples (6.12), before Peter's confession at Caesarea Philippi (9.18), and at his transfiguration (9.28–29).[15] It is Jesus' own praying which stimulates the request, 'Lord, teach us to pray', and the Lord's Prayer (11.1–4). The crucified Jesus continues to pray: 'Father, forgive them, for they know not what they do' (23.34) – 'Father into thy hands I commit my spirit' (23.46).[16] Luke's interest in prayer also appears in his introduction to the parable of the Unjust Judge: 'And he told them a parable, to the effect that they ought always to pray and not lose heart' (18.1).

(*iii*) **The Universality of Jesus** Although his nativity narrative stresses Jesus' Jewish origins, Luke emphasizes his universality. His birth in Bethlehem, in fulfilment of prophecy, is occasioned by an event in world history (2.1–2).[17] The beginning of John the Baptist's ministry is dated by reference to the reign of Tiberius. The genealogy in 3.23–38 traces Jesus' ancestry not only back to Abraham (as in Matthew) but to Adam, a universal figure. Jesus' rejection at Nazareth foreshadows the Jewish hostility to the gospel and the consequent turning to the Gentiles narrated in Acts (Luke 4.24–30). However, since this is to be one of the main themes of Acts, references to Gentiles or Gentile territory are played down or omitted in the Gospel itself. The gospel message is indeed 'a light for revelation to the Gentiles' (2.32), but the full story can only be told in Volume II (*see* Acts 13.46–47).

(*iv*) **The Return of Christ** Many of the early Christians fervently expected the return of Christ and the end of the world within their generation.[18] Luke discourages such hopes. In Mark 13.14–27, the desecration of the temple (described in mysterious apocalyptic language) immediately precedes the collapse of the universe and the coming of the Son of man with great power and glory. But Luke completely rewrites this section. He omits the apocalyptic imagery, and writes of the fate of Jerusalem and its inhabitants in AD 70 as a straightforward historical event (21.20–24). The collapse of the universe does not follow immediately, for Luke inserts a period of unspecified length which he describes as 'the times of the Gentiles' (i.e. the time of missionary work among the Gentiles?) that must first be 'fulfilled (21.24). He opposes not only false Christs who say 'I am he!' (as in Mark), but also those who say 'The time is at hand!', who might include Christians (21.8). The same concern is apparent in Acts 1.6–7.

MARK, GOSPEL ACCORDING TO The Gospel of Mark was traditionally regarded as a somewhat clumsy abbreviation of Matthew, of little real value. However, in the nineteenth century it was discovered that Mark was actually earlier than Matthew, and was Matthew's own chief source. As the earliest of the Gospels, Mark took on a new importance.[1]

1 Authorship The Gospel has nothing to say about its own authorship, and the title 'According to Mark' is not part of the original text. A tradition dating back at least to the second century states that a certain Mark wrote down what was taught orally by Peter. This tradition is probably of little value. The early church felt it important to ascribe apostolic authorship to all four Gospels, and so traditions about authorship are not motivated by pure historical concern. The Gospel of Mark does not appear to reflect the distinctive preaching of an individual, but the traditions about Jesus developed and handed down in communities. The link between Peter and Mark could be a deduction from I Peter 5.13, which links Peter with 'my son Mark'. Whoever the author was, he was probably a Gentile writing for Gentiles, because he has to explain Jewish customs (7.3–4) and does not observe the Jewish food laws (7.19).[2]

2 Date Mark is often dated before the destruction of Jerusalem in AD 70, but in fact it should probably be dated slightly later than that event. In Mark 13.2, Jesus clearly predicts the destruction of the temple: 'Do you see these great buildings? There will not be left here one stone upon another'. (Perhaps as a result of this saying, Jesus is in Mark 14.58 falsely accused of having said, '*I* will destroy this temple . . .'.) Some Christians before AD 70 believed that the temple would be desecrated immediately before the return of Christ (perhaps as a result of the Emperor Caligula's unsuccessful attempt to have a statue of himself erected in the temple in AD 40–1); but they do not seem to have believed that the temple would actually be destroyed. The very precise statement in Mark 13.2 therefore seems to date from a period after AD 70, which would make the Gospel as a whole later than is often thought. The approximate date may be about AD 75; Matthew and Luke, who use Mark independently of one another, would then have been composed sometime in the last quarter of the first century.

3 Structure In the case of Matthew and Luke it is possible to determine more or less which sources were at their disposal and how the evangelists used them in the construction of their Gospels. Because Mark is the earliest of the Gospels, such knowledge is impossible in this case. Whether he made use of written sources or relied mainly on oral tradition is unclear. Some deductions are possible: it seems likely that the events of Mark 1.21–39 and the parables of Mark 4 were already grouped together before Mark, and above all the passion narrative seems to have existed as a continuous story from the earliest times.

The Gospel falls into two clearly defined halves. The first is concerned with Jesus' ministry in and around Galilee, and the emphasis is on miracles and, to a lesser extent, on controversy with opponents. With the exception of the parables in chapter 4, there is little continuous teaching; indeed, by comparison with Matthew and Luke, Jesus' teaching is conspicuously lacking in Mark. At first, Jesus' spectacular miracles elicit astonishment from the disciples, but not faith. Thus, when Jesus walked on the water, 'they were utterly astounded, for they did not understand about the loaves, but their hearts were hardened' (6.51–52). The evangelist means that if the disciples had understood that Jesus' multiplication of the loaves proved him to be the Messiah, they would not have been so surprised when he walked on the water. Jesus harshly criticizes them for their failure to believe in 8.17–18: 'Do you not yet perceive or understand? Are your hearts hardened? Having eyes do you not see, and having ears do you not hear?' Again, the stupendous feeding miracles are seen as the main reason for faith in him (8.19–21). The breakthrough comes at Caesarea Philippi, where, in response to Jesus' question, 'Who do *you* say that I am?', Peter answers: 'You are the Christ' (8.29).[3]

The Caesarea Philippi incident is not only the culmination of the first half of the Gospel; it is the starting-point for the second. Immediately after Peter's confession, Jesus begins to teach the disciples about his forthcoming death (which has hardly even been hinted at in the first half): 'The Son of man must suffer many things, and be rejected by the elders and the chief priests and the scribes, and be killed, and after three days rise again' (8.31). From this point on, Jesus is steadily journeying towards Jerusalem. From Caesarea Philippi in the north, he moves southward through Galilee (9.30), into 'the region of Judaea' (10.1), along 'the road going up to Jerusalem' (10.32), passing through Jericho (10.46) and the villages next to the Mount of Olives (11.1), and eventually entering Jerusalem in triumph in 11.11. Repeated predictions of his death in Jerusalem (8.31, 9.10,12,31–32, 10.32–34, 38–39)[4] mean that the passion dominates the whole second half of the Gospel just as the miracles dominate the first half. The whole Gospel is structured around the paradoxical tension between power and weakness, revelation and hiddenness.

The contrast between the two halves of the Gospel, however, is not absolute. Weakness and hiddenness are also present in the first half, and power and revelation in the second.

4 *Theological Emphases* This tension between power and weakness is responsible for three of the most striking theological emphases of the Gospel of Mark: secrecy, suffering, and the enigmatic nature of the resurrection.

(*i*) **Secrecy** One remarkable feature of the Gospel of Mark is the stress on secrecy: Jesus repeatedly commands that his identity, his miracles and his teaching be kept secret. When the demons cry out, 'You are the Son of God!', Jesus orders them not to make him known' (3.11–12, *see* 1.34). When Peter at last recognizes him as the Christ, Jesus again commands that this be kept a secret (8.29–30).

Although many of the miracle stories stress the amazement of the crowds at what Jesus does, here too commands to secrecy are to be found, even in contexts where they seem quite inappropriate. When Jesus raises Jairus' daughter from the dead, he strictly commands that no-one should know about this (5.43); but because her death was public knowledge (5.38–40), it is hard to see how this command could be fulfilled. Jesus' teaching is likewise often secret. He does not explain his parables to the crowd, but only to the disciples in private (4.34). He contrasts the disciples, to whom 'has been given the secret of the kingdom of God', with 'those outside', for whom 'everything is in parables, so that they may indeed see but not perceive, and may indeed hear but not understand, lest they should turn again and be forgiven' (4.10–12).

This latter passage suggests that the key to Mark's secrecy theme is the notion of divine predestination: true knowledge of Jesus' identity, his miracles and his teaching is confined to the elect and withheld from the rest. Some such belief was held by many early Christians because they both recognized that the majority did not accept the gospel they proclaimed, and believed that God in his providence was in control of events. If people did not believe, then it must be because God had mysteriously withheld his revelation from them.[5]

This theme deeply affects the evangelist's whole presentation of Jesus. Despite his miracles, Jesus is not an unambiguous figure, but one who is open to misunderstanding and rejection. The misunderstanding may be hostile, as when the Pharisees ascribe his powers to the devil (3.22), or it may be well-meaning, as when the crowds conclude that he is John the Baptist, Elijah or one of the prophets (6.14–16, 8.28). Jesus himself rejects the opportunity offered him to remove himself from the realm of misunderstanding. When he is asked to perform an unambiguous 'sign', he refuses: 'Why does this generation seek a sign? Truly I say to you, no sign shall be given to this generation' (8.12).[6]

(*ii*) **Suffering and the Christ** The theme of suffering is abruptly introduced immediately after Peter's confession of Jesus as the Christ; Jesus 'began to teach them that the Son of man must suffer many things . . . and be killed' (8.31). Peter then 'began to rebuke him', but he answered, 'Get behind me Satan! For you are not on the side of God, but of men' (8.32–33). Peter's protest does not spring from his devotion to Jesus as an individual, but from his confession of him as the Messiah. The Messiah is the bringer of the new age, and it is inconceivable that the bringer of the new age should be overcome by the powers of the old. Yet this is what Jesus announces, and this is the paradox elaborated by the entire Gospel. The disciples must share in this suffering: 'If any man would come after me, let him deny himself and take up his cross and follow me' (8.34). When James and John ask for the places of honour in the kingdom of God, all Jesus will promise them is that 'the cup [of suffering] that I drink you will drink' (10.39).[7]

Mark's passion narrative is characterized by a stark emphasis on failure and defeat.[8] Jesus is betrayed by one of his own disciples, denied by another (the very disciple who had earlier acknowledged him as the Christ), and deserted by the rest. Mark, and the early Church generally, could easily have ignored such unpalatable facts; yet they did not. More remarkable still is the portrayal of Jesus himself. Jesus in Gethsemane does not show the calm demeanour which the early Church expected of its own martyrs; he 'began to be greatly distressed and troubled', and said, 'My soul is very sorrowful, even to death' (14.33–34). The contrast with the Gospel of John is particularly noteworthy: John omits the Gethsemane narrative, and has the soldiers who come to arrest Jesus fall to the ground, overwhelmed by his divine majesty (John 18.6). The 'distress' and 'sorrow' of Gethsemane reach their climax at the crucifixion with the terrible cry, 'My God, my God, why hast thou forsaken me?' (15.34) – the only utterance from the cross recorded by Mark, although 15.37 mentions a final wordless cry. Here too, later evangelists found this quite unacceptable. Thus, Luke turns the crucified Jesus into a model of true piety: praying for the forgiveness of his tormentors (23.34), looking forward to being in Paradise (23.43), and committing his soul to God (23.46). Mark, in contrast, does nothing to diminish the force of the great paradox: the bearer of the new age is overcome by the powers of the old.

(*iii*) **The Enigma of the Resurrection**[9] Of course, the death of Jesus is not the end of the story; a brief narrative, a mere eight verses long, tells of the events of Easter morning. But even here, the result is not triumph but bewilderment. The women encounter a mysterious young man dressed in white who informs them that Jesus is risen, and commands them to tell the disciples; but the women run away in terror and are too afraid to tell anyone. As presented by Mark, Easter is a riddle. He offers no proof that the tomb was empty because Jesus had risen from the dead and he does not tell us whether the young man's promise of a meeting with the risen Jesus in Galilee was fulfilled. Indeed, because the women failed to pass on the message, one might even assume that it could not have been fulfilled. The evangelist leaves the reader free to conclude that the young man might have been in error, or that he might have been deceiving the women. Of course, Mark himself believed that Jesus rose from the dead and that he appeared to his disciples, but it is nevertheless significant that he leaves the resurrection message with a question mark against it. The reader is confronted with a personal decision, for or against.

All this suggests that the contrast often drawn between the simplicity of Mark and the profundity of John is misleading. It is based on the mistaken assumption that only ideas can be profound, and not narratives.

MARRIAGE Perhaps because Jesus was unmarried, some of the early Christians considered whether they too should renounce marriage. Through remaining unmarried, one might devote oneself wholly to the cause of the kingdom of God, as Jesus did, and free oneself of the worldly desires and cares which hindered one's salvation. The fact that this path was generally rejected shows not just the social conservatism of the early Christians, but also the positive value they ascribed to the created order.

The possibility of Christian opposition to the institution of marriage is mentioned in I Tim. 4.1–5, which speaks in harsh language of those who 'depart from the faith' and who, inspired by demons, 'forbid marriage'. The author argues that 'everything created by God is good, and nothing is to be rejected if it is received with thanksgiving' (he has in mind here the foods forbidden by the heretics, as well as marriage).[1] He echoes here the teaching of Jesus on marriage, which again appeals to the creation story (Mark 10.6–9): marriage is part of the good created order that endures despite the 'hardness of heart' (v. 5) that has since entered the world. To live together in marriage is to fulfil the divine command-ment and to serve God.[2]

According to the New Testament, however, the world is not only created but also fallen. In I Cor. 7, Paul responds to the Corinthian suggestion that married couples should separate from one another, or at least abstain from sexual intercourse. The first possibility is rejected because of Jesus' prohibition of divorce (vv. 10–11). The second is ruled out because marriage is necessary to contain and restrict lust: 'Because of the temptation to immorality, each man should have his own wife and each woman her own husband. The husband should give to his wife her conjugal rights, and likewise the wife to her husband' (vv. 2–3). For the same reason, the suggestion that unmarried Christians should remain unmarried is treated with caution: Paul sees the force of the argument that one should devote oneself wholly to the service of the Lord (vv. 25–35), but he thinks that 'it is better to marry than to be aflame with passion' (v. 9, see v. 36). There is nothing in this context about the sanctity of marriage as part of the created order; it is viewed pragmatically as a remedy for lust in a fallen world. It is clear that Paul regards being single as a higher vocation than marriage, but he refuses to impose this as a law, as some at Corinth evidently wished him to do.[3]

Eph. 5.21–33 gives yet another view of marriage: it is justified not on the basis of the goodness of creation or pragmatic necessity, but on the basis of Christ's love for his Church. This view brings the element of subjection to the fore: because the Church is subject to Christ, wives must be subject to their husbands (v. 24). Yet subjection is not absolute, for husbands have a duty towards their wives: as Christ loved the Church and gave himself up for her, so husbands must love their wives (v. 25). Indeed, because Christ and the Church are 'one flesh' and one body, husbands should love their wives no less than they love themselves (vv. 28–32). This passage illustrates the early Christian tendency to attempt to serve God within the structures imposed by contemporary society, rather then rejecting those structures.

The varied views expressed in these and other passages lead one to doubt whether there is any single 'New Testament view of marriage'. As with other areas of ethics, the New Testament writers do not present their readers with detailed prescriptions about how to live their lives, but leave them to work out for themselves the precise implications of Christian commitment for daily life.

MARY MAGDALENE[1] The four Gospels disagree with one another about precisely which of the women visited the tomb of Jesus on Easter morning and they are agreed only on the fact that Mary Magdalene was one of them (or, in John, the only one). Mary Magdalene is mentioned in Luke 8.2 as a woman 'from whom seven demons had gone out' – that is, cast out by Jesus. She and the other women mentioned in 8.3 'provided for them [i.e. Jesus and the disciples] out of their means'. There is no evidence for the traditional view that she is to be identified with the 'woman of the city, who was a sinner' (evidently a prostitute) of Luke 7.36–50. She is introduced in Mark 15.40 as someone whose name would be familiar to the early Christian community, no doubt as the one who discovered that the tomb of Jesus was empty. Her reaction to this discovery is reported in various ways. In Mark 16.8 she and her companions flee from the tomb and are too frightened to tell anyone. In Luke 24.8–11 they tell the disciples, who do not believe (*see also* 24.22–24). In Matt. 28.8–10 they run from the tomb with fear and joy, and meet the risen Jesus on the way into the city (contrary to Luke 24.24: 'him they did not see'). In John 20.1–18 Mary's discovery of the empty tomb is at first a cause for grief ('They have taken away my Lord, and I do not know where they have laid him'), which is transformed into joy when the risen Lord appears to her.

The evangelists are therefore divided about whether Mary Magdalene was only the discoverer of the empty tomb or the first witness to the risen Lord. In the earliest tradition, represented by Mark, the former seems to be the case; this is confirmed by I Cor. 15.5–8, where Mary is not included in the list of witnesses to the resurrection.

MARY, THE VIRGIN[1]

In Matthew's nativity narrative, Mary plays a comparatively unimportant part. It is Joseph, and not Mary, who is the recipient of the Annunciation (1.18–25) and of other angelic messages (2.13,19–20); God deals with Mary only indirectly, through her husband, and she remains a passive figure. In Luke, the situation is reversed: Joseph is mentioned as Mary's betrothed in 1.27 and as going up to the home of his ancestors in 2.4–5, but otherwise it is Mary who plays the central role. Despite her initial doubts (1.29,34), she accepts the message of the Annunciation with the words, 'Behold, I am the handmaid of the Lord; let it be to me according to your word' (1.38). She is pronounced the most blessed of women by her relative Elisabeth (1.42) and praises God for his goodness to her in the *Magnificat* (1.46–55). She 'kept all these things [i.e. the angel's message to the shepherds], pondering them in her heart' (2.19), and is specifically addressed by the aged Simeon, who tells her that 'a sword will pierce through your own soul also' (2.34–35). After the child Jesus has amazed the teachers in Jerusalem with his learning, it is again said that Mary 'kept all these things in her heart' (2.51).

Apart from the nativity stories, Mary is mentioned only infrequently in the New Testament. The inhabitants of Nazareth describe Jesus as 'the son of Mary and brother of James and Joses and Judas and Simon'.[2] In a curious incident in Mark 3.21,31–35, Jesus' mother and brothers 'went out to seize him, for people were saying, "He is beside himself" '; but he refused to go with them, saying of his disciples, 'Here are my mother and my brothers! Whoever does the will of God is my brother, and sister, and mother'. In a related narrative, Jesus responds to the cry, 'Blessed is the womb that bore you, and the breasts that you sucked!', with the words: 'Blessed rather are those who hear the word of God and keep it!' (Luke 11.27–28). In John it is only Jesus' brothers who do not believe in him (7.5), whereas Mary (who is never named) is portrayed as believing in Jesus from the beginning (2.1–5) and remaining faithful to him until the end (19.25–27). There is a final reference to her in Acts 1.14, where she and Jesus' brothers join with the disciples in the days between the Ascension and Pentecost.

It is hard to form a consistent view of Mary from these passages; but a few general points may be worth noting.

(*i*) The tendency to ascribe special honour to Mary is already present in the New Testament, in Luke's nativity narratives and (to a lesser extent) in John. Mary is idealized as a model of devotion both to the will of God and to her own son. Yet she is not simply an individual figure, but the representative of the pious Israelites who have longed for the Messiah's coming and who now see that he is here at last. This is true above all in the *Magnificat*.

(*ii*) There is also a contrary tendency to play down the significance of Mary and of Jesus' family in general. Despite Elisabeth's acclamation, 'Blessed are you among women!' (Luke 1.42), Jesus himself rejects a similar acclamation of her from a woman in the crowd (Luke 11.27–28). Mark 3.21–35 links Jesus' family (including his mother) with his Pharisaic opponents. Historically, such passages may reflect the fact that James the brother of Jesus would have been unpopular in parts of the Church that honoured Paul (*see* Gal. 2.6,9,12).[3] Theologically, they express the conviction that Jesus is a figure of universal and ultimate significance who cannot be confined to a particular limited setting. Just as Jesus is the universal Lord and not just the Jewish Son of David (Mark 12.35–37), so as the universal Lord he is not just 'the son of Mary and brother of James and Joses and Judas and Simon' (Mark 6.3).

MATTHEW, GOSPEL ACCORDING TO
Matthew was traditionally thought to have been the earliest of the Gospels, but it is now recognized that the evangelist used the earlier Gospel of Mark as his own chief source, combining it with the sayings material found in 'Q' (the lost source used by both Matthew and Luke). Indeed, one might regard Matthew as a greatly enlarged second edition of Mark.[1]

1 Authorship and Date The Gospel has nothing to say about its own authorship. The tradition that its author was the apostle Matthew dates back to the second century and to the claim that Matthew compiled the sayings of Jesus, which were then translated by different people into Greek. A link between the Gospel and the apostle Matthew was discovered in Matt. 9.9, where Matthew (rather than Levi, as in Mark) is the name of the tax-collector called to be Jesus' disciple. The purpose of the early Christian discussions about authorship was to determine which books were authoritative, and the real origin of the claim that Matthew was the author of this Gospel was the belief that authoritative works had to have been written by apostles.

The author, however, was clearly a Jewish Christian. This is apparent from his attitude towards the Law, which is much more conservative than Mark's, and in his attacks on the Pharisees, which suggest that Pharisaic claims are still a problem for the community for which he is writing. Because the date of the Gospel of Mark seems to have been about AD 75,[2] one must assume that the Gospel of Matthew was written at some point in the final quarter of the first century.

2 Structure Matthew is the most carefully structured of all the Gospels. The evangelist has taken great pains to bring order to the chaotic diversity of the various traditions of Jesus.

(*i*) **Matt. 1–2** contains a genealogy of Jesus and stories relating to his birth.[3] This section is strikingly different from Luke's nativity narratives. Both accounts agree that Jesus was conceived by the Holy Spirit, that his mother was called Mary and his adoptive father Joseph, and that he was born in Bethlehem in the days of Herod the Great, but otherwise they have little in common. Matthew is especially concerned to show that Jesus is the fulfilment of Old Testament prophecy.

(*ii*) In **Matt. 3–4**, we read of the ministry of John the Baptist, the baptism and temptations of Jesus (all shared with Luke and taken from 'Q'),[4] and the beginning of Jesus' ministry (derived from Mark).

(*iii*) **Matt. 5–7** constitutes the collection of sayings known as 'the Sermon on the Mount'.[5] Matthew chooses to open his account of Jesus' ministry not with his miracles (as in Mark 1) but with his teaching. The Sermon on the Mount is based on a shorter discourse, found in 'Q' and preserved in Luke 6 (Luke's 'Sermon on the Plain'), which the evangelist has expanded with the addition of material from elsewhere in this lost source and some extra material of his own. The evangelist's orderly mind is seen in his attempt to group the material according to subject: for example, contrasts are drawn between the old Law and the teaching of Jesus (5.17–48), between true and false piety (6.1–18), and between God and earthly goods as the goal of human striving (6.19–34).

(*iv*) **Matt. 8–9** consists of narrative material mainly about Jesus' healing miracles, mostly drawn from Mark. Although the evangelist generally follows Mark's order, he is less strict in this respect than Luke. As in Luke, there is a tendency to abbreviate, which means that many of the stories are found in their fullest and most attractive form in Mark.

(*v*) In **Matt. 10–11** a discourse about mission, mainly drawn from 'Q', is followed by teaching (again from 'Q') about the relationship between Jesus and John the Baptist.[6]

(*vi*) **Matt. 12–17** returns to Mark's narrative, following Mark's order more closely than in Matt. 8–9. Because Mark's healing narratives have mostly been grouped together in Matt. 8–9, such stories are not prominent in this section. Additions and alterations to Mark are commonplace. For example, the evangelist has added extra parables to Mark's parable chapter (Mark 4, Matt. 13); he has provided a sequel to the story of Jesus walking on the water, in which Peter tries to do the same (14.28–33)[7]; and he has inserted the sayings relating to the authority of Peter to Mark's account of the confession at Caesarea Philippi (16.17–19).

(*vii*) **Matt. 18** consists of a discourse on church order, including teaching on the procedure for excommunication and the extent of forgiveness that is found only in Matthew. The parable of the lost sheep is here applied to the care of church leaders for their flock (vv. 12–14).[8]

(*viii*) In **Matt. 19–22**, the evangelist follows Mark's account of the final stages of Jesus' ministry, in Judaea and in Jerusalem. He adds material such as the parables of the labourers in the vineyard (20.1–16), the wedding feast (22.1–14), and the two sons (22.28–32).[9]

(*ix*) The discourses in **Matt. 23–25** consist of an attack on the scribes and Pharisees (Matt. 23), a revised version of the teaching on the end of the world in Mark 13 (Matt. 24), and a series of parables again relating to the end of the world (Matt. 25).[10]

(x) **Matt. 26–28** follows Mark's passion and resurrection narratives fairly closely, although with a number of additions.[11] For example, Matthew alone contains the narratives about Judas' repentance and suicide, Pilate's washing of his hands, the ineffectual guard at the tomb of Jesus, and the appearances of the risen Lord near Jerusalem and on the mountain in Galilee.

3 Main Theological Themes In his editing of the traditional material at his disposal, the evangelist shows a particular interest in a number of theological themes.

(i) **The Law** The evangelist is more conservative in his attitude towards the law than Mark. For this reason he omits the explanatory comment of Mark 7.19, 'Thus he declared all foods clean' (i.e. abolished the dietary laws) from his version of a particular saying of Jesus (Matt. 15.17). He places in a position of special prominence a saying about the eternal validity of the law: 'Think not that I have come to abolish the law and the prophets; I have come not to abolish but to fulfil them. For truly, I say to you, till heaven and earth pass away, not an iota, not a dot, will pass away from the law until all is accomplished' (5.17–18). He omits Mark's dangerously radical saying, 'The sabbath was made for man, not man for the sabbath' (Mark 2.27; compare Mark 2.23–28 with Matt. 12.1–8). He even accepts the authority of the teaching of the scribes and Pharisees: 'The scribes and Pharisees sit on Moses' seat; so practise and observe whatever they tell you, but not what they do . . .' (23.2–3).[12]

Yet there is an ambiguity about Matthew's attitude to the law. Despite the very conservative statements in 5.17–20, the following section consists of a series of contrasts between what was said 'to the men of old' (i.e. in the law) and what 'I say to you'. The content of most of these contrasts is in accordance with Jewish ethical teaching (e.g. the prohibitions of anger, lust, and revenge), but what is remarkable is the authority that is claimed: Jesus' 'I say to you' overrides the authority of the law itself. It is not clear how the evangelist reconciled these radical statements with the conservative tone of 5.17–20.

(ii) **The Fulfilment of Prophecy** Again and again, Matthew inserts some such phrase as, 'This took place to fulfil what was spoken through the prophet, saying . . .', followed by the quotation. All of the New Testament writers believed that Jesus was the fulfilment of Old Testament prophecy, but none of them takes such pains to emphasize this as Matthew. Jesus' conception took place in fulfilment of the prophecy (in the Greek translation of the Old Testament), 'Behold, a virgin shall conceive . . .' (1.23). Scripture predicted his birth in Bethlehem, his exile in Egypt, the massacre of the innocents, and his upbringing in Nazareth (2.6,15,17–18,23).[13] It likewise predicted many of the events and characteristics of his ministry: his association with the Sea of Galilee (4.14–16), his desire to keep his activity secret (12.17–21), the rejection he experienced (13.14–15), and his speaking in parables (13.35). Scripture also foretold the triumphal entry into Jerusalem (21.5), the praise of the children in the temple (21.16), and the thirty pieces of silver returned by Judas and used to buy the potter's field (27.9–10).

The evangelist sometimes takes his emphasis on fulfilment to extreme lengths. Zech. 9.13 predicted that the Messiah would enter Jerusalem 'mounted on an ass, and on a colt, the foal of an ass'. The parallelism is typical of Hebrew poetry, but Matthew takes it literally: Jesus entered Jerusalem mounted not on one animal but on two: an ass and a colt (21.2–7).

(iii) **The Church** In the four Gospels, the word 'church' occurs only in Matt. 16.17–19 and 18.17. In the former passage, Matthew explicitly presents Jesus as the founder of the Church: 'On this rock [i.e. Peter] I will build my church . . .'. The future tense suggests that Matthew, like the rest of the New Testament, sees the Church as the creation of the risen Lord, not the earthly Jesus. The evangelist stands in a tradition which regards Peter as the chief of the apostles[14] – a tradition which was disputed by the adherents of James (see Gal. 2.12), of Paul (see Gal. 2.11–14), and of the beloved disciple (see John 21.24, and other passages in which the beloved disciple is regarded as superior to Peter).[15] The authority given to Peter to 'bind and loose' (16.19) is not unique to him, because it is extended to all the disciples and, by implication, to all church leaders, in 18.18.

Despite the detailed instructions about excommunication in 18.15–18, the evangelist is aware that the Church on earth is bound to be imperfect. In the parable of the tares and its interpretation (13.24–30, 36–43), the point is that the tares cannot be separated from the wheat at present; there can be no such thing as a perfect Church on earth. The Church will be perfected only at the harvest (i.e. the last judgment), when the evildoers who have been infiltrated into the Church by the devil will be rooted out and destroyed.[16]

MIRACLES OF JESUS

MIRACLES OF JESUS The accounts of the ministry of Jesus in the Gospels contain three basic ingredients: teaching, controversy stories and miracle stories. Occasionally, the categories merge, as when a miracle (e.g. a healing on the sabbath) begins a controversy. The miracle stories involve healings, exorcisms, people being raised from the dead, and acts of power over inanimate nature. Most of the stories derive from Mark; Matthew and Luke add to Mark a great deal of teaching material but only a small number of miracle stories, such as the healing of the centurion's servant. However, John contains several independent miracle stories. In addition to the miracles linked with Jesus' ministry, there are references to miracles occurring in connection both with Jesus' birth and his death. Indeed, the New Testament proclamation stands or falls with the truth of the claim that Jesus was miraculously raised from the dead.

1 Miracles as Signs Perhaps the chief function of the miracle stories is to provide evidence for the Christian claim that Jesus is the Messiah. As John 20.30–31 puts it: 'Jesus did many other signs in the presence of the disciples, which are not written in this book; but these are written that you may believe that Jesus is the Christ, the Son of God, and that believing you may have life in his name'. The evangelist's view of the miracles as 'signs' shows that for him they are significant not in themselves but as pointers to Jesus' true identity. The same view is taken in the Synoptic Gospels. When Peter confesses that Jesus is the Christ (Mark 8.29), this is the conclusion towards which Jesus' miracles have all along been pointing – despite the disciples' failure to perceive this.[1] When John the Baptist sends messengers to ask, 'Are you he who is to come, or shall we look for another?', Jesus sends them back with a report about his miracles (Matt. 11.3–5).

There is also, however, a train of thought according to which miraculous *proofs* of Jesus' identity are not granted. True miracles may be performed by false Christs and false prophets (Mark 13.22), and conversely, Jesus' miracles may lead people to think that he is mad or possessed by a demon (Mark 3.21–22). In his answer to the latter accusation, Jesus refers to the success of other exorcists: 'If I cast out demons by Beelzebub, by whom do your sons cast them out? Therefore they shall be your judges' (12.27). Although this refutes the accusation, it has the effect of putting Jesus in the same category as other exorcists, thus compromising his uniqueness.[2] The exorcisms are therefore not unambiguous proofs that Jesus is the Christ – indeed, such proofs are deliberately withheld. When it is suggested to Jesus that he performs an unambiguous public miracle (throwing himself from the temple pinnacle so as to be rescued by angels), he rejects this as a temptation of the devil (Matt. 4.5–7). Similarly, when the Pharisees request 'a sign from heaven', he responds: 'Why does this generation seek a sign? Truly I say to you, no sign shall be given to this generation' (Mark 8.11–12).[3] Mark repeatedly presents Jesus as commanding that his miracles be kept secret (e.g. 1.44, 5.43, 7.36, 8.26); this suggests that in his view the relation between the miracles and knowledge of Jesus' messiahship is less direct than other passages might imply.[4] Finally, despite 20.30–31 (quoted above), John is disparaging about a faith based solely on miracles (2.23–25, 4.48, 20.29).

Thus, the miracles are seen by the New Testament as signs of Jesus' messiahship; they are intended to lead to faith in him. Yet they are *only* signs. They are pointers and not proofs, and a faith in him which is dependent on his miracles is not true faith at all.

2 The Development of the Tradition In some cases, it is possible to show that in a later form of a story, the miraculous element has been increased. In Mark 14.47, one of the disciples cuts off the ear of the high priest's servant; Luke 22.51 adds that Jesus miraculously healed it. In Mark the death of Jesus is accompanied by a supernatural darkness and the tearing of the temple veil from top to bottom (15.33,38), but in Matthew, there is also a violent earthquake, and many of the saints of Old Testament times are raised from the dead (27.51–54).[5] In Mark 16.5, the women meet 'a young man dressed in a white robe' in the tomb of Jesus, whereas Matthew tells of 'a great earthquake': 'An angel of the Lord descended from heaven and came and rolled back the stone, and sat upon it. His appearance was like lightning, and his raiment white as snow' (27.2–3).[6] In Mark, Jesus alone walks on the water (6.47–52), but Matthew adds that Peter too performed this feat, though with limited success (14.28–31). In the Synoptics, the people who are raised from the dead have only just died (Mark 5.21–43, Luke 7.11–17), but in John 11 Jesus deliberately waits until Lazarus has begun to decompose before going to raise him from the dead.[7]

Various Old Testament passages may also have influenced the development of the tradition about Jesus' miracles. Elisha performs miracles involving the resurrection of a child from the dead, the multiplication of food and the healing of a leper (II Kings 4–5). Jesus' stilling the storm recalls Ps. 89.9: 'Thou dost rule the raging of the sea; when its waves rise, thou stillest them'. His walking on the water recalls Ps. 77.19: 'Thy way was through the sea, thy path through the great waters; yet thy footprints were unseen'.[8]

We might conclude from the evidence of the gradual heightening of the miraculous element, and from the apparent influence of the Old Testament, that miracles played little or no part in the earliest tradition about Jesus and were the product of later Christian imagination. However, this conclusion would be mistaken. References to miracle-working activity are too deeply embedded in the Gospel tradition to be explained away as the result of later tendencies to create legends about Jesus. Legends were indeed created, but they do not produce an entirely new picture of Jesus, but one which reflects characteristics already present in the earliest tradition. The quest for a historical Jesus who is nothing more than an ordinary Jewish rabbi is a figment of the modern imagination. Jesus perceived himself and was perceived by others as a worker of miracles.

3 Miracles and the Modern World View Since the eighteenth century the miracles of Jesus have become increasingly problematic for those influenced by the standpoint of modern science. It came to seem unlikely that the creator of all should have disregarded the laws of nature that he had established. Some argued that Jesus possessed natural powers of a kind at present beyond our understanding, but in principle comprehensible. Others believed that natural events had been misunderstood and turned into miracles. Others still were inclined to regard all the miracle stories as pure legends.

For the early Christians, the miracles of Jesus were not isolated, self-contained events. They were closely bound up with belief in Jesus' absolute and ultimate significance, to which they were seen as pointers. These pointers or signs were not unambiguous; they did not compel belief, and requests for conclusive proofs of this sort were rejected. But they did at least raise the question of Jesus' identity and significance. Some answered this question with the hostile claim that he was mad or possessed by the devil (Mark 3.21–22); others, more sympathetic, identified Jesus with John the Baptist, Elijah or one of the prophets (Mark 6.14–15, 8.28) – figures of only relative significance. Peter's conclusion – 'You are the Christ' – was not the only possible conclusion from Jesus' miracles.

For all the differences between our modern view of the world and that of the early Christians, the main features of this analysis are still applicable. We are presented in the Gospel miracle stories with a mixture of legend and fact. Yet that does not mean that they can simply be discounted, for even legends may express true insights. These stories do not compel belief – they themselves assert that this would be contrary to their own nature – but they do at least sharply pose the question of Jesus' real significance. Is the Christian affirmation of his universal and ultimate significance justified, or is his significance in the course of human history only relative?

MOSES[1] The New Testament writers share the Jewish view that Moses' chief significance is as the author (under divine inspiration) of the law – that is, the Pentateuch, the first five books of the Bible. Within this collection of books, 'law' in the narrower sense holds pride of place: 'The law was given through Moses' (John 1.17), and to 'read Moses' (II Cor. 3.15) is to read the law. Yet for most of the New Testament writers, the law was no longer authoritative in the same sense that it was for Judaism; Jesus Christ had displaced the law as the chief centre of authority. There is, therefore, a shift of emphasis away from Moses the law-giver to Moses the prophet, who in word and deed looked forward to the coming of the Christ. The opposing conceptions of Moses are set side by side in John 5.45–47, where Jesus is addressing his Jewish opponents: 'It is Moses who accuses you, on whom you set your hope. If you believed Moses, you would believe me, for he wrote of me. But if you do not believe his writings, how will you believe my words?'

Moses is seen as writing about Jesus in an indirect sense when he writes about actions of his own which foreshadow Jesus. John 3.14–15 states: 'As Moses lifted up the serpent in the wilderness, so must the Son of man be lifted up, that whoever believes in him may have eternal life'. Here, Moses' action of setting up a bronze snake on a pole, which cured the Israelites of the snake-bites inflicted on them by the Lord, is (rather fancifully) seen as a prediction of the death of Jesus, who was lifted up on the cross to cure his people of sin and death. Paul writes that the Israelites 'were all baptized into Moses in the cloud and in the sea' (I Cor. 10.2), and here the relationship between Moses and the Israelites foreshadows Christian baptism with water and the Spirit, and the relationship this establishes between Christ and his people. In Acts 7.23–41 the Israelites' rejection of Moses prefigures their rejection of Jesus (compare 7.35 with 5.30–31).

This view of Moses inevitably means that he is inferior to Christ, and this is worked out in Heb. 3.1–6 in terms of a contrast between Christ the Son and Moses the servant. Indeed, in II Cor. 3 Moses (the 'minister of the old covenant') is inferior not only to Christ but also to Paul and other 'ministers of the new covenant'.

NAZARETH The New Testament is unanimous in presenting Nazareth as Jesus' place of origin, if not his birthplace. Indeed, Jesus was referred to as 'Jesus of Nazareth' during his lifetime and afterwards, mainly by those who were not his disciples. The influence of this expression was felt by Christians who wished to confess him as the Christ; Acts 3.6 and 4.10 speak of 'Jesus Christ of Nazareth'. Christians were referred to by some as 'the sect of the Nazarenes' (Acts 24.5).

Matthew refers to an Old Testament prophecy that spoke of the Messiah's upbringing in Nazareth: 'He shall be called a Nazarene' (2.23). However, these words do not appear in the Old Testament; the evangelist is perhaps thinking of Isa. 11.1, where the Messiah is called a 'branch' (Hebrew, *nezer*). Indeed, Nazareth is never mentioned in the Old Testament or in Jewish sources from the New Testament era. It is this problem that underlies Nathaniel's response to the claim that Jesus is the Messiah: 'Can anything good come out of Nazareth?' (John 1.46).

This verse has led to the conclusion that first century Nazareth must have had a particularly bad reputation; but this is incorrect. 'Anything good' is an indirect reference to the Messiah and the good things he will bring, and Nathaniel's problem is that he cannot believe in a Messiah from Nazareth: 'Is the Christ to come from Galilee? Has not the scripture said that the Christ is descended from David, and comes from Bethlehem, the village where David was?' (7.41–42). Nathaniel's doubts are overcome by Jesus' demonstration of supernatural knowledge (1.47–48). In their nativity stories, Matthew and Luke both attempt to reconcile the Old Testament prophecy about Bethlehem as the Messiah's birthplace with Jesus' well-known origins in Nazareth.[1]

According to Mark 6.1–6, Jesus was rejected in Nazareth, even by his own relatives[2]; as he put it, 'A prophet is not without honour, except in his own country, and among his own kin, and in his own house' (v. 4; *see also* the expansion of this story in Luke 4.16–30). Luke and perhaps Mark see this incident as an illustration of the rejection of Jesus by the Jewish people as a whole and the consequent turning to the Gentiles. John enlarges this theme still further: 'He came to his own home, and his own people received him not' means the same as 'he was in the world, and the world was made through him, yet the world knew him not' (John 1.10–11).

NICODEMUS According to John 3 Nicodemus was a Pharisee who was both sympathetic towards Jesus (v. 2) and uncomprehending of his teaching (vv. 4,9). The evangelist uses him to present Jesus as the bearer of a revelation that it is completely beyond the human mind to grasp. His coming to Jesus 'by night' (v. 2) may suggest that he, like others, keeps his discipleship secret 'for fear of the Jews' (*see* 9.22, 12.42–43, 19.38). However, he is at least prepared to oppose the injustice of his colleagues' determination to put Jesus to death: 'Does our law judge a man without first giving him a hearing and learning what he does?' (7.50–51). Later, he assists Joseph of Arimathea in the burial of Jesus, providing a huge quantity of 'myrrh and aloes' (19.39–40).[1] In earlier versions of this story, Joseph acts on his own and the spices are (belatedly) provided by the women.

PARABLES OF JESUS[1] Jesus' teaching is characterized throughout by the use of vivid pictorial language. Instead of saying, 'Avoid sin at all costs', he says, 'If your hand causes you to sin, cut it off ' (Mark 9.43). Instead of saying, 'When you give alms, do not let anyone know', he says, 'When you give alms, sound no trumpet before you' (Matt. 6.2). Frequently, this use of imagery is extended, and the result is a 'parable'. This may take the form of a full short story (for example the parable of the prodigal son); or the story may be very brief (for example, the woman and the leaven). In some cases, the word 'parable' seems to be appropriate for sayings in which there is no real 'story' at all. Thus, in Mark 2.22, Jesus says: 'No-one puts new wine into old wineskins; if he does, the wine will burst the skins, and the wine is lost, and so are the skins; but new wine is for fresh skins'. If a parable has to be a story, this saying can hardly be regarded as a parable, and yet it functions in exactly the same way as a parable by using an aspect of everyday life to shed light on the ways of God. Mark 3.23–27 uses the word 'parables' to apply even to brief sayings such as, 'If a house is divided against itself, that house will not be able to stand'.

1 Classification The parables of Jesus are so varied that it is difficult to classify them by subjects. The difficulty is increased by the distinction which must sometimes be drawn between the original intention of a parable and the way it was understood in the early Church. The following classification is not entirely satisfactory but at least gives some idea of the scope of the parables.

(*i*) **The Good News of the Kingdom** At the heart of Jesus' teaching is the proclamation of the kingdom of God: the establishing of God's reign on earth, beginning even now in a hidden way in the ministry of Jesus, and manifested in the future.[2] The contrast between present concealment and future manifestation is expressed in the parables of the mustard seed, the seed growing secretly (Mark 4.26–32), and the leaven (Matt. 13.33). As with other valuable things in life, sacrifices have to be made to obtain the kingdom; but the joy of possession means that one hardly notices this (Matt. 13.44–46: the parables of the hidden treasure and the pearl of great price).

(*ii*) **The Kingdom and the Judgment** The future manifestation of the kingdom means judgment as well as salvation.[3] The parable of the talents (Matt. 25.14–30, Luke 19.12–28) tells of servants to whom the master has entrusted the administration of his property; when he returns, will he not hold them accountable? The servant who is released from a crippling debt and yet refuses to show mercy to his own debtor is liable to extreme punishment (Matt. 18.23–35). The virgins who were unprepared for the bridegroom's delay were unable to attend the wedding feast (Matt. 25.1–13). They compare unfavourably with the unjust steward, whose prompt (though dishonest) action helped him to avert a crisis (Luke 16.1–9). In this world, the pure cannot be separated from the impure any more than the wheat can be separated from the tares; but at the harvest, the two will be separated (Matt. 13.24–30). Yet in the last resort, normal human standards do not apply in the judgment because the God of grace is like the eccentric owner of the vineyard who paid the part-time labourers as much as the full-time ones (Matt. 20.1–16).

(*iii*) **Controversy and the Kingdom** The good news of the kingdom is good news especially for the social outcasts despised by respectable society. The Synoptic Gospels constantly refer to the Pharisees' criticism of Jesus for his concern with such people, and Jesus replies in parables which show that God is like that. Luke 15 contains three parables (the lost sheep, the lost coin and the prodigal son), which the evangelist has rightly set in the context of Pharisaic criticism (vv. 1–2). In

Mark 2.17 Jesus responds to similar criticism with a brief parable: 'Those who are well have no need of a doctor, but those who are sick'.

2 The Development of the Tradition It is often possible to differentiate between the original meaning of a parable and its subsequent reinterpretation in the early Church. In Luke's version, the parable of the lost sheep is addressed to the Pharisaic critics of Jesus' attitude towards the tax- collectors and sinners (15.1–7), and very probably this was indeed the original context of the parable. The shepherd represents both God and Jesus as God's agent; or rather, he represents God working through Jesus as his agent. However, Matthew has placed the parable in a new context (18.12–14) – the pastoral care exercised by church leaders (18.15–18). When a church member goes astray, the leader must seek to bring him back, warning him first in private, then with one or two witnesses, and finally before the assembled church. If this fails, the shepherd is absolved of responsibility; the sheep is irretrievably lost and regarded as 'a Gentile or a tax-collector' (v. 17).

Sometimes, a comparison between two versions of the same parable reveals a tendency to make the parable express Christian beliefs about Jesus. Luke introduces his version of the parable of the talents (in Luke, the parable of the pounds) with the words: 'He proceeded to tell a parable . . . because they supposed that the kingdom of God was to appear immediately' (19.11). In other words, he emphasizes the theme of delay: the nobleman who goes into a far country to receive a kingdom and then return (v. 12) is a thinly-veiled reference to Jesus, who does not establish his kingdom immediately but first departs into heaven, with the promise of his future return. In Matthew, however, the master's departure and return is only implicitly related to Jesus.

Interpretations have sometimes been added to parables. The parable of the sower receives an interpretation in which every detail is significant: the seed is the word, the birds are the devil, the sun is persecution, the thorns are worldly pleasures and cares, and so on (4.13–20). In the case of Matthew's parable of the wheat and the tares, the parable itself seems to be an expansion of Mark's parable of the seed growing secretly (Mark 4.26–29, Matt. 13.24–30). As with the parable of the sower, a detailed interpretation of this new parable is also provided (13.36–43). This interpretation misses the point of the parables, which is not to provide allegorical descriptions of the state of the Church or of the last judgment, but to provoke thought about the action of God.

However, it is not only the original meaning of a parable (as far as this can be recovered) that is interesting. Part of the value of the parables for the early Church was their capacity to shed light on new problems that had not arisen in Jesus' own ministry.

PASSION NARRATIVES[1]
Most of the stories told in the Synoptic Gospels were originally isolated and unrelated to any broader context. Their order can be altered without affecting their meaning. The Passion narratives, however, are different: here, each incident derives its significance from the whole of which it is a part. We have here not a series of stories, but one continuous story.

Mark's is the earliest of the Passion narratives and it is followed fairly closely by Matthew, although with a number of important additions. Luke also probably follows Mark, although he has much more independent material than Matthew.[2] John, however, is probably wholly independent; the many points of contact with the Synoptic Gospels seem to spring from a widely known oral tradition, rather than from direct borrowing. But all four Gospels are clearly telling the same story, at least from the arrest of Jesus onwards. Because Mark's version already seems to stand at the end of a long process of development, it is likely that in its oral form the Passion narrative goes back to the earliest years of the Church's existence. Paul presupposes that his converts at Corinth were familiar with this when he introduces the Last Supper narrative with the words, 'The Lord Jesus, on the night when he was betrayed . . .' (I Cor. 11.23). The readers' knowledge of the events of that night would provide a context for the narrative.[3]

The early Christians did not tell the story of Jesus' Passion purely out of historical interest – although, believing as they did that in Jesus God had decisively acted in history, that was certainly one motive. The most important aspect of the story was that the death of Jesus was the death of the Messiah. Thus, the Passion narratives *interpret* the death of Jesus, as well as recounting the external events. Four elements of this interpretation are evident in all four versions, becoming still more notable in the later ones. First, it is emphasized that Jesus knew beforehand and in detail exactly what was going to happen to him. Secondly, the events are presented as the fulfilment of Old Testament prophecy. Thirdly, the manner of Jesus' death has to be in keeping with his Messiahship. Fourthly, the representatives of Roman power regard Jesus as innocent, and the Jews are seen as chiefly responsible for the crucifixion.

1 Mark These four emphases are already present in Mark, and must have shaped the development of the tradition from the earliest times.

(*i*) Jesus' detailed knowledge of forthcoming events in Jerusalem is apparent even before the Passion narrative begins, in Mark's three main Passion predictions (8.31, 9.31, 10.33–34). At the Last Supper and on the Mount of Olives, Jesus predicts his betrayal (14.18–21), his abandonment by his disciples (14.27), and his denial by Peter (14.29–31). However, all this does not mean that he is the helpless victim of fate, because part of the point of the Gethsemane story is to show that he went to his death in voluntary submission to the will of God.

(*ii*) It was held that the death of Jesus fulfilled the predictions of Scripture: 'The Son of man goes as it is written of him . . .' (14.21, *see also* 14.49). The disciples' desertion is presented as the fulfilment of Zech. 13.7, quoted in Mark 14.27: 'You will all fall away; for it is written, "I will strike the shepherd, and the sheep will be scattered" '. Although there are no more explicit quotations like this, the Old Testament is a constant influence on the narrative. For example, Ps. 22.18 states, 'They divide my garments among them, and for my raiment they cast lots'; Mark 15.24 sees this as fulfilled by the soldiers at the cross. Ps. 22.7–8 describes how 'all who see me mock at me', saying, "He committed his cause to the Lord; let him deliver him . . ."; this seems to underlie the account of the mocking of the crucified Jesus in Mark 15.29–32.

(*iii*) The manner of Jesus' death has to be in keeping with his Messiahship. It is accompanied by portents: as he hangs dying on the cross, a darkness covers the land

(15.33), and at the moment of death the temple veil is torn from top to bottom (15.38).

(*iv*) The Jews are held responsible for Jesus' death. In 15.1–15, Pilate does his utmost to release Jesus, but is prevented from doing so by the Jewish crowd's fanatical determination to have him crucified.[4] For the early Christians, it was important that the representative of Roman authority should have regarded Jesus as innocent, despite ordering him to be crucified; they were anxious to dispel the impression that Jesus was a political rebel. Jewish hostility to Christian preaching made the Jewish people the natural scapegoat for the crucifixion.

2 Matthew The importance of these four tendencies is clear from Matthew's additions to Mark.

(*i*) In Mark, Jesus predicts his betrayal but does not specifically identify Judas as the betrayer. Matt. 26.25 clarifies this point: 'Judas, who betrayed him, said, "Is it I, Master?" He said to him, "You have said so" '. Thus, Jesus' foreknowledge is shown to be complete.

(*ii*) The fulfilment of Scripture extends in Matthew to the amount of money paid to Judas, and to what was done with it. Zech. 11.12 states, 'They weighed out as my wages thirty shekels of silver', and Matt. 26.15 portrays the chief priests as doing just that. Zech. 11.13 states, 'I took the thirty shekels of silver and cast them into the treasury in the house of the Lord'. Matt. 27.15 describes how Judas 'threw down the pieces of silver in the temple'.

(*iii*) In Matthew, the death of Jesus is accompanied not only by a great darkness and the tearing of the temple veil, but also by an earthquake, the splitting of the rocks, and the resurrection of the saints of Old Testament times, who emerged from their tombs and appeared to many after Jesus' resurrection (27.51–53).[5]

(*iv*) Matt. 27.24–25 adds to Mark the account of Pilate's washing of his hands, with the declaration, 'I am innocent of this man's blood'. The Jews respond: 'His blood be on us and on our children!' Responsibility for the crucifixion lies wholly with the Jews (including future generations) and not at all with the Romans.

3 Luke Here too, the four tendencies which are already present in Mark are heightened in Luke's additions and alterations.

(*i*) Luke adds a saying showing that Jesus foresaw both Peter's denial and his subsequent repentance: 'Simon, Simon, behold, Satan demanded to have you, that he might sift you like wheat, but I have prayed for you that your faith may not fail; and when you have turned again, strengthen your brethren' (22.31–32).

(*ii*) In Luke, Jesus stresses the need for Scripture to be fulfilled still more strongly than in Mark: 'I tell you that this scripture must be fulfilled in me, "And he was reckoned with transgressors"; for what is written about me has its fulfilment' (22.37). The evangelist perhaps sees the fulfilment of this passage in Jesus' crucifixion together with two criminals.

(*iii*) No further miracles at Jesus' death are reported, but Luke's concern that Jesus' death should be in keeping with his Messiahship is apparent in his version of the words from the cross. Mark (followed by Matthew) reports only one such saying: 'My God, my God, why hast thou forsaken me?' Jesus dies with a loud (presumably wordless) cry. Luke evidently regards all this as incompatible with Jesus' dignity, and he therefore presents the suffering Jesus as a model of piety. The 'cry of dereliction' is omitted, and its place is taken by a prayer for the forgiveness of Jesus' tormentors (23.24), and by the promise of paradise for the repentant thief (23.43). The loud cry at Jesus' death consists of the pious prayer, 'Father, into thy hands I commit my spirit' (23.46).[6]

(*iv*) In Luke, Jesus' innocence is confirmed not just by Pilate but also by Herod Antipas (23.6–15), who is rightly regarded as another representative of Roman power. Pilate's statement of Jesus' innocence is more explicit than in Mark: 'After examining him before you, behold, I did not find this man guilty of any of your charges against him; neither did Herod, for he sent him back to us. Behold, nothing deserving death has been done by him' (23.14–15).

4 John The Fourth Gospel differs from the Synoptics in its account of the events preceding Jesus' arrest, but from that point on follows their order of events fairly closely. The same four tendencies are apparent here.

(*i*) As in Matthew, Jesus specifically identifies Judas as his betrayer – a lengthy account of this is given in 13.21–30. The long discourses in John 14–16 and the prayer in John 17 are all based on Jesus' foreknowledge of his imminent return to heaven through his death, resurrection and ascension. Here, he teaches the disciples about the new situation in which he will be absent from them.

(*ii*) John's narrative contains more direct quotations from Scripture than the others (for example in 19.24,28,36). The evangelist's interest in this theme is apparent in his quotation from Ps. 22.18 in 19.24: 'They parted my garments among them, and for my clothing they cast lots'. This is taken to refer to two separate events. The soldiers first 'took his garments and made four parts, one for each soldier'. But why then the reference to casting lots? The answer is that 'the tunic was without seam, woven from top to bottom; so they said to one another, "Let us not tear it, but cast lots for it to see whose it shall be" '.

(*iii*) The evangelist presumably feels that the Gethsemane episode is not in keeping with Jesus' dignity as the divine Son of God, and he therefore omits it. His account of the arrest of Jesus stresses his awesome power: when Jesus makes himself known to those who have come to arrest him, 'they drew back and fell to the ground' (18.6).

(*iv*) Pilate's attempts to have Jesus released are much more prolonged in John than in Mark (29 verses in John, 15 in Mark). The effect is to emphasize Pilate's conviction of Jesus' innocence and the Jews' determination to crucify him. Pilate gives in only when the chief priests claim that he is being disloyal to Caesar, and that they themselves are simply acting out of loyalty (19.12,15). The evangelist would no doubt expect his readers to recall the Jewish revolt of AD 66–70, which exposed the falsehood of this protestation of loyalty.

The presence of these tendencies in all four versions of the Passion narrative does not mean that whenever one of them is present, the narrative is fictional. For example, the early Christians saw Judas's betrayal as a fulfilment of Old Testament prophecy (*see* John 13.18, quoting Ps. 41.9), but the correspondence between the two does not mean that Judas's action is pure fiction. However, in many cases it does seem likely that theological rather than historical considerations have led to the creation of particular aspects of the narratives.

PASSOVER[1] Probably the most important feast in the Jewish calendar, the Passover commemorated the Israelites' liberation from Egypt, and especially God's 'passing over' of the Israelite houses with the blood of a lamb on the doorposts. Each year, Jewish families would flock to Jerusalem to share in the Passover ritual, which had as its highlight the sacrifice of the Passover lambs (one for each family) in the temple, followed by a solemn meal. The huge numbers of pilgrims led to political tensions at Passover time, and extra soldiers were drafted in to try to prevent the violent incidents that still sometimes took place. No doubt this general feeling of tension was a factor in the events leading to Jesus' crucifixion.

In the New Testament the Passover is mainly significant for its connection with Jesus' death. However, the Gospels do not make it clear precisely what this connection was: the Synoptics find it in the Last Supper (seen as the Passover meal [Mark 14.12–16, Luke 22.15–16]), whereas John finds it in the crucifixion, which he claims took place at the time when the Passover lambs were being slaughtered (*see* 18.28 and especially 19.36, which quotes from the Passover regulations). It is therefore difficult to know whether Jesus' death took place the day after Passover or on the day itself; there might be theological reasons for both views. Paul identifies Christ in his death with 'our Passover lamb' (I Cor. 5.7), and does not link the Lord's Supper narrative with the Passover meal (I Cor. 11.23–25).[2] This may suggest that here John's view is historically correct, because Paul is writing perhaps 20 years before the earliest of the evangelists.

PAUL Paul has been the subject of widely differing assessments. To some, he is the most faithful interpreter of Jesus; to others he has seemed so far removed from Jesus that he is virtually the second founder of Christianity. No-one, however, can doubt his immense significance in the course of early Christian development. Paul was largely responsible for the fateful decision to address the Christian gospel primarily to Gentiles rather than to Jews – a decision that eventually led to an almost complete break between the Church and the Jewish community. Yet he did not understand his apostolic commission solely in terms of preaching; for him, it also included theological reflection that sought to work out the implications of what God had done in Christ. Here too Paul has had a lasting influence. The study of his letters deeply influenced the sixteenth century Reformation, the eighteenth century origins of Methodism, and the twentieth century revolution in theology undertaken by Karl Barth.

1 Paul and Acts One of the initial problems in studying Paul is that the way he presents himself in his own letters is often very different from the way in which he is presented in Acts. Acts is in some ways a valuable source for reconstructing the course of Paul's life, but it can often be somewhat misleading.

(*i*) **Paul the Persecutor** Did Paul persecute the Church in Jerusalem? Acts claims that he did; he was implicated in the martyrdom of Stephen, and immediately afterwards 'a great persecution arose against the church in Jerusalem', as Paul dragged suspected Christians away to prison (Acts 8.1–3). Yet Paul himself implies that before his conversion he was unknown to the Christians of Judaea. Writing of a time three years after his conversion, he says: 'And I was still not known by sight to the churches of Christ in Judaea; they only heard it said, "He who once persecuted us is now preaching the faith he once tried to destroy" ' (Gal. 1.22–23). In other words, the Judaean Christians had only second-hand knowledge of Paul from Christians elsewhere whom he had persecuted.

(*ii*) **Paul's Conversion** Paul insists that his conversion experience was an appearance of the risen Christ in exactly the same category as the other resurrection appearances (I Cor. 15.5–8). This is the basis for his claim to be an apostle (I Cor. 9.1). However, Acts places the appearance of Jesus to Paul on the road to Damascus in a different category from the appearances of the risen Lord to the disciples; the latter took place only during the 40 day period between the resurrection and the ascension (1.3). It is consistent with this that (with the exceptions of 14.4, 14) Paul is generally denied the title of 'apostle'.[1]

(*iii*) **Paul and the Jerusalem Church** In Gal. 2.11–21 Paul tells of a quarrel between himself on the one hand and the leaders of the churches of Jerusalem and Antioch on the other, about the position of Gentiles within the Church (despite the apparent agreement just reached, according to Gal. 2.1–10). James had instructed Peter, Barnabas and the Jewish Christians of Antioch to withdraw from fellowship with Gentile Christians who did not observe the full Jewish law, and Paul accused them of distorting an essential element of the gospel – the equality of Jews and Gentiles in Christ. However, in Acts 15.36–40, the quarrel is played down: nothing is said about any disagreement with James and Peter, and the disagreement with Barnabas is over the trivial question of John Mark's competence for missionary work. In 15.22–31 (*see* 16.4), Paul himself becomes one of the 'men from James', entrusted with the task of imposing certain Jewish dietary regulations on Gentile converts. In reality, he vehemently opposed such people.[2]

(*iv*) **Paul and the Law** Paul has Timothy circumcised (Acts 16.3), observes a Jewish vow (18.18), submits to a ritual of purification in the temple (21.20–26), and at his various hearings repeatedly stresses his absolute loyalty to the law. He claims that he still lives as a strict Pharisee (23.6, 26.5) and that contrary to popular opinion he has never in any way offended against the Jewish law (25.8, 28.17). He is thus a Pharisee who believes that the Messiah has come, but whose conversion to faith in Jesus makes no difference to his attitude towards the law. This is far removed from Paul's own view:[3] he regarded his life as a Pharisee as past (Phil. 3.4–8), and was prepared to abandon the practice of the law in order to increase his effectiveness as a missionary (I Cor. 9.21).

These examples (which could be multiplied) show that one cannot treat Acts uncritically as a historical source for Paul's life and work.

2 The Course of Paul's Life Paul's letters, rather than Acts, must be regarded as the main source for reconstructing the course of his life.

(*i*) **Early Life**[4] According to Acts, Paul was born in Tarsus, in Cilicia, but received a Pharisaic education in Jerusalem under Gamaliel (21.39, 22.3). He was also born a Roman citizen (16.37, 22.25–29), which suggests that his family sought to combine loyalty to their traditional culture with service towards the wider community. Paul confirms that he had lived as a Pharisee (Phil. 3.5), claiming that 'I advanced in Judaism beyond many of my own age among my people, so extremely zealous was I for the traditions of my fathers' (Gal. 1.14). Yet he must also have received some sort of Greek education because he writes idiomatic and highly individual Greek. Indeed, the early link with Jerusalem is somewhat doubtful, for Paul himself never speaks of it. The letters seem to reflect a more extensive exposure to Greek culture than Acts suggests.

(*ii*) **Persecution and Conversion** Paul admits that his zeal for Judaism led him to persecute the Church (I Cor. 15.9, Gal. 1.13, Phil. 3.6) – he does not tell us where, but the reference in Gal. 1.17 to a return to Damascus suggests that this was the region of his persecuting activities. Nor does he ever tell us exactly what he had found objectionable in the Christian claim; probably it was the identification of a crucified man with the Messiah (*see* I Cor. 1.23). We know nothing of any events leading up to his conversion because he ascribes it purely to the power of Christ; attempts to explain his conversion are sheer speculation as all evidence is lacking.

(*iii*) **Early Missionary Work**[5] Paul speaks of early missionary work in Arabia, a first visit to Jerusalem to visit Peter three years after his conversion, and further missionary work in Syria and Cilicia (Gal. 1.18–24). A reference in II Cor. 11.32–33 to the hostility of King Aretas of Arabia presumably belongs to this earliest period. There is some evidence that at this stage of his career he was still preaching primarily to Jews rather than to Gentiles; the view that he began his Gentile mission immediately after his conversion is probably an over-simplification. The transition to work among the Gentiles must have taken place at some point during the 14 years between Paul's first and second visits to Jerusalem (Gal. 2.1). Paul and other Jewish Christians at Antioch seem to have reflected on their failure to gain many Jewish converts and to have concluded that God was calling them to preach to Gentiles instead. In order to ensure the success of their preaching, they did not insist on Gentile submission to objectionable parts of the Jewish law such as circumcision and the dietary requirements.

(*iv*) **Controversy with Jerusalem**[6] Paul speaks of 'false brethren' who 'slipped in to spy out our freedom which we have in Christ Jesus' (Gal. 2.4). He is probably referring to Christians from Jerusalem who arrived at Antioch to investigate the disturbing reports about the radical view of the law now being taken there. Paul, his colleague Barnabas and a Gentile convert (Titus) went up to Jerusalem to argue their case before the chief apostles there. He claims that they accepted his position (Gal. 2.6–10), but James' subsequent attempt to force Gentiles to adopt the Jewish way of life (Gal. 2.11–14) suggests that the agreement may not have been as clear-cut as Paul asserts. At any rate, the latter passage implies that James' attempt was successful, for Paul tells of his protest (vv. 14–21) but does not claim that it had any effect. It seems that he had to leave Antioch as a result of this defeat.

(*v*) **Missionary Work in Asia Minor and Greece** Paul's typically defiant response to this setback was to found Gentile congregations that did not observe the Jewish law. He did so first in Galatia, and then in various Greek cities as he travelled from northern to southern Greece: the churches of Philippi and Thessalonica in the north and Corinth in the south were the most important of these.[7] The events of this 'second missionary journey' are described in Acts 16–18 and in scattered hints in Paul's letters to these churches. For example, we learn that he had founded the churches of Galatia while he was delayed there by illness (Gal. 4.13–15), that he had been 'shamefully treated at Philippi' (I Thess. 2.1), that the Philippian Christians began sending him financial aid shortly after he had left them (Phil. 4.15–16), and that he preached the gospel in Corinth 'in weakness and in much fear and trembling' (I Cor. 2.3). The first letter to the Thessalonians belongs to this period, and it may well have been at Corinth that Paul received the ominous news that the 'men from James' had infiltrated his churches in Galatia.[8]

(*vi*) **Missionary Work in Ephesus** According to Acts, Ephesus was Paul's base for three years.[9] At Ephesus, he wrote the first great letter to the Corinthians, in response to news and a letter brought by a delegation from Corinth. Here he speaks of 'a wide door for effective work' and 'many adversaries' (16.9) at Ephesus, and in 15.32 even seems to contemplate the possibility of 'fighting with wild beasts' in the arena there. If Philippians and Philemon date from this period (as they probably do),[10] this suggests that Paul was imprisoned for a time in Ephesus and was in danger of losing his life (*see also* II Cor. 1.8–9, with its references to being 'utterly and unbearably crushed', and to 'the sentence of death'). As well as these difficulties in Ephesus, Paul's relationship with the Corinthians was under severe strain. After a disastrous second visit, during which his authority had been challenged, he wrote them an angry letter (probably preserved at least in part in II Cor. 10–13). He tells us in II Cor. 2.12 of an anxious but fruitless wait for their response at Troas; he eventually received the good news of a reconciliation across the Aegean in Macedonia, and immediately wrote them a final, mainly conciliatory letter (II Cor. 1–9).[11]

(*vii*) **The Final Visit to Jerusalem**[12] The idea of a collection by Gentile Christians for the Christians of Jerusalem was first suggested by the chief apostles (Gal. 2.10), but fell into abeyance after Paul's break with them. However, Paul later revived the idea, in order to try to persuade the Jerusalem Church that the Gentile churches really had received the grace of God despite their not observing the Jewish law. This collection caused him many problems, not least because the Corinthians at one stage suspected him of dishonesty. However, the collection was eventually completed: the letter to the Romans was written at Corinth when Paul was ready to set sail with it to Judaea (Rom. 15.25). Whether the peace-offering was accepted by the Jerusalem Church is not clear, but the fact that Acts suppresses any reference to it may suggest that it was not. While in Judaea, Paul was placed under arrest; the story is graphically told in Acts 21–26.

(*viii*) **Paul's Last Days** Acts ends with Paul under house arrest in Rome awaiting the outcome of his appeal to Caesar. He had earlier hoped that after spending some time in Rome he would be able to preach the gospel in Spain (Rom. 15.24), and later tradition states that he fulfilled this objective before being arrested again and finally executed in Rome by Nero. However, the evidence for a release followed by a second arrest is extremely slender, and it is much more likely that Paul's appeal to Caesar led directly to his execution.

3 The Theology of Paul Paul is a highly creative but somewhat disorderly thinker who likes to approach the same subject (e.g. the law) from all sorts of different angles, without being too concerned to achieve any systematic coherence. However, his theology at least has a coherent centre, and it is closely related to his own life work of establishing Gentile Christian communities which did not observe the Jewish law: that centre is Jesus Christ as the universal Lord of Jew and Gentile alike. Almost everything in his theology is related to this single theme of the universality of Christ, which Paul constantly had to defend against his various opponents. The following examples must suffice, but they cannot convey the full richness and variety of his explorations of this theme.

(*i*) **Christ and Adam** Paul is aware of the traditional Jewish Christian view of Jesus, which regards him as the Messiah sent to fulfil God's promises to the Jewish people (*see* Rom. 15.8). However, his own view is that Jesus was sent to resolve a universally human problem, rather than a specifically Jewish one. This is the reason why in Rom. 5 and I Cor. 15 he sets Jesus against the background of Adam's sin, which brought death into the world: 'As by a man came death, by a man has come also the resurrection of the dead. For as in Adam all die, so also in Christ shall all be made alive' (I Cor. 15.20–21). Nor is salvation from the universal plight symbolized by Adam a purely future thing (as this passage might suggest): in Rom. 5.17 Paul claims that one may *already* 'receive the abundance of grace and the free gift of righteousness' which delivers one from the sin and death engendered by Adam.

(*ii*) **Justification**[13] In the course of his controversies with Jewish Christianity, Paul insisted again and again that we are justified by faith not by works: 'We ourselves, who are Jews by birth and not Gentile sinners, yet who know that a man is not justified by works of the law but through faith in Jesus Christ, even we have believed in Christ Jesus, in order to be justified by faith in Christ, and not by works of the law, because by works of the law shall no-one be justified' (Gal. 2.15–16). To seek to be justified by works of the law is to 'live as a Jew' (2.14) and to insist on the absolute validity of the distinction between Jews and 'Gentile sinners'. To seek to be justified by faith is to acknowledge that Jews no less than Gentiles stand in a position of guilt before God (*see* 2.17), and can only be accepted by God 'through faith in Jesus Christ'. Thus, Jews and Gentiles are 'one in Christ Jesus' (3.28).

(*iii*) **Promise and Law**[14] The Judaism opposed by Paul lays great stress on promise and law: the promise to Abraham and to his seed ensures final salvation for the Jewish community, and the gift of the law means that only within the Jewish community is God's will truly obeyed. Paul, however, holds that salvation and true obedience are to be found outside the Jewish community, in the congregations of Gentile Christians he has founded, and he therefore gives the themes of promise and law a universal content, severing their exclusive link with the Jewish community. The promise to Abraham was a promise to the whole human race: 'In you shall all the nations be blessed' (quoted in Gal. 3.8) – 'I have made you the father of many nations' (quoted in Rom. 4.17). The true 'seed of Abraham' is Christ and those who belong to Christ (Gal. 3.16,19,29). On the other hand, the law is indeed the exclusive possession of the Jewish community, yet it places that community in the same position of guilt before God as the Gentiles. The law pronounces a curse on all who disobey it, and because it is disobeyed by Jews who know it as well as by Gentiles who do not, the curse applies to all alike (Gal. 3.10, Rom. 3.10–20). The fulfilment of the universal promise must free us from the universal curse imposed by the law.

(*iv*) **Christian Living** Paul makes only occasional use of the Jewish law in his ethical instruction – for example, in Gal. 5.14 and Rom. 13.8–10, where he sees the whole law summarized in the commandment to love one's neighbour as oneself. In general, his view is that Christ as the universal Lord must determine the pattern of Christian living. In Phil. 2.1–11, Paul therefore bases his appeal, 'Let each of you look not only to his own interests, but also to the interests of others' (v. 4) on the example of Christ, who in his incarnation 'emptied himself, taking the form of a servant' (v. 7).[15] The same argument is used in II Cor. 8.9 to encourage generous contributions to Paul's collection for the Jerusalem Church. Yet, though the *motivation* for Christian living is quite distinctive, this does not always mean that its *content* is distinctive. Paul allows that a Jewish Christian who observes the law may honour the Lord by doing so, just as a Gentile Christian who does not observe the Jewish law may equally honour the Lord. The important thing, as Christ is the Lord of Jews and Gentiles alike, is that Christians from whatever background should accept one another, even while they maintain differences of practice (Rom. 14.1–15.13).

PEACE The New Testament uses many different terms to describe the content of salvation: redemption, justification, the Spirit, eternal life, grace, love, joy, peace, and so on.[1] These are not so much separate aspects of salvation as the same salvation seen from different angles. Thus, the entire content of salvation is summed up in the term 'peace', just as it is in the other terms. God is the God of peace (I Thess. 5.23, Heb. 13.20), and Jesus Christ is the bringer of his peace to earth. God 'preached good news of peace by Jesus Christ' (Acts 10.36), and even during his earthly ministry, Jesus sent out his disciples to proclaim peace (Luke 10.5–6). The risen Christ likewise is the bringer of peace; he appears to his disciples with the words, 'Peace be with you' (John 20.19,21,26), and through his apostles 'came and preached peace to you who were far off and peace to those who were near' (Eph. 2.17).

In Eph. 2.14–18 peace means the end of hostility both between man and God and between Jew and Gentile: Christ 'is our peace, who has made us both one' and has 'reconciled us both to God'. Peace at the earthly level is not simply a consequence of peace with God; the two things are inseparable, and one is inconceivable without the other.[2] But peace is the divine solution not only to the problem of conflict but also to the problem of anxiety: 'Have no anxiety about anything . . ., and the peace of God, which passes all understanding, will keep your hearts and your minds in Christ Jesus' (Phil. 4.6–7).

PENTECOST[1] The Feast of Weeks received the name 'Pentecost' (from the Greek word for 'fifty') because it was celebrated 50 days after Passover. It celebrated the presentation of the first fruits of the harvest.[2] The chief significance of Pentecost in the New Testament is that it was on this day that the gift of the Spirit was first bestowed (Acts 2.1–4). In Rom. 8.23 Paul speaks of 'the first fruits of the Spirit' (i.e. the Spirit as the beginning of the full salvation which is yet to come), and it may be that there is a deliberate reference here to the feast at which the Spirit was bestowed.

Luke sees the bestowal of the Spirit as the fulfilment of John the Baptist's prophecy of a baptism with the Spirit and with fire; this accounts for the 'tongues of fire'.[3] The coming of the Spirit establishes the Church; it brings together the crowds, and it enables Peter to 'speak the word of God with boldness' (*see* 4.31), with the result that three thousand of his hearers are converted. It is at first sight strange that his audience consists of Jews who originate from every part of the known world ('Parthians and Medes and residents of Mesopotamia . . .', 2.9–11). The point of this is partly to confirm that the apostles were genuinely speaking in other languages – a fact doubted by some, who suspected the influence of alcohol (2.13). Yet the main point is that the event of Pentecost is a sign of the destiny of the gospel to reach the whole human race – those regarded as 'barbarians' as well as the inhabitants of the Roman world.

The New Testament everywhere assumes that the Spirit is the gift of the risen Lord (e.g. John 7.39), but there is no real concern with the question of when and in what circumstances it was first given. However, John 20.22 does provide an alternative account of the bestowal of the Holy Spirit; the risen Jesus breathes on his disciples and says, 'Receive the Holy Spirit', in fulfilment of the promises given in John 14–16.

PETER In the earliest list of the twelve disciples, the first place is occupied by 'Simon whom he surnamed Peter' (Mark 3.16). Matt. 16.17 preserves his original name, 'Simon Bar-Jona' (i.e. 'son of Jona'). He is referred to in Acts 15.14 as 'Simeon' (*see also* II Peter 1.1). 'Petros' is the Greek translation of the Aramaic 'Cepha', preserved in John 1.42 and on several occasions in Paul, and means 'Rock'. This explains Matt. 16.18: 'You are Peter [*Petros*], and on this rock [*petra*] I will build my church . . .'. Although John 1.42 suggests that this name was bestowed on Simon when he first met Jesus, Matt. 16.17 states that it was occasioned by Simon's confession of Jesus as the Christ at Caesarea Philippi. It is possible that it actually derives from the fact that in the earliest tradition Simon was the first person to see the risen Christ (I Cor. 15.5, *see* Luke 24.34).

(*i*) **Peter's Call** There are three different accounts of Peter's call. The oldest is in Mark 1.16–20: Jesus sees Simon and his brother Andrew fishing, and calls them to follow him with the words, 'Follow me and I will make you become fishers of men'. Luke 5.1–11 develops this into a rather more elaborate story in which Peter's call follows a miraculous catch of fish that almost sinks his boat. In John 1.40–42, Peter is brought to Jesus by his brother Andrew, who announces, 'We have found the Messiah'.

(*ii*) **Peter as Spokesman for the Twelve** Together with James and John,

Peter is a member of the 'inner circle' of Jesus' disciples, present with him on special occasions (e.g. at the transfiguration and in Gethsemane).[1] But his main function in the Gospel narratives is to be the spokesman for the twelve. For example, after Jesus' saying about the difficulty of entering the kingdom of God, it is Peter who responds on behalf of the disciples: 'Lo, we have left everything and followed you' (Mark 10.28). The most significant example of this takes place in the incident at Caesarea Philippi (Mark 8.27–33), where Peter first confesses that Jesus is the Christ, then rebukes him when he announces his forthcoming sufferings, and is himself sharply rebuked.[2] There is no good reason for denying that this narrative is essentially historically accurate. The saying identifying Peter with Satan (v. 33) is so harsh that it could hardly have been invented by the early Church.

(*iii*) **Peter's Denial** As with the Caesarea Philippi incident, the story of Peter's denial (which occurs in all four Gospels) is so unflattering to the chief of the apostles that it is likely to be essentially historical. The evangelists differ about the details. In Mark, Peter denies Jesus first as he warms himself at the fire, and second at the entrance (14.66–70); John reverses the order (18.17–18,25). In John, an unnamed disciple who knew the high priest enables Peter to enter (18.15–16); this is possibly another reference to 'the disciple whom Jesus loved', who is always in a position of superiority to Peter.[3] Luke adds the words, 'And the Lord turned and looked at Peter' after the third denial (22.61), but does not explain how Jesus was in a position to do so. It is remarkable that the Church that preserved the saying, 'Whoever denies me before men, I also will deny before my Father who is in heaven' (Matt. 10.33), should also have preserved the story of the denial by the chief of the apostles. The fact that the story was not suppressed shows that the early Christians were interested in the historical facts; it also shows that part of the point of the Passion narratives is to emphasize (and not to cover up) the utter humiliation and isolation of Jesus.

(*iv*) **Peter and the Risen Lord** In I Cor. 15.5, Paul states that it was Cephas (i.e. Peter) to whom the risen Lord first appeared. There is a brief reference to this event in Luke 24.34: 'The Lord has risen indeed, and has appeared to Simon!' It is strange that in the various appearance stories in Matthew, Luke and John, there is no explicit account of this appearance. However, it is possible that the sayings of Jesus to Peter recorded in Matt. 16.17–19 (inserted by Matthew into the Caesarea Philippi narrative) originally belonged to the context of the resurrection.

(*v*) **Peter in the Early Church** In Acts 1–12, Peter is seen as the chief of the apostles: he preaches to the inhabitants of Jerusalem, he boldly defends the faith before the Sanhedrin, he performs spectacular miracles, and he inaugurates the mission to the Gentiles. Later in Acts he is somewhat overshadowed by James the Brother of the Lord (12.17, 15.6–21). Paul implies that when he first visited Jerusalem, three years after his conversion, Peter was the chief of the apostles (Gal. 1.18). On his second visit, 14 years later, the main responsibility for the mission to Jews still lies with Peter (Gal. 2.7–8), and yet James is mentioned before him in the list of 'pillars' of the Church (Gal. 2.9). In Gal. 2.11–14, Peter submits to James' authority when he abandons his previous practice of eating with Gentile Christians; he receives a vehement rebuke from Paul for doing so.[4] I Cor. 1.12 and 3.22 suggests that Peter had his supporters at Corinth (although there is little evidence in the rest of the letter that Peter's brand of Jewish Christianity was a reality there), and I Cor. 9.5 mentions that he was accompanied by his wife in his missionary work. His death is referred to in mysterious language in John 21.18–19; the tradition that he was martyred in Rome is almost certainly correct.

PETER, FIRST LETTER OF

PETER, FIRST LETTER OF I Peter is a general letter addressed to 'the exiles of the Dispersion in Pontus, Galatia, Cappadocia, Asia and Bithynia' (1.1). Although the term 'dispersion' would normally apply to Jews not resident in Palestine, it probably refers here to Christians, 'exiled' from their heavenly home and 'dispersed' in the world. The letter is a general meditation on Christian hope and conduct, and does not address itself to any specific problems of the recipients (except the imminence of persecution).

1 Authorship The letter claims that its author is Peter (1.1), writing with the help of Silvanus, Paul's former colleague (5.12), from 'Babylon' that is, Rome (5.13)[1] – the earliest evidence of a tradition linking Peter with Rome. It is possible that Peter really did write the letter, but there are considerable difficulties in such a view.

(*i*) I Peter is written in good Greek with quite a wide vocabulary, and such language would surely have been beyond the reach of the former Galilean fisherman.

(*ii*) According to Gal. 2.7–8, Peter was entrusted with the mission to the Jews, and his submission to James at Antioch (Gal. 2.11–14) shows his continued sense of responsibility for this task. Yet I Peter (which would have to have been written no more than ten or twelve years later) knows nothing of this. It is addressed to Gentile Christians (1.18, 2.10, 4.3–4), and accepts that the Jewish people as a whole are irretrievably hard of heart (2.7–8).

(*iii*) At various points, I Peter shows the influence of Paul: for example, in the view that Gentile Christians have taken the place of the Jews as God's people (2.7–10), in the view of the State (2.13–14; *see* Rom. 13), and in the reference to 'dying to sin' (2.24, *see* Rom. 6). Gal. 2.11–21 does indeed show Paul trying to influence Peter, but it is unlikely that he succeeded. Like other New Testament letters, I Peter is therefore likely to be pseudonymous – written under the name of a great figure of the past. This practice was extremely widespread in early Christian literature, and although it was sometimes attacked (*see* II Thess. 2.1–2), it was motivated not so much by dishonesty as by a sense of continuity with the apostolic preaching.

2 Main Themes I Peter is a somewhat discursive work, and it is difficult to divide it up into distinct sections with clearly defined themes. Nevertheless, certain emphases do stand out as significant.

(*i*) **The Old Testament as a Christian Book** In 2.4–10, the author quotes or alludes to various Old Testament passages in order to show that the Jewish rejection of Jesus Christ and the Gentiles' faith in him were announced beforehand through the prophets; Christians now constitute God's chosen people, and the Old

Testament is their charter. In 1.10–12, the author claims that the oracles inspired by the Holy Spirit concerning the suffering and glory of the Christ were intended for the benefit of Christians ('you'). Even the prophets themselves did not understand them as Christians now can.[2] The author also uses the Old Testament in the context of moral instruction, quoting from Ps. 34 in 3.10–12.

(*ii*) **Christ as the Source of Hope** After the introduction, the main body of the letter opens with a hymn of praise: 'Blessed be the God and Father of our Lord Jesus Christ! By his great mercy we have been born anew to a living hope through the resurrection of Jesus Christ from the dead' (1.3). The resurrection is the source of the hope for 'an inheritance which is imperishable, undefiled, and unfading' (1.4); this is the true home from which the readers are at present in exile (1.1, 2.11). The author is aware that a vivid sense of Christian hope will help the readers to 'abstain from the passions of the flesh which wage war against your soul' (2.11), and to endure the coming persecutions (1.6–7, 4.12–13, 5.8–11).

(*iii*) **Persecution**[3] Persecution is to be understood as a necessary test of the genuineness of faith (1.6–7). At present, it does not appear to be too severe. The author mentions the possibility of Gentiles 'speaking against you as wrongdoers' (2.12), and of their 'abuse' when Christians no longer join with them in 'licentiousness, passions, drunkenness, revels, carousing and lawless idolatry' (4.3–4); but such manifestations of unpopularity are hardly the same as being thrown to the lions. However, the author expects a much more intense persecution to begin shortly. Its author is to be the devil, who 'prowls around like a roaring lion, seeking some one to devour' (5.8); that is, the devil seeks to force people into apostasy out of fear of the persecution. This persecution is to be world-wide: 'The same experience of suffering is required of your brotherhood throughout the world' (5.9). But it will only last 'a little while' (5.10) because it is merely the dark prelude to the final revelation of the glory of Christ (4.13,17–18). This idea of a final great persecution before the end is also expressed in Matt. 24.9–13 and Rev. 7.14, 12.17, and 13.7–10.

PETER, SECOND LETTER OF The author of this letter is allegedly 'Simeon Peter, a servant and apostle of Jesus Christ', and its recipients are 'those who have obtained a faith of equal standing with ours' (1.1). The letter is intended as a final testament: because Peter's death is at hand, 'I will see to it that after my departure you may be able at any time to recall these things' (1.15) – that is, through this letter. 'Peter' warns that after his death false teachers will arise to despoil the church both by their conduct and by their doctrine.

1 Authorship The authorship of II Peter was disputed within the early Church; many felt that the apostle could not have been its author. These doubts re-emerged at the time of the Reformation, and today there are very few scholars who believe that Peter was the author.

(*i*) Peter is written in an extraordinarily verbose and inflated Greek style. Assuming that Peter spoke the language at all (as he probably did), one would expect him to write a much simpler Greek influenced by Aramaic idioms.

(*ii*) There is no reference to Peter's life-work, the mission to the Jews (*see* Gal. 2.7–8). It is Christian heresy that is the problem, rather than Judaism.

(*iii*) II Peter 2–3 describes the abhorrent conduct and doctrine of 'false teachers' or 'scoffers' whose emergence is still future: 'There *will be* false teachers among you, who *will* secretly bring in destructive heresies . . .' (2.1); 'Scoffers *will* come in the last days' (3.3); 'You therefore, beloved, knowing this *beforehand* . . .' (3.17). In other words 'Peter' is portrayed as writing prophetically about the last days, and not about the present situation (*see* Jude 17–18, expanded in II Peter 3.1–5). Yet it is clear from the lengthy description of their errors that these false teachers are a present reality from the standpoint of the author of the letter. Indeed, the present tense is often used in describing them (e.g. in 2.10–22, 3.5,16–17), which shows that the 'prophetic' element is purely fictional.[1]

(*iv*) II Peter 2 closely resembles the Letter of Jude, and one author has clearly used the work of the other.[2] For various reasons (e.g. the omission of Jude's references to Jewish apocryphal works), it seems that it is II Peter which has used Jude, rather than the other way round. The apostle Peter would surely not have needed to plagiarize in this way.

2 The Heretics and the Author's Response[3] The false teachers are described in lurid terms, and it is difficult to be sure what they really taught. We learn in 2.19 that they promise their adherents freedom, which in this context must mean freedom from all moral constraints. They 'despise authority' and 'revile the glorious ones' (2.10–12) – the spiritual beings to whom the government of the world has been committed. They also 'scoff' at the traditional belief in the return of Christ, on the grounds that 'all things have continued as they were from the beginning of creation' (3.4). They 'twist to their own destruction' the letters of 'our beloved brother Paul', who unfortunately included in them 'some things hard to understand' (3.15–16). They likewise misunderstand 'the other scriptures' (3.16) because they fail to realize that Scripture is not to be interpreted privately (1.20–21). All this suggests a group who invoke the authority of Paul for their belief in 'freedom' and their stress on their present exaltation with Christ. We know from other sources that Paul was indeed used in this way by certain 'heretics'.

The author combats this position in a number of ways. He argues that holiness of life is necessary to 'escape from the corruption that is in the world because of passion' (1.3–11). He asserts that his eyewitness testimony to the risen and exalted Christ proves that 'we did not follow cleverly devised myths when we made known to you the power and [future] coming of our Lord Jesus Christ' (1.16–18).[4] He threatens his opponents with 'pits of nether gloom' where they are to be 'kept until the judgment' (2.4), and warns his readers of the grave danger of being taken in by their seductive propaganda (2.2–3,14,18–22, 3.17). He claims that the Lord has delayed the coming of Christ for a while, to allow as many as possible to repent; yet the delay does not make it any less certain (3.8–15).[5]

PHARISEES There exists a large body of rabbinic literature dating from about AD 200 onwards, which includes a number of traditions which go back beyond the catastrophic destruction of Jerusalem in AD 70, into the New Testament era. However, because Judaism after the revolt of AD 66–70 underwent a transformation, it is often difficult to use these later texts to shed light on the New Testament. For this reason, the New Testament and Josephus, the first century historian, are valuable additional sources for understanding the Pharisees, although one must constantly make allowances for bias.

It seems that the Pharisaic movement originated in about the middle of the second century BC, with the aim of applying the law more rigorously to everyday life. The name 'Pharisee' may derive from the verb 'to separate', in which case the Pharisees were 'the separated ones' – a term perhaps used by their priestly (Sadducee) opponents to brand them as schismatics. Or it may derive from the word for 'Persian'. The Pharisees, unlike the Sadducees, believed in the resurrection of the dead (*see* Acts 23.8),[1] a doctrine derived from the Persian religion of Zoroastrianism and not found in the Old Testament except in one or two very late passages. For this reason, their opponents might well have called them 'Persians', who brought foreign innovations into the ancient religion.

Pharisaism was a lay movement, and one of its aims was to 'build a fence around the Torah' (that is, the law), by surrounding it with detailed prescriptions that enabled one to know exactly what constituted obedience to the law and what did not. For example, the law commanded that the Sabbath be kept holy and that one abstained from work on it. Yet what constituted 'work'? To what extent was it legitimate to engage in everyday activities like preparing food? How far could men walk on the Sabbath? What should be done in emergencies, when, perhaps, life could be saved by disregarding the Sabbath? Because it was believed that the prosperity of the whole community depended to a large extent on its success in keeping the law, it was obviously important to know exactly what the law entailed. The Pharisees devoted themselves to such matters in exhaustive detail, and the oral tradition built up in this way came to have as great an authority as the law itself.

Attacks on the Pharisees, such as Matt. 23, probably reflect the worsening relations between Pharisees and Jewish Christians at the time when the Gospel of Matthew was written. However, much of the material is likely to be authentic teaching of Jesus; his own view of the law seems to have been worked out in opposition to the Pharisees'. In contrast to them, Jesus' view of the law is characterized by humanistic concern and a sense of the immediacy of God's will.[2] There is no need for the detailed Sabbath prescriptions because 'the Sabbath was made for man, and not man for the Sabbath' (Mark 2.27). The Sabbath must not stop people satisfying their hunger (Mark 2.23–26) or doing good (Mark 3.4). Excessive concern with ritual washing before meals (Mark 7.1–5) ignores the fact that food cannot defile one, but only the thoughts of the heart (7.14–23).

The Pharisees have of course had an exceptionally 'bad press' from Christians; Matthew's identification of all Pharisees as hypocrites (23.13, etc.) has been treated as though it were sober fact. Recent work on this subject has rightly tried to redress the balance. Although Jesus' understanding of the will of God is thought to be the more satisfactory, their differing views should not be regarded as a conflict between his own 'common sense' and the Pharisees' exaggerated casuistry. It was the Pharisees who – in the situation of the time – represented 'common sense', and Jesus who proposed radical solutions that left many questions unanswered.

PHILEMON, LETTER OF PAUL TO Paul's letter to Philemon is little more than a short note about a single practical problem, and it says much for the devotion Paul could inspire that this letter was first preserved and then accepted into the corpus of his writings. It is written to 'Philemon our beloved fellow worker and Apphia our sister [Philemon's wife] and Archippus our fellow soldier [his son?] and the church in your house' (vv. 1–2). Paul is writing from prison (vv. 1,9), where he has been visited by a runaway slave belonging to Philemon, called Onesimus. Under Paul's influence, Onesimus became a Christian (vv. 10,16) and presumably asked him to intercede with his master on his behalf. Paul appeals to Philemon to forgive Onesimus and promises to repay anything he owes his master (vv. 18–19) – although because Philemon is indebted to him for his conversion, he does not think it likely that this offer will be accepted (vv. 19–21). There is also a hint that Paul would like Philemon to allow Onesimus to return in order to look after him in prison (vv. 13–14,21).

The letter is of interest for two main reasons. First, it gives an exceptionally vivid portrayal of a particular incident in the life of the early Church. One would like to know more: for example, did Onesimus initially seek out Paul in Ephesus[1] because he regretted his action, and thought (rightly) that Paul was the man to help him? Secondly, it shows how the institution of slavery was accepted by the early Christians but at the same time transformed.[2] Philemon is to receive Onesimus back 'no longer as a slave but more than a slave, as a beloved brother . . .' (v. 16). He is to be welcomed in the same way that Paul himself might expect to be welcomed (v. 17). Although slavery is not abolished, in Christ 'there is neither slave nor free' (Gal. 3.28); the old distinction has been robbed of its absoluteness.

PHILIP The New Testament knows of three (or possibly four) men with this name.

(i) **Philip the Tetrarch**[1] On the death of Herod the Great in 4 BC, his territories were divided between three of his sons, who were known as 'tetrarchs'. Philip received areas in the northern and eastern parts of Palestine; he is described in Luke 3.1 as 'tetrarch of the region of Ituraea and Trachonitis'. His rule lasted until AD 34. Caesarea Philippi was built by him and named after him. According to Mark 6.17, Herod Antipas (the tetrarch of Galilee) married Herodias, 'his brother Philip's wife', but it seems likely that the evangelist has confused the real first husband of Herodias (an obscure son of Herod the Great, also called Herod) with the better known Philip.

(ii) **The Apostle Philip** Like most of the twelve, Philip is simply a name in the Synoptic Gospels (Matt. 10.3, Mark 3.18, Luke 6.14) and in Acts (1.13). He comes into his own, however, in the Gospel of John,[2] which tells of his call (1.43–44), his bringing of Nathanael to Jesus (1.45–46), his involvement in the feeding of the five thousand (6.5–7), his assistance of certain 'Greeks' who 'wished to see Jesus' (12.20–22), and his request at the Last Supper, 'Show us the Father, and we shall be satisfied' (14.8–9). Here and elsewhere, the Fourth Gospel is concerned to give a more prominent role to certain of the disciples – Andrew, Judas 'not Iscariot', Thomas, as well as Philip – than they have in the Synoptics.

(*iii*) **Philip the Evangelist** Although Acts 6.1–6 narrates the appointment of seven men 'to serve tables', two of them (Stephen and Philip) make their names as evangelists rather than as waiters.[3] Philip, forced to flee from Jerusalem by the persecution which followed Stephen's martyrdom, is responsible for the conversion first of many of the Samaritans and then of an Ethiopian court official (Acts 8). There is also a reference to his preaching the gospel in the Greek cities on the Mediterranean coast, from Azotus to Caesarea (8.40). Acts 21.8–9 tells us that he entertained Paul and his companions some years later, and that he had four unmarried daughters who were prophetesses. It is strange that Luke presents Philip as the first missionary to non-Jews but plays down the fact – presumably because he wishes to attribute this momentous step to Peter (Acts 10–11, *see also* 15.7–9). Because apostolic authority is necessary to give legitimacy to such activity, Peter and John have to come from Jerusalem to complete Philip's work in Samaria (8.14–24).[4]

PHILIPPIANS, PAUL'S LETTER TO Philippians has often been regarded as the most attractive of Paul's letters. Much of it breathes an air of serene joy which is not always present in Paul, although characteristically this is interrupted by forthright polemic in chapter 3.

1 Place of Origin Traditionally, Rome has been regarded as the most likely place of origin for Philippians, although Caesarea (in Palestine) has also had its advocates. Paul is writing from prison (1.7,13), facing the possibility of the death sentence (1.20–27, 2.23), and we know from Acts that Paul was indeed imprisoned in both those places. However, Paul tells us in Rom. 15.24 that after he has visited Rome he intends to travel on to Spain, whereas in Phil. 1.27 and 2.24, he expresses his hope of visiting Philippi as soon as he is released. If Philippians was written at Caesarea or Rome, Paul must have abandoned the long-cherished plan to visit Spain (*see also* II Cor. 10.16). It is perhaps more likely that Philippians was written during an imprisonment in Ephesus, because we know that Paul actually did visit Philippi immediately after leaving Ephesus (II Cor. 7.5, 8.1). Although it is impossible to prove that Paul was ever in prison there, his references to frequent imprisonments not mentioned in Acts (II Cor. 6.5, 11.23) and to particular troubles at Ephesus (I Cor. 15.32, 16.8–9, II Cor. 1.8–10) make it highly likely.[1]

2 Circumstances Paul states in II Cor. 11.7–11 that although he consistently refused to accept help from the Corinthians, he had even while at Corinth received a gift delivered by 'the brethren who came from Macedonia'. This occasion is recalled in Phil. 4.15, where Paul reminds the Philippians how, 'in the beginning of the gospel, when I left Macedonia, no church entered into partnership with me in giving and receiving except you only'.[2] For a while, this 'partnership' lapsed (4.10), but when news of Paul's imprisonment reached Philippi, a further gift was sent. Paul writes to the Philippians to acknowledge receipt of the gift (4.18).

Paul also takes the opportunity to bring the Philippians up to date with his own news. He is still in prison, but the Philippians must not be despondent about this but recognize that 'what has happened to me has really served to advance the gospel' (1.12). The threat of the death sentence is still real, and although Paul believes that God has further work for him to do and will therefore ensure his release (1.19–26), he delays sending Timothy to the Philippians until he knows the outcome of his case (2.22–24).[3] In his troubles, Paul has not had the whole-hearted support of the local Christian community. Some continue his proclamation of the gospel out of love for him; but others 'preach Christ out of envy and rivalry. . . , out of partisanship, not sincerely but thinking to afflict me in my imprisonment' (1.15–17, see also 2.21). Epaphroditus's health has been a further problem: having delivered the Philippians' gift, he became ill and almost died, and news of this had already reached Philippi. But now he is well enough to return (2.25–29).

3 Main Theological Themes The fact that Philippians is so closely bound up with circumstances in Paul's life does not lessen its religious importance. For him, life and theology were inseparable.

(*i*) **The Humiliation and Exaltation of Christ**[4] In a famous passage (2.5–11), which may well be an originally independent hymn, Paul speaks of the incarnation, death and resurrection of Christ. In his view, this is a story marked by contrasts.. The one who was originally, before the incarnation, 'in the form of God', has now 'taken the form of a slave' – not just in becoming man but above all in enduring crucifixion, the slave's punishment. Yet because of his obedience, 'God has highly exalted him', and every tongue will eventually confess him no longer as a slave but as Lord. This passage is important for three main reasons. First, it shows that belief in the incarnation was not a late development in early Christian thought; it is not found only in the Fourth Gospel. Secondly, it exemplifies the importance of paradox in Paul's theology: the one who is outwardly an unfortunate man who endured the death of a slave is in fact eternally in the form of God and now also the Lord of heaven and earth. Thirdly, the incarnation here is not simply a mystery to be contemplated but a pattern to be imitated; the passage occurs in the context of the exhortation, 'Let each of you look not only to his own interests, but also to the interests of others' (2.4).

(*ii*) **Justification by Faith**[5] In Phil. 3, Paul attacks the emissaries of Jewish Christianity, fearing their arrival at Philippi and warning the Philippians to reject them. The warning takes on all the more urgency in the light of the possibility of Paul's death. His opponents claim that the coming of the Messiah makes no difference to Israel's privileged position. If Gentile Christians wish to participate in the benefits brought by the Messiah, then they must become converts to Judaism and submit to the Jewish law. Paul describes how he had once been a zealous Jew, with still more reason to glory in his privileges than his opponents (3.4–6), but in the light of the revelation of God in Jesus Christ, he has utterly renounced his Jewish past which he now regards as 'loss' and as 'refuse' (3.7–8). In Jesus Christ is to be found a righteousness and a promise of the final resurrection that is independent of Judaism. Here, the contrast between loss of privileges and the hope of 'the upward call of God in Christ Jesus' (v. 14) forms a parallel to the pattern of humiliation and exaltation in the hymn to Christ (2.5–11).

PILATE[1] Sources outside the New Testament give us a certain amount of information about Pontius Pilate. He was the Roman governor of Judaea from

AD 26 to 36, and in several recorded incidents he showed notable insensitivity towards Jewish religious scruples and a cruelty that eventually led to his recall to Rome. One Jewish writer speaks of Pilate's fear of Jewish ambassadors to the Emperor Tiberius exposing 'the rest of his conduct as governor by stating in full the briberies, the insults, the robberies, the outrages and wanton injuries, the executions without trial constantly repeated, the ceaseless and supremely grievous cruelty'.

The Gospels present Pilate as declaring Jesus innocent and wishing to release him, and this becomes more pronounced in later versions.[2] In Matthew, Pilate is warned of Jesus' innocence by his wife's dream, and absolves himself of all responsibility for Jesus' death (27.19,24); and in John, he desperately tries to secure Jesus' release, abandoning the attempt only when he is accused by the chief priests of disloyalty to Caesar (18.28–19.16). There are considerable historical problems here,[3] and it seems that the Gospels' portrayal of Pilate is motivated by the desire that the crucified Jesus should not be perceived as a rebel against Roman authority.

PRAYER[1]
The practice of prayer was extremely widespread both in the Jewish and in the Gentile world of the New Testament era. The early Christians took over this practice as a matter of course, but understood it in the light of the distinctive message they proclaimed.

In Matt. 6.5–15 the prayer Jesus taught his disciples is contrasted with prayer as practised by Pharisees and Gentiles. The Pharisees regard prayer as a public act that serves to increase their reputation for piety; but Jesus' disciples are to pray in private. The Gentiles 'heap up empty phrases', thinking 'that they will be heard for their many words'; but Jesus' disciples are to pray simply, in the words of the Lord's Prayer. The first case involves a distinction between religious piety and everyday, public life in the world; the second substitutes the heavenly Father of Jesus for the unreliable gods of the pagan world who need to be cajoled into action.

The willingness of the Father to answer prayer is stressed in the brief 'parable of the friend at midnight' that follows Luke's version of the Lord's Prayer (11.5–8). The parable is typical of Jesus' deliberately exaggerated style, which seems to be intended to shock. All of us try to help out our friends when they ask us a favour; and when their request is inconvenient, we may still give in if they persist, if only to get some peace and quiet. If we behave like this, how much more will God (11.13). The accompanying promises ('Ask and it will be given you; seek, and you will find; knock, and it will be opened to you', 11.9) are hard to interpret because the early Church was well aware that as a matter of fact not all specific requests were answered. Jesus himself in Gethsemane (Mark 14.36) and Paul with his 'thorn in the flesh' (II Cor. 12.7–10) are examples of this. The Letter of James seems to be aware of this problem when it attributes the failure of prayer to selfishness: 'You ask and do not receive [contrast Luke 11.9, quoted above], because you ask wrongly, to spend it on your passions' (4.3). The solution to the problem is probably that in Luke the promises occur in the context of the Lord's Prayer, which is a general prayer for the coming of God's kingdom, for sustenance, forgiveness and preservation from sin. In this context, the promises that prayer will be fulfilled are not a blank cheque for any kind of request, but an affirmation that ultimately God will 'vindicate his elect, who cry to him day and night' (Luke 18.1–8). The prayer for the coming of the kingdom of God will be heard.

The New Testament gives no support to the view that the only effect of prayer is a subjective change in the one who prays; nor does it understand prayer as contemplation which has as its goal a mystical union with the ineffable ground of our being. The reason for this is that it sees God as personal and involved in his world. This is not simply the result of primitive and naive religious thought, but an inevitable conclusion from the early Christians' belief that God had sent his Son into the world.

PREDESTINATION

The term 'predestination' conjures up the Calvinist theory in which the elect are destined for salvation and the damned for eternal punishment by God's unchangeable will, and without any reference to their own good or bad deeds. There are passages in the New Testament which seem to speak in these terms; but they must be understood in their context in early Christian thought, and not turned into an all-embracing world view.

Underlying language about predestination is the doctrine of grace, according to which salvation is the result of divine initiative and not human.[1] For Paul, the faith of his converts is evidence not of their own good sense and wisdom, but of God's choice (I Thess. 1.4–5, I Cor. 1.23–24).[2] This call is beyond human capacity to control, and so the belief arises that those who respond to the gospel do so because they have been predestined to do so by God: those who are called are 'called according to his purpose' – that is, because they are 'predestined' (Rom. 8.28–30).[3]

If faith has its origin only in divine grace, then lack of faith must stem from the withholding of divine grace. In Mark 4.11–12, this withholding of grace is no less God's act than the bestowal of grace: Jesus' mysterious parables were told so that 'those outside' the circle of disciples 'may indeed see but not perceive, and may indeed hear but not understand; lest they should turn again and be forgiven'. Paul develops this theory in Rom. 9 while attempting to explain why the Jews, the chosen people, have rejected the gospel, whereas Gentiles have accepted it. The answer to this problem is simply that it was God's will that it should be so; if anyone objects that this is unfair, the response is, 'Who are you, a man, to answer back to God?' (v. 20).

However, the New Testament does not consistently take this predestinarian position. The conclusion of the argument begun in Rom. 9 is that in the end God's mercy will encompass all (11.25–32).[4] The need for genuine, active obedience as a condition of salvation is constantly stressed (e.g. Rom. 2.1–11, 8.13, Gal. 5.21, 6.7–8).[5] The various views somehow belong together, but they cannot be combined into a single, rationally coherent position because Christian knowledge is fragmentary (Rom. 11.33–36, I Cor. 8.2, 13.11–12) and subordinate to faith, hope and love (I Cor. 13.13).

PRODIGAL SON, PARABLE OF

Luke sets this parable in the context of the Pharisees' criticism of Jesus for 'receiving sinners and eating with them' (15.1–2). Jesus tells the parables of the lost sheep, the lost coin, and the prodigal son to defend his own conduct.[1] The point of the first two parables is that God seeks what is lost, and Jesus' mission is the means by which he does this. Jesus is God's representative; where Jesus is, there God is too.[2] The parables do not teach general truths about God, but relate specifically to the mission of Jesus. In the case of the much longer parable of the prodigal son (15.11–31), a link with the activity of Jesus is also present. The father welcomes his younger son home, prepares a feast for him, and is criticized for his actions by the elder son. This precisely fits the setting described in 15.1–2: Jesus welcomes home the 'tax collectors and sinners', shares a feast with them, and is criticized for doing so by the Pharisees.[3] The point of the parable is therefore that the action of Jesus is identical to the action of God. What Jesus does, God does; God is acting through Jesus in welcoming home his disobedient children, and the Pharisees' criticism is directed ultimately at God. As the Fourth Gospel puts it, 'He who does not honour the Son does not honour the Father who sent him' (John 5.23, *see also* 15.23).

The parable points to two ways in which the original relationship between the father and his sons is distorted: the first is the younger son's desire for complete independence, and the second is the elder son's failure to understand the father's goodness. These are the distortions – the sin of the tax collector and of the Pharisee respectively – which it is the purpose of Jesus' mission to expose and heal.

REDEMPTION[1] The Greek word originally meant the buying back of a slave or captive, making him free through payment of a ransom. The New Testament can sometimes see Christ's death as a ransom. According to Mark 10.45, 'The Son of man came . . . to give his life as a ransom for many' (*see also* I Tim. 2.6). The Corinthians are reminded that they were 'bought with a price' (I Cor. 6.20, 7.23), and I Peter 1.18–19 explains this in more detail: 'You were ransomed from the futile ways inherited from your fathers . . . with the precious blood of Christ'. Nothing is said about any recipient of the ransom payment; at this point the metaphor breaks down. However, the word 'redemption' is often used simply to mean 'deliverance', with no reference to any payment. The hope for 'the redemption of Jerusalem' (Luke 2.38) means the hope that her captivity will be brought to an end. 'The redemption of our bodies' (Rom. 8.23) means the eventual deliverance of the body from sin and death.

REPENTANCE[1] The word is generally used for a definitive, once-for-all turning away from an old way of life in order to adopt a new one. It is used fairly frequently in the Synoptic Gospels and Acts, but not in Paul and John. John the Baptist preaches 'a baptism of repentance for the forgiveness of sins' (Mark 1.4), and here repentance refers to a final conversion which immediately precedes the coming of the Lord in judgment. Jesus' preaching of 'the gospel of God' seeks the twofold response, 'Repent and believe' (Mark 1.14–15); Peter likewise urges his hearers to 'repent and be baptized' in his Pentecost speech (Acts 2.38). Although in one sense repentance is a human action, it is nevertheless dependent on God. Peter stresses this in his address to the Sanhedrin in Acts 5.31: 'God exalted him [Christ] at his right hand as Leader and Saviour, to give repentance to Israel and forgiveness of sins'. When the Jerusalem Church is finally persuaded that Peter did right to preach the gospel to Cornelius the Gentile centurion, 'they glorified God, saying, "Then to the Gentiles also God has granted repentance unto life" ' (Acts 11.18).[2] Through Jesus Christ, God 'now commands all men everywhere to repent' (Acts 17.30), and this commandment is a sign of his grace. Repentance is thus seen not as a general religious duty, but as a specific response to the grace of God manifested in Christ.

RESURRECTION[1] At the heart of the New Testament is the claim that Jesus has been raised from the dead. By the truth or falsehood of this claim the Christian gospel stands or falls: 'If Christ has not been raised, then our preaching is in vain and your faith is in vain' (I Cor. 15.14). The resurrection of Jesus is not, however, seen as an isolated event, but as the beginning of the general resurrection of the dead, which is to follow the return of Christ and which is to lead to the final judgment. The risen Christ is thus 'the first fruits of those who had fallen asleep' (I Cor. 15.20), so that 'by a man has come . . . the resurrection of the dead' (I Cor. 15.21). The resurrection of Jesus is inseparable from the general resurrection.

For all its startling novelty, Christian belief in the resurrection of Jesus is therefore a modification of Jewish belief in the resurrection. The relationship between the Christian and Jewish views is apparent in Acts, where Paul is on trial before the Sanhedrin. Paul cries out, 'Brethren, I am a Pharisee, a son of Pharisees; with respect to the hope and the resurrection of the dead I am on trial' (23.6), thus neatly dividing his accusers between Sadducees who deny the resurrection and Pharisees who believe in it (23.7–10).[2] The Paul of Acts regards his own belief in the resurrection as a modification of the Pharisaic view; he believes that it has already begun in Jesus, but otherwise he and his non-Christian Pharisaic opponents are agreed (*see also* 26.5–8). The Gospels, too, testify to the widespread Jewish belief in the resurrection of the dead. There is nothing specifically Christian about Jesus' response to the Sadducees' rationalistic problems with the resurrection (Mark 12.18–27); the discussion takes place within the framework of Jewish belief.

Here and elsewhere, the New Testament takes over ideas from its environment, both Jewish and Gentile, but it rarely leaves these ideas untouched. In the case of the resurrection of the dead, Christian faith in the risen Jesus leads to a major modification, indeed, a transformation, of the Jewish belief. In order to understand this central early Christian belief, it is necessary first to examine the New Testament's witness to the resurrection of Jesus, and secondly to consider its wider implications.

1 The Earliest Form of Resurrection Faith It is certain that from the beginning of the Church's existence, belief in the resurrection of Jesus was central. What is not so clear, however, is the precise nature of the earliest faith in the risen

Lord. The four Gospels all date from about the last quarter of the first century, and even Paul was writing two decades or so after the crucifixion. This, therefore, leaves room for the possibility that the earliest belief in the resurrection was not necessarily identical to later belief. In individual cases, this is clear; for example, it is unlikely that Matthew's story of the guard at the tomb was part of the earliest tradition because it seems to have been developed in order to counter a Jewish objection to the resurrection ('the disciples stole the body').[2] The story of the discovery of the empty tomb develops considerably between Mark and John.[3] All such developments, however, do not really affect the fundamental content of the resurrection faith.

A more important possibility is the theory, accepted by many modern scholars, that the later stories make the resurrection much more of a physical event that the earliest tradition.[4] On this view, belief that the tomb of Jesus was empty was of little significance to the earliest Christians. In addition, they did not distinguish the resurrection of Jesus from his ascension, and so believed that the appearances of the risen Lord were not earthly events but appearances in visionary form from heaven. On this view, in the earliest resurrection faith Jesus was 'raised' directly into heaven, and it was from there that he appeared to his followers as the risen Lord who had conquered death. It was the spiritual experiences of his 'risenness' which were fundamental, and these were much later expressed in legends that to some extent misrepresented the original experiences by turning them into physical events.

This view is obviously influenced by the modern difficulty with traditional belief in the resurrection. It shifts the emphasis away from the miraculous to religious experience, from the objective to the subjective, and from the physical to the spiritual. This shift of emphasis may or may not be necessary for modern Christian faith; the question here is whether the evidence advanced in favour of the hypothesis is sufficient to support it at a purely historical level. Was the earliest form of resurrection faith as this hypothesis claims?

The stories of the appearances of the risen Lord in Luke and John take place during an interim period between the resurrection itself and Jesus' ascension into heaven, a period which according to Acts 1.3 lasted 40 days, although in Luke 24 it seems to last only one day.[5] In their view, it is the risen but still earthly Jesus who appears to his disciples. Although they do not specifically refer to the ascension, Matthew and Mark take the same view. In Matthew's first resurrection appearance story, the women take hold of his feet and worship him (28.9); the reference in Mark 14.28 and 16.7 to Jesus' going before his disciples to Galilee also suggests that the risen Jesus appears to his disciples on earth. Resurrection and ascension are clearly differentiated (in Luke and John, explicitly, in Matthew and Mark, implicitly), and despite their strangeness the appearances of the risen Lord are earthly, physical events. Indeed, this is deliberately emphasized in the repeated references to the physical body of the risen Lord. Despite his apparent ability to vanish and reappear at will, he invites the disciples to touch him to prove he is not a spirit, and he eats and drinks with them (Luke 24.38–43, John 20.24–29, Acts 10.40–41).

Because the resurrection appearances can only take place during the 40 day period between the resurrection and the ascension, Paul's conversion on the Damascus road (described three times with minor differences in Acts 9, 22, and 26) is not seen as a resurrection appearance like the others. Paul sees 'a light from heaven, brighter than the sun' (26.13) and he hears the voice of the exalted Christ. Strictly speaking, this does not make Paul a 'witness to the resurrection' because the true witnesses 'ate and drank with him after he rose from the dead' (Acts 10.41) – that is, during the temporary period of renewed earthly life before the ascension. The physical, earthly appearances are distinguished from Paul's more visionary experience. For this reason, the term 'apostle' is generally not applied to Paul because an apostle must have seen the risen Lord between his resurrection and his ascension (1.21–22).

Paul, however, regards his conversion experience as an appearance of the risen Lord just as the others were. In I Cor. 9.1, he writes: 'Am I not an apostle? Have I not seen Jesus our Lord?' Paul here bases his claim to apostleship on having seen the risen Lord. A more important passage for his view of the resurrection, however, is I Cor. 15.3–8, referred to above. He states that he had taught the Corinthians the tradition he had received, that Christ died for our sins, was buried and was raised, 'and that he appeared to Cephas, then to the twelve. Then he appeared to more than five hundred brethren at one time, most of whom are still alive, though some have fallen asleep. Then he appeared to James, then to all the apostles. Last of all, as to one untimely born, he appeared also to me'. Here, it seems that, unlike the author of Acts, Paul regards his conversion experience as an appearance of the risen Lord just like the others.[6] It is the last in the series of appearances, but it unquestionably belongs to that series. The conclusion has often been drawn from this that Paul regards all the resurrection appearances as he regards his own: appearances in visionary form of the exalted Lord from heaven, rather than earthly appearances during a short period between the resurrection and the ascension. Because Paul is writing perhaps 20 years before the earliest of the Gospels this early, 'visionary' view of the resurrection appearances of Jesus must be differentiated from the later more 'physical' view.

Such conclusions must remain hypothetical, however. Paul does not explicitly say that all the appearances were exactly the same in nature as his own; he simply asserts that he was the recipient of an appearance of the risen Jesus no less genuine than the others, even though it was later. Because he is defending the authenticity of his own apostleship, one would not expect him to draw attention to any differences between his own experience and the others, although the obscure reference to himself as an 'aborted foetus' (or 'miscarriage') may suggest that he is aware of such differences. In fact, the traditional list of resurrection appearances which he quotes in I Cor. 15.5–7 may imply that the distinction between resurrection and ascension was recognized from the earliest period. The existence of such a list must mean that the early Church believed that the series of appearances was in principle closed; it was impossible for further appearances to occur. Visionary experiences were still possible (see Rev. 1), but they were not regarded as belonging to the same category. The fact that the series of appearances is regarded as closed may mean that, from an early date, they were regarded as belonging to a unique and unrepeatable time – the time between the resurrection and the ascension.

It seems plausible to many people that, in the earliest view, Jesus was physically raised directly into heaven, from where he appeared to his followers in visions which an objective observer might reject as 'subjective' but which they were convinced were utterly objective. Much of the evidence is consistent with this hypothesis; but it would be an exaggeration to claim that the hypothesis was proved beyond reasonable doubt. People's conclusions on this matter may well be influenced more by their general theological outlook than by the fragmentary historical evidence.

2 *The Theological Significance of the Resurrection of Jesus* For the early Christians, the resurrection of Jesus changed everything: 'The old has passed away, behold, the new has come' (II Cor. 5.17). There is virtually no area of their thought which is unaffected by it, so that a full discussion of its significance would have to encompass the whole of New Testament theology. But the following points stand out as particularly important.

(*i*) **The Living Christ** In early Christian thought the fact that Jesus has been raised means that the resurrection of the dead is not a purely future entity, as in Jewish belief; there is an important sense in which Christians already share the risen life of Christ. In Gal. 2.19–20, Paul writes, 'I through the law died to the law, that I might live to God'; although he still lives 'in the flesh', in another sense Christ 'lives in me'. In his death, Christ left behind the old realm of sin, death and the law, and entered the new realm of life in the presence of God. The Christian already shares in this transference, through baptism (which of course presupposes faith) in which the old life 'dies' and the new begins (Rom. 6.1–4). This idea is further worked out in the probably post-Pauline letters to the Ephesians and the Colossians. God has 'made us alive together with Christ . . . and raised us up with him, and made us sit with him in the heavenly places' (Eph. 2.5–6; *see* Col. 2.12–13).[7]

However, Paul is strongly opposed to the idea that Christians already share *fully* in the risen life of Christ, and attacks those of his Corinthian converts who take this view: 'Already you are filled! Already you have become rich! Without us you have become kings! And would that you did reign, so that we might share the rule with you!' (I Cor. 4.8). There follows a description of the sufferings endured by Christ's apostles, which are a sign that the life of the resurrection has certainly not yet arrived in all its fullness (vv. 9–13). The character of the present age is determined neither by Jesus' crucifixion alone (which would make the general resurrection purely future), nor by his resurrection alone (which would make the resurrection purely present), but by both together: the new age is present only in a paradoxical manner while the old continues. Thus, even where Paul speaks of union with Christ in his resurrection, there is an emphatic future element: 'If we have died with Christ, we believe that we shall also live with him' (Rom. 6.8, *see also* v. 5).[8]

(*ii*) **The Return of Christ**[9] Belief in the resurrection of Christ implied belief in his return. Although he is at present absent from his followers, that absence is only temporary, for at his coming they will 'meet the Lord' and thereafter 'always be with the Lord' (I Thess. 4.17, *see also* II Cor. 5.6–9). Yet his absence was not complete, as it was for the disciples between his death and resurrection; in his resurrection and in the gift of the Spirit, he is already present. In the Gospel of John, the return of Christ thus takes a threefold form: he returns in his resurrection, in the gift of the Spirit, and in his future coming. The paradox of his presence while absent is expressed in the often veiled language of the Last Supper discourses of John 13–17.[10]

Jesus speaks of his departure in 13.36: 'Where I am going you cannot follow me now; but you shall follow afterward'. Jesus will 'go and prepare a place for you', and when he has done so, 'I will come again and take you to myself, that where I am you may be also' (14.3). The promise is repeated in 14.18: 'I will not leave you desolate; I will come to you'. This sounds straightforward: in his death, resurrection and ascension Jesus returns to the heavenly world from which he came, and leaves the disciples behind – but he will one day return so that they may be reunited. And yet, the reunion is not a purely future event (as in I Thess. 4.17 and II Cor. 5.6–9). In one sense, Jesus has already returned in his resurrection and the consequent gift of the Spirit. 'I will come to you' is in its context in 14.18 a promise not of the manifestation of Christ to the whole world at his final coming, but a secret return known only to the disciples (14.19–23). The promise is fulfilled in the appearance of the risen Lord to his disciples in 20.19–23, in which 'he breathed on them, and said to them, "Receive the Holy Spirit" '.

(*iii*) **The Resurrection of the Dead** Christ is 'the first fruits of those who have fallen asleep' (I Cor. 15.20), and his resurrection is thus seen as the guarantee of the final resurrection. In I Cor. 15 Paul defends the doctrine of the future resurrection against critics at Corinth who find it incredible (v. 12).[11] He concedes that resurrection does not mean that the body which is restored to life is precisely the same as the body which died (vv. 35–50), but insists that despite the distinction an identity remains. Paul here is writing in opposition to the view that, because there is no life after death, we should 'eat and drink for tomorrow we die' (v. 32). Yet he is also implicitly opposing the typically Greek view that there is no salvation for the body, and that immortality (if it exists at all) is the destiny only of the human soul. (A Christian form of this view was perhaps held by Paul's Corinthian opponents.) Thus, both the resurrection of Christ and the future general resurrection are in some sense 'physical'. This raises the question of why this should be so important to Paul. Elsewhere, he shows a remarkable freedom in criticizing and reinterpreting traditional views. But in this case, is he merely repeating a traditional view in conservative fashion? Might he not have abandoned his concern for the salvation of the 'body' without damaging the structure of his thought?

The reason why resurrection matters to Paul is implied in the quotation from Ps. 8 in I Cor. 15.27: 'For God has put all things in subjection under his feet'. In its original setting, this passage is speaking of the present position of man, to whom God gave dominion over the created order (*see* Gen. 1.28). But for Paul, man is not a lord but the slave of hostile, anti-divine powers, and he there applies this passage to the exalted Christ: he is the one in whom the destiny for which man was created is fulfilled. At the general resurrection, those who are 'in Christ' will share in his rule over creation. To speak (as some of the Corinthians perhaps did) of the immortality of the soul would be to imply a fundamental split within the created order: the soul alone is to be saved, whereas the rest of creation (including the body) is written off as unimportant or even as evil. Because for Paul the God who redeems is also the creator, such a view is unacceptable. Redemption must be the destiny of the whole created order, including the body (Rom. 8.18–25), and it is this destiny which is already anticipated in the resurrection of Christ. This is the underlying reason why Paul tenaciously defends the doctrine of resurrection, for all its difficulties. To deny it is to deny the goodness of the world God created; to affirm it is to affirm that the goodness of the world will finally be manifested when it attains its ultimate destiny.

RETURN OF CHRIST

RETURN OF CHRIST For the New Testament writers, history is not a meaningless process constantly moving on into a wholly uncertain future; rather, it moves towards the goal appointed for it by God – the return of Christ. That goal has been disclosed in advance in the resurrection of Jesus, and it is this that gives the early Christians their joyful certainty of his return.[1]

The idea of this return is already expressed in several of Jesus' 'Son of man' sayings: 'Whoever is ashamed of me and of my words in this adulterous and sinful generation, of him will the Son of man also be ashamed, when he comes in the glory of his Father with the holy angels' (Mark 8.38). It seems that in the earliest tradition, this coming was expected to be sudden: 'As the lightning flashes and lights up the sky from one side to the other, so will the Son of man be in his day' (Luke 17.22). His coming will be as sudden as the flood which overwhelmed the contemporaries of Noah, or as the fire and sulphur which rained down on Sodom (Luke 17.26–30). At least in the early decades, it was believed that his coming would be within the present generation, and that many if not all Christians would live to see it. I Thess. 4.13–18 indicates that Paul had not previously warned the Thessalonians of the possibility that some of their number would die before the Lord's return, so eagerly had he taught them to 'wait for God's Son from heaven, whom he raised from the dead, Jesus, who delivers us from the wrath to come' (1.10). Even in I Thessalonians he still distinguishes between 'we who are alive, who are left until the coming of the Lord' and 'those who have fallen asleep' (4.15). The same stress on the imminence of Christ's return recurs in I Cor. 7.29 ('The appointed time has grown very short'), and Rom. 13.12 ('The night is far gone, the day is at hand').

At a slightly later date, it became clear that the continuation of history was a fact to be reckoned with. In the discourse ascribed to Jesus in Mark 13, the end does not come suddenly, but is preceded by a series of 'signs' (e.g. 'wars and rumours of wars', v. 7), culminating in a great act of apostasy (vv. 14–23) which will usher in the coming of the Son of man with power and glory (vv. 24–27); many Christians seem to have seen the desecration of Jerusalem in AD 70 as that act of apostasy. But still Christ did not return; and so in Luke's version of the discourse, there is a gap of unspecified duration between the destruction of Jerusalem and the coming of the Son of man (21.24).[2]

It has often been suggested that the failure of the hoped for return of Christ to materialize when expected created a severe problem for the early Christians. There is some evidence for this, although the point should not be exaggerated. The death of the 'beloved disciple', who had been expected to survive until Christ's return, apparently caused something of a crisis (John 21.22–23); and II Peter 3.4 speaks of certain heretics who mockingly ask, 'Where is the promise of his coming?' When in John 16.16–19 the disciples are presented as utterly bewildered at Jesus' promise that they will see him again 'in a little while', the evangelist may have in mind Christians of his own day who felt that the 'little while' before Christ's return was becoming unduly protracted. His answer is that already in the resurrection and the bestowal of the Spirit, the promise of Christ's return is fulfilled, and that this makes its ultimate fulfilment certain. The author of II Peter attributes the delay to God's patience and his desire that as many as possible should repent (3.9). I Tim. 6.14–15 is content to state that 'the appearing of our Lord Jesus Christ' will take place 'at the proper time'.

REVELATION, BOOK OF

REVELATION, BOOK OF The Book of Revelation has always been a puzzle to the Church. There were many Christians in the early centuries who felt that it should be excluded from the canon on the grounds that its obscure and bizarre imagery encouraged heresy and fanaticism, since anything could be read into it. Some recent writing has approached Revelation more sympathetically by stressing its considerable literary power. The author writes highly unusual and sometimes incorrect Greek, and yet his imaginative power is undeniable.

1 Authorship The author introduces himself simply as 'John' (1.4); evidently he is already well-known to his readers. We cannot rule out the possibility that the apostle John is meant; we know that he was an authoritative figure in the early Church (Gal. 2.9), and it might be argued that the book is in keeping with John's reported desire to call down fire from heaven to destroy the unbelieving Samaritan villages (Luke 9.54).[1] On the other hand, the author does not claim apostolic authority, and the reference to 'the twelve apostles of the Lamb' as the foundations of the heavenly Jerusalem (21.14) may suggest that the twelve are now figures of the past. We can at least be reasonably certain that the author of Revelation was not the author of the Fourth Gospel or of the Johannine letters. As perceptive critics in the early Church rightly noted, differences of style and outlook make it inconceivable that these works should have had the same author.[2]

2 The Recipients Revelation is written in the form of a letter (1.4–5), and chapters 2–3 consist of a series of exhortations dictated by the living Christ to the seven churches. It is this section that teaches us most about the first readers of the work. Several of the churches have problems with heresy.[3] The Ephesians have rejected certain would-be apostles, and 'hate the works of the Nicolaitans' (2.2,6); the two groups are no doubt identical. The church at Pergamum has not done so well, because some of its members 'hold the teaching of the Nicolaitans', which is identified as 'eating food sacrificed to idols and practising immorality' (2.14–15); the same is true at Thyatira (2.20–23). Evidently the author is a Jewish Christian who is bitterly opposed to Pauline freedom from the law.[4] But heresy is not the only problem. The churches of Smyrna and Philadelphia are being opposed by the local synagogues, whom the author describes as 'the synagogues of Satan' (2.9, 3.9). The church at Pergamum has suffered a martyrdom (2.13). The churches of Sardis and Laodicea have become comfortable and lukewarm (3.1,15–16). In one way or another, each of the churches seems to the author to be in a state of crisis.

3 The Future The main subject of Revelation is the future: 'The revelation of Jesus Christ' has been given 'to show to his servants what must soon take place . . . For the time is near' (1.1,3). In 4.1 the author is transported into heaven with the words, 'Come up hither, and I will show you what must take place after this'. The author's symbolism is so complex that it is impossible to be sure exactly what he thought was to take place; and the situation is further complicated by the fact that he evidently makes use of different traditions which are not always compatible with one another.

(*i*) In Rev. 5.1–8.1, the revelation of the future occurs through the opening of a scroll with seven seals. First, four angelic horsemen bring war, famine, and pestilence; they are followed by an earthquake, the destruction of sun, moon and stars, and the Day of Wrath. This chapter is based on the apocalyptic discourse in Mark 13, where similar signs precede the coming of the Son of man.[5] Between the sixth and seventh seal there is a passage which tells of the salvation of 'a great multitude which no man could number', who 'come out of the great tribulation' (the evils described in chapter 6) and who stand before the throne of God (7.14–15).

(*ii*) In Rev. 5.1–8.1 apparently there is a fairly complete description of the events which are to culminate in the salvation of the elect. But in 8.2–11.19, we have what seems to be an alternative scenario: a series of disasters inaugurated by seven angels with seven trumpets, whose lurid horrors include giant locusts with human faces. These woes are a punishment for the Gentiles' idolatry and other sins (9.20–21). Once again, the woes culminate in the establishing of God's kingdom: 'The kingdom of the world has become the kingdom of our Lord and of his Christ, and he shall reign for ever and ever' (11.15).

(*iii*) A new series of visions introduces the figures of the dragon and the two beasts.[6] The dragon is the devil, who has been expelled from heaven and is permitted for a while to persecute God's people on earth (Rev. 12). The figure of the first beast derives from Dan. 7, where four successive pagan empires are portrayed as four beasts. In Rev. 13 the beast represents the Roman empire, which is seen as inspired by Satan (13.2); its godless arrogance is apparent in the worship it claims for itself (13.4, 11–16, 14.9) – no doubt a reference to the emperor cult.[7] Yet this is not simply the Roman state of the author's time. The emperor is a superhuman Antichrist figure, and his agent is able to perform miracles (13.13–14); an earlier version of this tradition occurs in II Thess. 2.

(*iv*) In 14.8, we have the first reference to 'Babylon': 'Fallen, fallen is Babylon the great, she who made all nations drink the wine of her impure passion'. Much of the rest of the book is dominated by the contrast between the two cities: Babylon (i.e. Rome), which is doomed, and the heavenly Jerusalem. Revelations 18–19 contains lamentations and songs of praise for the fall of Babylon, and in Rev. 21–22, its place is taken by the new Jerusalem. Throughout this long section, additional material concerning yet more dire catastrophes, the last judgment, and so forth, makes the picture both confused and vivid.

ROMANS, PAUL'S LETTER TO

Romans is probably the last of Paul's letters, written at Corinth just before the journey to Jerusalem which led to his arrest and eventual death (15.25–28). It has been seen as his final testament, summarizing all the main themes of his theology and standing above the particular circumstances and problems which usually preoccupied him. However, the comparatively general nature of its contents should not lead us to conclude that it is a purely theoretical work. Its main theme is the very practical problem of the status of Gentile Christians who do not observe the Jewish law; Paul defends the legitimacy of their position against their Jewish or Jewish Christian critics.

1 The Purpose of Romans Paul states in 1.9–15 and 15.22–29 that he is hoping to visit the Roman Christians after he has delivered the collection to the Church of Jerusalem. Romans must therefore be in some sense a preparation for that visit; and yet it seems a rather elaborate way for Paul to announce his forthcoming arrival. We must take into account the fact that Paul was a highly controversial figure in the early Church, regarded with considerable suspicion by those who disapproved of his policy of refusing to impose the law on his Gentile converts.[1] This policy, it was held, was a recipe for moral anarchy; disregarding the divine commandments concerning circumcision or the food laws might lead to neglect of other commandments concerning, for example, adultery or idolatry. Paul was in effect preaching that God's grace made salvation quite independent of one's behaviour. Paul shows that he is aware of this criticism in Gal. 5.13–6.10, and he specifically refers to it in Rom. 3.8, where he mentions that some people slanderously accuse him of teaching, 'Let us do evil that good may come'. Rom. 6 contains his answer. A second criticism of Paul's policy was that it led him to turn his back on his own people, teaching that the glorious privileges of Israel had been transferred to the Gentiles. This was an act both of apostasy and of betrayal. Paul responds to this charge when he opens his discussion in Rom. 9–11 of the place of Israel in God's plan with the strongest possible protestation of his love for his own people and his grief that they have not believed the gospel (9.1–5, *see also* 10.1).[2] Thus, part of his reason for writing at such length is to prepare the way for his intended visit by explaining his position and refuting the charges made against him. The fact that there were large numbers of Jewish Christians in Rome made this especially necessary.

As Rom. 16 shows, however, there were Gentile as well as Jewish Christians in Rome, and 14.1–15.13 suggests that there was considerable tension between them. Those who observe the laws concerning diet and the Sabbath 'pass judgment' on those who do not; those who do not observe such laws 'despise' those who do (14.1–5). Instead of this hostility, the two groups must 'welcome one another' (15.7), recognizing that Christ came for the salvation of both Jews and Gentiles alike and therefore worshipping together (15.6). Scripture speaks of Jews worshipping alongside Gentiles, and Gentiles worshipping together with Jews (15.9–12); the two groups in Rome should take note. The problem would be greatest for the Jewish Christians, required to recognize the legitimacy of Gentile Christians who did not observe the law, and this is presumably the reason why throughout the letter there is such a stress on the place of the Gentiles in God's plan. Salvation is indeed 'for the Jew first', but it is 'also for the Greek' (1.16). Gentiles who believe as Abraham did are descendants of Abraham and heirs to the promise of salvation, whereas Jews who do not believe are unrelated to Abraham and subject to the wrath of God (Rom. 4).[3]

2 Main Theological Themes Romans may be seen as a systematic defence of the proposition that God has responded to the problem of universal human guilt by setting forth Jesus Christ as the universal solution, for both Jews and Gentiles alike.

(*i*) **Universal Guilt** The theme of the first main section of the letter (1.18–3.20) is not so much 'all have committed acts of sin' (*see* 3.23) as 'all are without excuse for their sin' (*see* 1.20). The argument seeks to expose the means by which Gentiles and Jews alike seek to evade and excuse the fact of their sin. In Rom. 1, Paul refutes the view that Gentiles are able to claim exemption from God's judgment on the grounds of their ignorance of God and of his will. The Gentiles cannot claim that they did not know the true God, for their idolatry is the result not of ignorance but of the wilful suppression of the truth about God given through the natural order (1.18–23). Three times Paul emphasizes that the sins which resulted from this basic sin of idolatry were the direct result of that deliberate decision to ignore the Creator and to serve the creature (1.24–25,26,28). The chapter closes with an emphatic assertion that the sins of the Gentiles are not sins of ignorance but acts of wilful rebellion (1.32); Gentiles, therefore, cannot evade God's judgment by pleading their ignorance.

On the other hand, Jews cannot evade God's judgment by pleading their elect status (2.1–3.20). The Jew regards himself as a member of a nation marked out by God for special favour. The two great signs of this privileged position are the law and circumcision, and the Jew of Rom. 2 holds that possession of these guarantees his salvation, even if his actual conduct is no better than that of the Gentiles. Against this claim, Paul argues that God is impartial and must judge Jews and Gentiles alike. The Gentile who, taught by nature, obeys God's will is in a better position than the Jew who does not. In the last resort, the law does not differentiate Jews from Gentiles at all, but places Jews in the same position of guilt before God as the Gentiles. The result is that 'the whole world is held accountable to God' (3.20). The Roman Jewish Christians should, therefore, not set themselves apart from the Gentiles.

(*ii*) **The Righteousness of God**[4] Rom. 3.21–22 marks a dramatic turning-point in the argument: 'But now the righteousness of God has been manifested apart from law, although the law and the prophets bear witness to it, the righteousness of God through faith in Jesus Christ for all who believe'. Earlier in the argument, the phrase 'the righteousness of God' has referred to God's activity in maintaining his covenant promises (3.5),[5] and that seems to be the case here too: God has always promised salvation to his people (hence, 'the law and the prophets bear witness to it'), and now at last that promise has been fulfilled in 'the redemption which is in Christ Jesus' (3.24). 'The righteousness of God', the fulfilment of God's covenant promise of salvation, is concerned with making people righteous, removing them from the position of guilt in which they previously stood and placing them in a right relationship with God. 'Faith' is the means by which this takes place, and it is the nature of faith to be universal: 'There is no distinction' – that is, between Jew and Gentile (3.22). Because this is the case, the 'boasting' of a special, privileged status in which the Jews had engaged is quite inappropriate for God is the God of the Gentiles as well as of the Jews, and justifies Jews and Gentiles in the same way, by faith (3.27–30). Faith is not a general attitude of trust towards God, but is oriented specifically towards Jesus Christ (3.22) and his cross (3.25).

Jewish Christians, in Rome and elsewhere, should therefore withdraw their objections to Gentile Christians who do not live by the law, recognizing that God has provided for the salvation of Jews and Gentiles alike through faith in Jesus Christ and not through the law.

(*iii*) **Law and Spirit**[6] It is essential for Paul to give as full an account as possible of his attitude towards the law, because this is the point at which he and his Gentile followers are most fiercely criticized by Jewish Christians. These people claim that Gentile freedom from the law leads its advocates into sin, because the law is the divinely-appointed means for the restraint of sin. In Rom. 7–8, Paul argues that, on the contrary, the law actually leads people into sin, and that freedom from the law is therefore necessary to promote freedom from sin and obedience to the will of God. This at least appears to be the main point in an extremely complex and many-sided argument.

The law-Spirit contrast is introduced in 7.5–6: 'While we were living in the flesh, our sinful passions, aroused by the law, were at work in our members to bear fruit for death. But now we are discharged from the law . . . so that we serve not under the old written code but in the new life of the Spirit'. In 7.7–12, Paul defends the view that the law provoked sin by distinguishing between its origin – it is the good and holy law of God – and its effect. 'Sin' (understood here as a demonic power) used the good law to create 'in me all kinds of desire'. Paul seems to have in mind Gen. 3, where the serpent (represented here by Sin) uses God's commandment to persuade the man and woman to sin. Verse 7.13–25 is the lament of one who longs to keep the law but is powerless to do so because of 'sin which dwells within me'.[7] The law is powerless to help resolve this situation that it has unwittingly been used to bring about. Rom. 8 proclaims the advent of a new power – that of the Spirit – that brings freedom from 'sin which dwells within me' and the possibility of fulfilling the law's just demand. This new power is available because in the death of his Son, God has 'condemned sin in the flesh' (v. 3); he has made himself responsible both for sin and for the condemnation by which sin is removed.

SABBATH[1] One of the main causes of controversy between Jesus and the Pharisees was his attitude towards the Sabbath. The Pharisees criticized his disciples for plucking heads of grain as they walked through a corn-field on the Sabbath, on the grounds that this constituted threshing, and that threshing was work. Jesus defended them, citing first a scriptural example, that of David and then the general principle: 'The sabbath was made for man, and not man for the sabbath' (Mark 2.23–27). However, in the following verse the general principle is apparently restricted: 'So the Son of man is lord even of the sabbath'. The early Church was perhaps alarmed at the radical implications of the saying of v. 27 (which Matthew and Luke therefore omit), and sought to restrict freedom from sabbath regulations to Jesus himself ('the Son of man').[2]

All four Gospels contain different accounts of healing miracles on the sabbath. In Mark 3.6, a man with a withered hand is healed, and Jesus asks his critics: 'Is it lawful on the sabbath to do good or to do harm, to save life or to kill?' Matthew inserts a more specific argument into this context: 'What man of you, if he has one sheep and it falls into a pit on the sabbath, will not lay hold of it and lift it out? Of how much more value is a man than a sheep!' (12.11–12). Luke tells a similar story about the healing on the sabbath of 'a woman who had had a spirit of infirmity for eighteen years' (13.10–17). In John 5.1–18, Jesus heals the paralysed man at the pool of Bethesda, with the result that 'the Jews persecuted Jesus, because he did this on the sabbath' (v. 16). A second sabbath healing takes place in John 9, where the blind man receives his sight on the sabbath (v. 14). However, for the fourth evangelist the main dispute between Jesus and his opponents was about his identity and not about the sabbath, and he therefore adds that the real reason why the Jews sought to kill him was that 'he not only broke the sabbath but also called God his own Father, making himself equal with God' (5.18).

SADDUCEES[1] The term 'Sadducee' is probably derived from the name of the high priest during the reign of David, Zadok. To be a legitimate high priest, it was necessary to prove descent from Zadok. The link between the Sadducees and the high priesthood is implied in Acts 5.17, where 'the party of the Sadducees' is identified as 'the high priest and all who were with him'. However, the Sadducees represented not just particular family interests but a distinctive theological position. One of their main disagreements with their great rivals, the Pharisees, is summed up in Acts 23.8: 'The Sadducees say that there is no resurrection, nor angel, nor spirit; but the Pharisees acknowledge them all'. The Sadducees' denial of the resurrection is also mentioned in Mark 12.18–27, where they come to Jesus with a problem intended to show how foolish belief in the resurrection really is. Because they also rejected the Pharisaic oral interpretation of the law, their motive seems to have been conservatism: they sought to preserve the Jewish religion as it had been before it was corrupted by the foreign doctrine of the resurrection and by the other innovations of the Pharisees.

SALVATION[1] The Greek verb translated 'save' does not initially have particular religious connotations, but simply refers to rescue from any threat. The disciples cry out, 'Lord, save us!', when their boat is in danger of sinking in a storm (Matt. 8.25). The crucified Jesus is taunted with the words, 'Save yourself, and come down from the cross' (Mark 15.30). And yet, in the New Testament the verb (and even more the noun, translated 'salvation') is generally used in a religious sense. Jesus 'will save his people from their sins' (Matt. 1.21). He came 'not to judge the world but to save the world' (John 12.47). When Jesus visits the repentant tax collector Zacchaeus, he says, 'Today salvation has come to this house' (Luke 19.9).

'Save' and 'salvation' became extremely common terms in early Christian vocabulary to summarize the entire content of what God had done, was still doing, and would do in the future, through Jesus Christ. The presupposition underlying its use is that humanity was in a state of dire peril apart from Christ, from which a rescue was needed. These terms can be linked with the coming of Jesus Christ into the world: 'Christ Jesus came into the world to save sinners' (I Tim. 1.15), but more commonly, they have a future aspect. Paul speaks of 'the hope of salvation' (I Thess. 5.8), and the author of I Peter reminds his readers of the 'salvation' which awaits them, 'ready to be revealed in the last time' (1.5).

SAMARIA[1] This region, situated between Galilee in the north and Judaea in the south, was inhabited by people who practised a form of Judaism not recognized by the Jewish authorities. They observed the Law of Moses, and they had their own sanctuary on Mount Gerizim (*see* John 4.20), but they rejected the authority of the later parts of the Jewish canon. As John 4.9 succinctly puts it, 'Jews have no dealings with Samaritans', and so it is striking that they are on the whole portrayed so positively in the New Testament. It is mainly Luke who is responsible for the preservation of traditions concerning Samaritans. Despite the Samaritan villages' refusal to receive Jesus, because he was on his way to Jerusalem, Jesus rebukes James and John who wish to call down fire from heaven upon them (Luke 9.52–55). The Samaritan in the parable shows more understanding of the will of God than the Jews who pass by on the other side (10.29–37). Of the ten lepers cleansed by Jesus, only one, a Samaritan, returns to give thanks (17.11–19). In Acts 8.4–25, Luke tells of the conversion of 'a city of Samaria' through Philip the evangelist, assisted by Peter and John who come from Jerusalem to confer apostolic legitimacy on his work. However, despite his pro-Samaritan attitude, Luke seems to have only a hazy idea of where Samaria actually is, because he portrays Jesus on his way up to Jerusalem as passing *between* Galilee and Samaria (17.11).

SANCTIFICATION[1] To sanctify something is to make it holy, not in a moral sense but by transferring it from the ordinary, profane realm to the realm belonging to God. Thus, all Christians have been 'sanctified', taken out of the profane world and placed in the sphere of the Holy Spirit. The Corinthians are addressed as those who are 'sanctified in Christ Jesus', and thus as 'saints' (I Cor. 1.2); this took place at baptism, when 'you were washed, you were sanctified, you were justified in the name of the Lord Jesus Christ and in the Spirit of our God' (I Cor. 6.11). However, this does not mean that their conduct was especially 'holy' from a moral viewpoint because the whole point of this section of I Corinthians is the complaint that their present way of life is not sufficiently different from their previous conduct as pagans. 'Sanctification' thus takes place in conversion and baptism, and is the bestowal of a new standing before God; it must issue in new patterns of conduct, but it is not itself identical to that new conduct. This religious, indeed cultic, sense of 'sanctification' is particularly in evidence in the Letter to the Hebrews, where to be 'sanctified' means not to be morally pure (though this will be a consequence of it) but to be cleansed from one's old life through the sacrifice of Christ so as to be able to come into the presence of God (9.13–14, 10.10,14,29, 13.12). Sanctification is something that is done to one, not something one does for oneself. As I Cor. 1.30 puts it, Christ is 'our sanctification'.

However, the Greek verb translated 'sanctify' is closely related to the words usually translated 'holy' and 'holiness', and here a moral sense is more prominent: 'God has not called us for uncleanness, but in holiness' (I Thess. 4.8); 'As he who called you is holy, be holy yourselves in all your conduct' (I Peter 1.15).

SANHEDRIN[1] The word 'Sanhedrin' is an Aramaic form of the Greek word, *synedrion*, meaning 'a council', and it is in this Greek form that it occurs in the New Testament. 'The Council' met twice a week in the temple, and was composed of 71 priests, Pharisees, and 'elders' from the leading families, under the presidency of the High Priest. It legislated on all aspects of religious life (for example, the liturgical calendar), and functioned as a court for crimes against the law. It also had a political function, working together with the Roman authorities. It had its own police force, referred to disparagingly in Mark 14.43 as 'a crowd . . . from the chief priests and the scribes and the elders', but more correctly in John 18.3 as 'a band of soldiers and some officers from the chief priests and the Pharisees'.

Several aspects of the trial of Jesus before the Sanhedrin are puzzling. For example, the death penalty could not be pronounced at night, contrary to Mark 14.64. Yet Mark 15.1 also mentions a meeting in the morning after Jesus' arrest, and in Luke 22.66–71 Jesus' trial takes place in the morning. Judging from the Sanhedrin's normal procedures, Luke's account is more likely to be correct. In addition, Jesus' accusers say in John 19.31, 'It is not lawful for us to put any man to death'; yet it seems that the Sanhedrin normally had power to inflict the death sentence.

The Sanhedrin is also portrayed as hostile to the Church in Acts. However, the early Christians acknowledged that its members were not all bad: Joseph of Arimathea, Nicodemus, and Gamaliel are all seen in a positive light.[2]

SHEEP AND GOATS, PARABLE OF[1] Matt. 25.31–46 is not really a parable at all, but a straightforward description of the last judgment, which will involve a separation 'as a shepherd separates the sheep from the goats' (v. 32). The criterion of the judgment is whether or not people have welcomed and cared for the King's 'brethren', who are his representatives: 'Truly, I say to you, as you did it [or did it not] to one of the least of these my brethren, you did it [or did it not] to me' (vv. 40,44). The passage has often been regarded as a general commendation of acts of charity: in the last resort what matters is not what you believe, but what you do to feed the hungry, visit the prisoners, and so forth.

This interpretation, however, is very unlikely to be correct. Who are Christ's 'brethren'? Matt. 10.42–44 seems to provide the answer: 'He who receives you receives me . . . And whoever gives to one of these little ones a cup of cold water because he is a disciple, truly I say to you, he shall not lose his reward'. It is acts of mercy done to *disciples* – here, itinerant evangelists are meant – which are done to Christ himself, and so merit a reward. The passage shows that Matt. 25 is not speaking of acts of mercy in general, but acts of mercy to Christ's disciples *because* they are disciples. The risen Christ sends his disciples into all the world to preach his gospel (Matt. 28.19–20), and the judgment is determined by the reception they receive. This is, of course, not a complete statement of the criterion of the judgment; it merely draws attention to one aspect of it.

SILAS/SILVANUS The same person is referred to in Acts as 'Silas' and in various of the letters as 'Silvanus'. He makes his first appearance in Acts 15.22, where together with a certain 'Judas called Barsabbas' he is sent by the Jerusalem Church to accompany Paul and Barnabas as they take the 'Apostolic Decree' back to Antioch. This whole narrative is full of historical problems, and Luke's tendency to link all the main characters in the Gentile mission with Jerusalem may be

motivated more by theological than by historical considerations.[1] However, the fact that he accompanied Paul on his so-called 'second missionary journey' (Acts 15.36–18.22) is confirmed by Paul's letters. Together with Timothy, Silvanus is a co-writer of Paul's letters to the Thessalonians (I Thess. 1.1, II Thess. 1.1), which must mean that he had played a part in the founding of the Church at Thessalonica as Acts claims.[2] In II Cor. 1.19, Paul speaks of 'the Son of God, Jesus Christ, whom we preached among you [i.e. at Corinth], Silvanus and Timothy and I', and this again agrees with Acts. He is also seen in I Peter 5.12 as the secretary to whom Peter dictated the letter; but Peter's authorship of this work (and therefore Silvanus' involvement) is doubtful.[3] He is commended there as 'a faithful brother as I regard him'; here, Christian tradition rejects the conclusion that might have been drawn from Gal. 2.11–21, that there was a permanent rift between Paul and his supporters on the one hand and Peter on the other.

SIMEON Luke's nativity narrative relates the births of John the Baptist and of Jesus to a small group of pious Jews, loyal to the law and eagerly awaiting the Messiah's coming.[1] One of these is Simeon (Luke 2.25–35), to whom it has been revealed 'that he should not see death before he had seen the Lord's Christ' (compare Mark 9.1). The Spirit reveals to him that the infant Jesus is the Christ, and he utters the famous hymn known as the *Nunc Dimittis* and also addresses Mary in prophetic language. Several of the themes of Luke's two volume work are announced for the first time here in veiled language: the necessity for the Christ to suffer, the unbelief of Israel, and the consequent salvation of the Gentiles. The figure of Simeon is used by Luke to stress that there is nothing arbitrary or accidental in the history he is beginning to relate.

SIMON MAGUS Acts 8.9–24 tells the story of 'a man named Simon who had previously practised magic in the city and amazed the nation of Samaria' (v. 9), who believed Philip's preaching and was baptized, but who incurred the wrath of Peter when he offered money for the power to bestow the Holy Spirit.[1] Luke probably includes the story in his narrative because he wishes to differentiate the Holy Spirit from the various claims to magical and miracle-working powers of which the Ancient World was full. Simon regards the apostolic bestowal of the Holy Spirit merely as a higher form of the magical arts which he himself practises, which as a magician he must acquire for himself. There is a hint in v. 10 that Simon was regarded as more than simply a magician ('This man is that power of God which is called great'), and later Christian tradition sees him as the father of all heresies, who taught that he himself was the incarnation of the supreme deity. It is impossible to tell which, if any, of the various ideas later ascribed to Simon were actually taught by him. He remains an enigmatic figure.

SIN[1] The New Testament takes over from the Old Testament and Judaism the idea that human life is subject to God's command, and that certain actions constitute transgressions of that command. By and large, the early Christians agreed with Judaism about what those actions were. Thus, Paul quotes four of the ten commandments ('You shall not commit adultery, You shall not kill, You shall not steal, You shall not covet') in the context of Christian ethical instruction (Rom. 13.9). Some writers simply repeat Jewish ideas on the subject of sin; others seek to reinterpret the subject in the light of the gospel. Rather than attempting an overall view of the New Testament's teaching on this matter, it seems best simply to draw attention to a few notable points.

(*i*) There is a strong stress on the inward motivation as well as the outward action. In Matt. 5, Jesus extends the prohibitions of murder and adultery to the hatred and lust from which the actions spring. The Pharisees 'outwardly appear righteous to men', but that is not enough, because inwardly they are 'full of hypocrisy and iniquity' (Matt. 23.28).[2] In Rom. 7.7–25, the fundamental commandment of the law is the prohibition of desire – that is, the inward motivation which leads to external actions.

(*ii*) Sin is generally seen as rebellion against God. In Rom. 1.18–32, the Gentiles' sin is due not to their ignorance of the will of God, but to their rejection of his revelation of himself in the natural order. This rebellion is traced back to Adam in Rom. 5.12–21. However, a somewhat different view is expressed in Rom. 7.14–25, where sin is seen as in the last resort involuntary. The speaker laments the fact that 'I do not do what I want, but I do the very thing I hate' (v. 15), and concludes, 'It is no longer I that do it, but sin which dwells within me' (v. 17). Here, sin is not simply individual acts of wrongdoing, but a quasi-demonic power that has taken over the speaker and forced him to obey its dictates, contrary to his will.[3]

(*iii*) In the Gospel of John, sin is identified almost exclusively with unbelief – failure to believe in Jesus as the Son of God. Before the coming of the light into the world, sin is therefore not a full reality: 'If I had not come and spoken to them, they would not have sin; but now they have no excuse for their sin' (John 15.22, *see also* v. 24). This is perhaps the most radical attempt in the New Testament to reinterpret the concept of sin from the standpoint of God's revelation in Jesus Christ. God's command is expressed not in the multiplicity of demands in the law, but in Jesus' call to faith in himself. Sin is therefore unbelief. It is exemplified by the Pharisees, to whom Jesus says: 'If you were blind, you would have no guilt; but now that you say, "We see", your guilt remains' (9.41).

SLAVERY As with other social institutions, the New Testament generally avoids two extremes in its approach to slavery. One is the conservative approach that uses religion to reinforce the authority of particular social institutions; the other is the revolutionary approach which seeks to abolish the institutions in question.

The conservative approach is rejected on the grounds that the relationship of master and slave is transcended in the gospel's proclamation of human equality in Christ: in Christ, 'There is neither slave nor free' (Gal. 3.28). 'He who was called in the Lord as a slave is a freedman of the Lord', and similarly 'he who was free when called is a slave of Christ' (I Cor. 7.22); the difference between slave and free is of only relative significance because the ultimate truth about people is to be found 'in Christ'. Paul's letter to Philemon exhorts him to accept back Onesimus, the runaway slave, 'no longer as a slave but more than a slave, as a beloved brother' (v. 16).[1] Christian masters must no longer threaten their slaves, knowing that he who is both their master and yours is in heaven, and there is no partiality with him' (Eph. 6.9, *see also* Col. 4.1). Thus, the status quo is accepted but at the same time undermined and transcended.

The revolutionary approach is also rejected; the early Christians do not inhabit a fantasy world in which normal social institutions have ceased to exist. Paul does not particularly approve of slavery; he permits slaves to seek their freedom by legitimate means, and he warns his readers not to submit to slavery voluntarily (I Cor. 7.21,23). Yet he teaches that 'everyone should remain in the state in which he was called', and if that means remaining as a slave, 'Never mind!' (I Cor. 7.20–21). This is not a demand for submission to an unjust fate; the emphasis is on the 'call', which transforms the present situation into an opportunity for the service of Christ.[2] Slaves who serve their earthly masters well are thus 'slaves of Christ, doing the will of God from the heart, rendering service with a good will as to the Lord and not to men' (Eph. 6.6–7).

SON OF GOD[1]

The entire contents of Christian proclamation can be summarized in the claim that Jesus is the Son of God. Immediately after his conversion, Paul is said to have proclaimed Jesus in the synagogues of Damascus, saying, 'He is the Son of God' (Acts 9.20). In II Cor. 1.19 he sums up his preaching at Corinth in a similar way, referring to 'the son of God, Jesus Christ, whom we preached among you'. The sole purpose of the Gospel of John is 'that you may believe that Jesus is the Christ, the Son of God, and that believing you may have life in his name' (20.31). The title 'Son of God' is of the greatest importance for the New Testament writers as they seek to convey the full significance of Jesus.

(*i*) **The Origins of the Title** Jesus referred to God as *Abba* ('Father'),[2] and in the Synoptic Gospels is occasionally said to have referred to himself as 'the Son' (e.g. Matt. 11.27, Mark 13.32). It is likely that the latter sayings arose from early Christian faith and were not uttered by Jesus himself, but they preserve the insight that there was a uniqueness in the relationship between Jesus and his Father that makes the term 'Son' appropriate for him. It is only through him that others too can know God as *Abba*.

Several of the titles ascribed to Jesus derive from individual Old Testament passages: for example, the main source for the title 'Lord' was evidently Ps. 110.1 ('The Lord said to my Lord, "Sit at my right hand . . ." ').[3] The same is apparently true of 'Son of God', which seems to have entered early Christian usage from Ps. 2.7: 'I will tell of the decree of the Lord; he said to me, "You are my son, today I have begotten you" '. This passage is echoed in the divine words at Jesus' baptism ('You are my beloved Son', Mark 1.11), and is directly quoted in connection with the resurrection in Acts 13.33 and Heb. 1.5, 5.5 (*see also* Rom. 1.4, which again links Jesus' sonship with his resurrection).

(*ii*) **Paul** The most common title Paul ascribes to Jesus is not 'Son of God' but 'Lord'. However, the two titles have a rather different function. 'Lord' is used in implicit contrast to the position of the earthly Jesus, who 'took the form of a slave' (Phil. 2.7); the contrast is clearer in Greek, where *Kyrios* means both 'Lord' and 'master'. Thus, Jesus becomes Lord at his resurrection.[4] 'Son of God' is, however, a more comprehensive title, used not only of the risen and exalted Jesus but of every stage in his existence. He is already 'the Son of God' in his heavenly state before his incarnation, and it is as such that he takes human form: God 'sent his own Son in the likeness of sinful flesh' (Rom. 8.3); he 'sent forth his Son, born of woman, born under the law' (Gal. 4.4). He is God's Son during his earthly life as a descendant of David (Rom. 1.3), and he is God's Son in his crucifixion (Rom. 8.32). His sonship is manifested in power in his resurrection (Rom. 1.4), and the appearance of the risen Jesus to Paul is therefore a revelation of God's Son (Gal. 1.16). It is 'the Son' to whom all things will eventually be subjected (I Cor. 15.28).

(*iii*) **John** In Paul, Jesus' sonship means both that he is 'in the form of God' and that he is distinguished from God. God is uniquely related to Jesus; where Jesus is, there God is in all his fullness; but Jesus is not explicitly *identified* with God. The situation is clarified in the Fourth Gospel, in which Jesus' status as Son of God means that he can appropriately be acknowledged as 'God' (1.1, 20.28). In one sense, he is subordinate to the Father ('The Father is greater than I', 14.28), but only in the sense that the relationship between Father and Son naturally implies an element of subordination. In another sense, they are equal; the Jews seek to stone Jesus 'because he called God his own Father, making himself equal with God' (5.18, *see* 10.33).

SON OF MAN

In Dan. 7.13–14, the prophet sees a vision: 'And behold, with the clouds of heaven there came one like a son of man, and he came to the Ancient of Days and was presented before him. And to him was given dominion and glory and kingdom that all peoples, nations and languages should serve him . . .'. The phrase, 'one like a son of man' means 'a figure resembling a human being', for in the Old Testament, 'son of man' is identical to 'man': 'What is man that thou art mindful of him, or the son of man that thou dost care for him?' (Ps. 8.4). Later in Dan. 7, it becomes clear that, as the grotesque beasts have represented the four pagan empires, so the figure of the son of man represents 'the people of the saints of the Most High', to whom world-dominion is to be given (v. 22).[1] Here is the fulfilment of the promise of Gen. 1.28: man gains dominion over the beasts.

In early Christian usage, 'Son of man' is found almost exclusively in sayings attributed to Jesus. Many of these clearly show the influence of Dan. 7.13, for example Mark 13.26: 'Then they will see the Son of man coming in clouds with great power and glory'. The 'Son of man' is no longer simply a symbolic representation of 'the saints of the Most High', as in Daniel; he is a concrete figure who is to come to judge the world and to save his people. The future 'coming of the Son of man' was a central belief for the earliest Christians, and it is referred to again and again in the teaching ascribed to Jesus.[2]

However, 'the Son of man' also occurs in contexts where there is no reference to his future coming. In Mark 2.10, Jesus cures the paralytic 'that you may know that the Son of man has authority on earth to forgive sins'. In Matt. 8.20, he uses the phrase with reference to his own homelessness: 'Foxes have holes, and birds of the air have nests, but the Son of man has nowhere to lay his head'. In another group of sayings, the phrase is used in connection with his death and resurrection. This is the case in Mark's three main passion predictions (8.31, 9.31, 10.33), in each of which it is announced that 'the Son of man' must suffer and on the third day rise from the dead. In Mark 10.45, 'the Son of man' is used with reference both to Jesus' ministry and to his death: 'The Son of man also came not to be served but to serve, and to give his life as a ransom for many'. Thus, 'Son of man' is used in three main contexts: the future coming of Jesus, his earthly ministry, and his death and resurrection.

The influence of Dan. 7.13 means that 'Son of man' is used in part as a messianic title, alongside 'Christ', 'Lord', 'Son of God', and so on. In Aramaic (the language spoken by Jesus), however, it was sometimes used to refer to the speaker in an indirect way; 'I' might be replaced by 'the Son of man' in the same way as in English 'I' can be replaced by 'one'. This means that when Jesus speaks of himself as the Son of man, no direct messianic claim is made: 'The Son of man has nowhere to lay his head' means 'I have nowhere to lay my head'. Yet because Jesus elsewhere refers to himself as the messianic Son of man who is to come with the clouds and great glory, the early Christians must have seen a hidden messianic claim even in sayings where 'Son of man' is used in the conventional Aramaic way. At one level, 'the Son of man' simply means 'I'; at another level, the point is that in the earthly ministry of Jesus, the future Son of man who is to judge the world has already come among us. The ambiguity and indirectness of the messianic claim is typical of Jesus.[3]

SOWER, PARABLE OF

The early Church tended to treat Jesus' parables as allegories.[1] It was thought that every detail was significant, although in fact the parables make only a few main points. The parable of the sower (Mark 4.1–20) is a good example of this tendency because it is accompanied by a detailed explanation which is generally regarded as the work of the early Church. Every detail in the parable is given a precise interpretation. For example, the birds who devour the seed sown on the path (v. 4) stand for Satan (v. 15); the sun which scorches the seed sown on rocky ground (v. 5) stands for 'tribulation and persecution' (v. 17); the thorns which choke the seed (v. 7) stand for worldly attitudes (v. 19). In this way, the parable is turned into a coded message whose purpose, as Mark explains (vv. 10–12), is to conceal the truth from outsiders and to reveal it only to the chosen few.[2] The interpretation (vv. 14–20) uses many terms that are prominent in early Christian vocabulary but occur rarely if at all elsewhere in the teaching of Jesus, and it seems to reflect experiences of church life over a comparatively lengthy period.

The conclusion has often been drawn from this that the early Church has missed the point of the original parable, which was to affirm the certainty of the final harvest (i.e. the kingdom of God), despite the apparently wasted labour of the present. Yet the stress in the parable falls not on the contrast between the present and the future, but on the different types of ground. The early Church was therefore probably right to regard this as a parable about responding to the word of God (see Matt. 7.24–27); it challenges the hearers to decide what sort of ground they are. The interpretation finds a much more precise meaning in every detail than was originally intended, but it remains essentially true to the meaning of the parable.

SPIRIT/HOLY SPIRIT The early Christians did not believe that the Holy Spirit was active at all times and in all places; they believed that the Spirit was the gift of the risen and exalted Lord to his Church.[1] Thus, in John 7.39 the evangelist comments on Jesus' promise, 'If anyone thirst, let him come to me and drink', explaining that he said this about the Spirit and that 'as yet the Spirit had not been given because Jesus was not yet glorified'. Whether the Spirit is bestowed at one of the resurrection appearances (John 20.22) or on the Day of Pentecost (Acts 2), only the risen Lord makes this possible. Despite the fact that Jesus received the Holy Spirit at his baptism, the Gospels are unanimous that the gift is not shared with the disciples until after the resurrection.

1 The Experience of the Spirit For the early Christians, the Spirit was primarily an experience rather than a doctrine. One enters into this experience at baptism, through which one becomes a member of the Christian community: 'By one Spirit we were all baptized into one body – Jews or Greeks, slaves or free – and all were made to drink of one Spirit' (I Cor. 12.13). However, the Spirit also brings people to the point of submitting to baptism – that is, in bringing them to faith. Paul teaches that only through the Holy Spirit are those who listen to his preaching able to discern in it the word of God rather than the word of man (I Cor. 2.4–5, I Thess. 1.5, *see* 2.13).[2]

What is the nature of this experience? Paul can appeal to it as something with which his readers are sure to be familiar: 'Did you receive the Spirit by works of the law, or by hearing with faith?' (Gal. 3.2). To simplify a complex issue, the Spirit is the means by which the Christian gospel is subjectively appropriated by the individual. Thus, the Spirit brings about the experience of revelation, in which one perceives oneself as the beneficiary of God's saving act in Christ.

(i) **The Spirit, the Father and the Son** In Gal. 4.4, Paul states that 'God has sent the Spirit of his Son into our hearts, crying, "Abba, Father!" '; in Rom. 8.15–16, this cry is similarly understood as the result of 'receiving the Spirit of sonship'.[3] An important element in receiving the Spirit at baptism was therefore the glad recognition of God as Father. This acknowledgement is of course made repeatedly in the course of Christian life and worship, but it begins in baptism. Paul has in mind not a formal acceptance of a doctrine, but a divine act in which the one being baptized becomes a son or child of God for the first time, and gratefully acknowledges the fact.

Another important element of early Christian baptism was that 'you confess with your lips that Jesus is Lord' (Rom. 10.9).[4] Like the confession of God as Father, this too was seen as possible only through the Holy Spirit: 'No-one can say "Jesus is Lord" except by the Holy Spirit' (I Cor. 12.3). The Spirit is the means by which the statements of Christian tradition are appropriated and come to express the individual's own sure conviction. In this way, the unbelief which can see in the gospel only 'an offence' or 'folly' (I Cor. 1.23) is contradicted and overcome.

(ii) **The Fruit of the Spirit** In a famous passage in Gal. 5.22–23, Paul lists the qualities the Spirit produces: love, joy, peace, patience, kindness, and so on. He does not mean that wherever (for example) kindness is found, it is the work of the Holy Spirit; that would change the Spirit into a vague and generalized power for good in the world, and that is not the New Testament view. Paul is referring to the

Spirit which is present within the Christian community, continually enabling its members to recognize God as Father and Jesus as Lord; it is this recognition, enabled by the Spirit, which produces love, joy, peace and so forth. Elsewhere, Paul speaks in similar terms of the Holy Spirit as bringing certainty of God's love (Rom. 5.5), righteousness, peace and joy (Rom. 14.17) and hope (Rom. 15.13). In Rom. 8.23–27 Paul describes the dark side of the hope inspired by the Spirit, which is a dissatisfaction with the way things are, a longing for the promise of freedom to be fulfilled, expressed in sighs and groans; this too he attributes to the Spirit (*see also* II Cor. 5.4–5). In each case, these things spring from the Spirit's work in enabling people to hear anew the message of the gospel, not as a series of external doctrines to which one must submit but as a true expression of one's own mind.

(*iii*) **The Gifts of the Spirit**[5] Paul thanks God that his preaching to the Corinthians was 'confirmed' by the 'spiritual gifts' which they received, gifts of 'speech and knowledge' (I Cor. 1.4–7). The fundamental recognition that 'Jesus is Lord', made possible by the Spirit (I Cor. 12.3), calls forth a variety of responses from the members of the congregation, and Paul lists some of these in I Cor. 12.8–10: the utterance of wisdom and of knowledge, faith (i.e. 'the faith that moves mountains', 13.2), gifts of healing, miracles, prophecy, distinguishing spirits, speaking in tongues, and interpreting tongues. The precise meaning of some of these expressions is unclear, and it seems doubtful whether Paul differentiated between, for example, the utterance of wisdom and the utterance of knowledge as precisely as this list might imply. Other lists elsewhere indicate that for him the variety of activity inspired by the Spirit is endless (I Cor. 12.27–30, Rom. 12.6–8). The essential criterion which indicates whether a particular activity is genuinely inspired by the Spirit is 'the common good' (I Cor. 12.7). Whatever promotes the common good is a gift of the Spirit; whatever does not is not a gift of the Spirit.

2 The Spirit and the Trinity It is often said that the doctrine of the Trinity is to be found nowhere in the New Testament; instead, it is the result of a misguided attempt to combine Greek philosophical ideas with early Christian beliefs. It is true that the New Testament does not formally teach the later view that God is three persons in one essence, but it does state that the God who confronts us in the gospel does so in threefold form, as the Father, the Son and the Spirit. This threefold form is apparent in the summary of Paul's view of the Spirit given above, that the Spirit is the means by which one comes to acknowledge God as Father and Jesus as Lord. It is apparent in Paul's statements in Gal. 4.4–6: 'God sent forth his Son', and 'God has sent forth the Spirit of his Son into our hearts . . .'. Even Matthew, the most Jewish of the evangelists, speaks of baptism in the name of the Father, the Son and the Holy Spirit (28.19).

However, it is the Fourth Gospel which comes closest to a formal doctrine of the Trinity. It is true that in the prologue (John 1.1–18) the Spirit is not mentioned, because the subject is the eternal relationship between the Father and the Son, God and the Word who is himself God. However, in 14.16 Jesus promises the disciples 'another Counsellor to be with you for ever' (the Greek word, *parakletos*, could also be translated, 'advocate'). This 'Spirit of truth' will in one sense take the place of Jesus, continuing the teaching that he has begun (16.12–13); in another sense, he will manifest the presence of the exalted Jesus and the Father to the disciples

(14.21–23).[6] It is the Father who sends the Spirit, at the request of Jesus (14.16,26); if it can be said that Jesus himself 'sends' the Spirit, he does so 'from the Father' because the Spirit 'proceeds from the Father' (15.26). Nothing is directly said here about any eternal relationship of the Spirit to the Father and the Son, corresponding to the eternal relationship of the Father and the Son with one another,[7] but such a view is perhaps implied in these statements.

The doctrine of the Trinity took as its starting-point the universal New Testament belief that God the Father is manifested through the Son and the Spirit. It then took a further step: because God has revealed himself as Father, Son and Spirit, he must be Father, Son and Spirit in himself and eternally. The idea of an eternal relationship between the Father and the Son is to be found only in a few parts of the New Testament, and an eternal presence with them of the Spirit is nowhere explicitly mentioned. Yet it was felt that God in his revelation must ultimately be the same as God as he is in himself. Otherwise, one would leave open the possibility that God might elsewhere and at other times manifest himself in quite different ways; or one might seek a higher knowledge of God as he is in himself, and leave behind the lower and inadequate grade of knowledge attested to in the New Testament. Both paths were taken in the early centuries of church history, and it was in order to rule them out that the doctrine of the Trinity insisted that God is in himself no other than he is in his revelation: Father, Son and Spirit. In one sense, this goes beyond the letter of the New Testament (especially in the case of the Spirit). In another sense, it is the result of an enquiry into the ultimate grounds of the revelation to which the New Testament bears witness.

STATE For all the New Testament writers, 'the State' meant the power of Rome, and it is assessed in a variety of ways.

(*i*) **The Gospels** In the Gospels, the State makes its presence felt primarily in the passion narratives. Although it was the Romans who crucified Jesus, it is the Jews whom the evangelists blame for this, because (they claim) it was their fanaticism which compelled the Roman governor to crucify a man he rightly regarded as innocent.[1] This presentation is not motivated by a positive attitude towards the State as such, but by the need to explain that Jesus was not really a political rebel, despite the fact that he was crucified. However, John's passion narrative does include some reflections on the power of the State. Pilate reminds Jesus that he has the authority to put him to death, and Jesus replies that the State's authority is God-given; those who clamour for his death pervert the gift of God by using it as the instrument of their rebellion against God (John 19.10–11).

Jesus' attitude towards the State is apparent in Mark 12.13–17, where he rejects the view that the State's authority over the chosen people is unlawful and should be resisted.[2] At the same time, he also speaks of a higher duty than one's duty to the State: 'Render to Caesar the things that are Caesar's, and to God the things that are God's'. The State cannot claim the absolute allegiance of its subjects as though it were itself divine.

(*ii*) **Paul** The discussion of the State in Rom. 13.1–7 seems to be an attempt to provide a theological foundation for the cryptic saying of Jesus' quoted above. Why should the servants of Christ and of God 'render to Caesar the things that are

Caesar's'? Paul's answer is that the State has been 'instituted by God' (v. 1), and that its individual representatives are 'God's servants for your good' (v. 4). To be punished by the State for wrong-doing is to be punished by God (vv. 2,4). The State, like the family, is one of the ordinances decreed by God, and its command is therefore God's command. It is a remarkable example of the combination of conservatism and radicalism in Paul that in the same context he can proclaim the nearness of the Day of the Lord, which will bring the State to an end (13.11–14). His point is presumably that Christians should not anticipate the end by rejecting the authority of the State here and now.

(*iii*) **Acts** In the Acts narrative, the Roman authorities are on the whole portrayed positively. Part of the point of this is to assert Paul's innocence of the Jewish charge that he is a trouble-maker whose view of the Jewish law makes him a disruptive influence wherever he goes. The Roman officials to whom this charge is brought, Gallio, Felix and Festus,[3] all agree that the dispute in question is an internal Jewish affair over which the State has no jurisdiction. The parallel with the Gospels' portrayal of the trial of Jesus is clear: Paul, like Jesus, is rightly declared to be innocent by the Roman authorities; his arrest and trial is solely due to the malevolence of his Jewish enemies, who are the true trouble-makers. However, Luke's view of the State is not simply determined by the need to clear Paul's good name; he seems to present it as the providential instrument for the protection and spread of the gospel. Paul in Acts 19.21 announces his intention of preaching the gospel in Rome, and Acts 28 tells how this ambition was eventually fulfilled. The intervening chapters tell how in Judaea it was Roman power which rescued Paul from a violent mob and from his enemies in high places; it is the power of the State which ensures that the gospel is preached in Rome. Luke hints at the possibility of a harmonious relationship between Church and State.

(*iv*) **Revelation**[4] A quite different view of the State is taken in the Book of Revelation. The Antichrist ('the beast') is to be a Roman emperor who, inspired by the devil, will be 'allowed to make war on the saints and to conquer them' (13.7). Aided and abetted by a second beast, he will force all peoples to worship him on pain of death (13.11–17). Satan and the two beasts are a blasphemous parody of the true Trinity. Like Jesus, the first beast 'seemed to have a mortal wound, but its mortal wound was healed' (v. 3); like Jesus, the second beast resembled a lamb and performed signs and wonders (vv. 11,13–14). In Rev. 17–18, Rome is portrayed as 'the great harlot', 'drunk with the blood of the saints', whose overthrow is near. The author is speaking not of the present Roman State, but of a future incarnation of evil in the State. Nevertheless, he believes that the State already betrays the satanic characteristics which will become fully manifest with the appearance of the Antichrist.

STEPHEN

Acts 6–7 describes the brief career of Stephen as an evangelist before his martyrdom at the hands of the Sanhedrin.[1] In Acts 6.1–6, he is the first-named of the seven men appointed by the apostles to deal with practical matters such as the care of poor members of the Jerusalem congregation. In fact, 6.8–15 tells how he made a name for himself not in the service of the poor but in preaching the gospel in the synagogue of the Hellenists – Jews from the Greek-speaking world now resident in Jerusalem. It has been argued that Luke is in this section covering up a serious theological controversy between Aramaic-speaking and Greek-speaking Christians at Jerusalem; this theory assumes that Stephen was the leader of the latter group. This is uncertain, however, as the only evidence in Acts 6–7 that Stephen held radical theological views is found in the accusation of false witnesses that he taught that Jesus would destroy the temple and change the law (6.13–14); but the term 'false witnesses' means that – that is, they were lying.

When requested to defend himself against this charge, Stephen responds with a long and apparently irrelevant summary of Old Testament history from Abraham to Moses, which concluded abruptly with a denunciation of the present Jewish leaders (Acts 7). Whatever tradition he may have at his disposal, the speech in its present form is Luke's composition, and we must therefore ask what his purpose is in inserting it at this point. The emphasis seems to be on Israel's rejection of Moses, God's servant. Luke is about to tell how the gospel was first preached to the Gentiles because of Israel's persistent refusal to accept it, and he therefore wishes to show that this Jewish disobedience is nothing new but has existed ever since the time of Moses. God has finally lost patience with his people, and therefore turns to the Gentiles instead. Stephen thus serves as a mouthpiece for Luke to express his view of the origins of the Gentile mission and its theological justification.

SUFFERING The New Testament speaks of 'suffering' as a constant factor in Christian life. In Mark, Jesus' first prediction of his own suffering is followed by a call to the disciple to be prepared for suffering: the disciple must 'deny himself and take up his cross and follow me', which means that he must not be 'ashamed of me and of my words in this adulterous and sinful generation' (8.34,38).[1] In Rom. 8.17, suffering is an indispensable part of Christian living, so that it can be seen as a condition of final salvation: we are 'fellow heirs with Christ' only 'provided we suffer with him in order that we may also be glorified with him'. According to II Tim. 3.12, 'All who desire to live a godly life in Christ Jesus will be persecuted'.

The New Testament is therefore full of exhortations not to abandon one's Christian commitment when one is called upon to suffer for it. Paul speaks in I Thess. 3.1–10 of his previous fear that the Thessalonians will have abandoned their new-found faith in the face of persecution, and his present joy now that Timothy has returned to Athens bringing the good news of their faithful endurance; he exhorts them to remember that 'afflictions' are to be 'our lot'.[2] The main purpose of I Peter is to encourage the recipients 'not to be surprised at the fiery ordeal which comes upon you to prove you, as though something strange were happening to you' (4.12).[3] The author to the Hebrews reminds his readers of the persecutions they once joyfully endured (10.32–34), and exhorts them to return to the true Christian discipleship they then manifested, following the example of Christ: 'Let us go forth to him outside the camp, and bear the abuse he endured. For here we have no lasting city, but we seek the city which is to come' (13.13–14). The interpretation of the parable of the sower reflects sadly on those who 'when they receive the word, immediately receive it with joy', but 'when tribulation or persecution arises on account of the word, immediately they fall away' (Mark 4.16–17).

The suffering of which the New Testament writers speak is not generally persecution by the State; the Book of Revelation is an exception to this, but there the State persecution is still future. It arises from the inevitable tension between Christians and the society in which they live; Christians have renounced many of the norms and beliefs of that society and adopted new norms and beliefs, and resentment and hostility is the almost inevitable result. This is clearly expressed in I Peter 4.4: 'the Gentiles' (i.e. non-Christians) 'are surprised that you do not now join them in the same wild profligacy, and they abuse you'. Such 'suffering' might take a wide range of forms: awareness of disapproval, 'abuse', exclusion from particular areas of life, physical violence, court proceedings, and so on. It is regarded as inevitable because anyone who accepts and lives by a gospel which is 'a stumbling block to Jews and folly to Gentiles' (I Cor. 1.23) cannot avoid some form of tension with 'those outside'.

However, 'suffering' is a broader term than 'persecution'. In Rom. 8.18–25, Paul speaks of a Christian suffering which is an expression of the suffering of the whole created order through its 'bondage to decay', as it awaits the fulfilment of the promise of freedom. All forms of suffering spring from the tension between the promise of the world to come and the reality of the present world.[4]

SYNAGOGUE

SYNAGOGUE The origins of the synagogue are unknown, but are obviously related to the new prominence of the law in Jewish thought and life after the Exile. In Acts 15.21, James can assume that there have long been synagogues in all the main cities of the Roman world: 'From early generations Moses has had in every city those who preach him, for he is read every sabbath in the synagogues'. In Greek-speaking areas, the Scriptures were read in the Greek translation known as the Septuagint, produced in Alexandria during the third and second centuries BC. In Palestine itself, where Aramaic was spoken, the Scriptures were read in the original Hebrew, and a translator was present. A synagogue could be established wherever there were at least ten adult Jewish males. Each congregation had a 'ruler' (Acts 18.8,17) or 'rulers' (Mark 5.22, Acts 13.15), but the position might be held by laymen with no special training.

In the New Testament it is Luke who gives us the most vivid pictures of synagogue worship. Luke 4.16–30 tells the story of Jesus' visit to the synagogue in Nazareth: he stands up to read, is given the book of Isaiah, reads a passage from chapter 61, hands the book back to the attendant, and sits down to deliver a homily.[1] Presumably this combination of reading and preaching was standard procedure. In Acts 13.14–15, Paul and Barnabas visit the synagogue in Pisidian Antioch, and here again readings are followed by a homily: 'After the reading of the law and the prophets, the rulers of the synagogue sent to them, saying, "Brethren, if you have any word of exhortation for the people, say it" '. So Paul delivers an address (on this occasion, standing up).

According to Acts, it was Paul's normal custom to begin his missionary activity in the local synagogue, and only to preach to the Gentiles after being rejected by the Jews. This seems to conflict with Paul's letters, where he presents himself exclusively as 'apostle to the Gentiles' (Rom. 1.5, 11.13, 15.15–16, Gal. 1.16); occasional references to preaching activity among Jews (I Cor. 9.20, II Cor. 11.24) may refer to an earlier stage in his career as a Christian missionary. While Paul deliberately set up Gentile Christian congregations in separation from the synagogue,[2] elsewhere Jewish Christians continued to live as members of the synagogue for as long as it remained possible (*see* Acts 26.11, John 9.22, 12.42, 16.2, James 2.2).

SYNOPTIC PROBLEM

The Gospels of Matthew, Mark and Luke are commonly called the 'Synoptic Gospels'. The term 'synoptic' implies that they can be viewed together because they have so much material in common. The so-called 'Synoptic Problem' arises from the existence of this common material, which requires an explanation. Matthew and Luke include within their own Gospels almost the entire contents of Mark, and they also share with one another a great deal of material relating Jesus' teaching.[1] In general, the material common to all three Gospels occurs in the same order in all three, and this virtually rules out the possibility that the Gospels are independent of one another and rely solely on oral tradition. So the question arises of how the Synoptic Gospels are related to one another.

It was traditionally believed that Matthew was the earliest of the Gospels, and that Mark used Matthew, concentrating on narrative and omitting much of the teaching material. This view has been almost universally abandoned, and it is now held that Mark is the earliest of the Gospels, and that both Matthew and Luke have used Mark as the basis for their own work. In a sense, Matthew and Luke should both be seen as expanded second editions of Mark. The reasons for this conclusion are complex, but they relate to the many differences between Mark on the one hand and Matthew and Luke on the other when reporting what is obviously the same story. Again and again, Matthew and Luke seem to represent a later form of the narrative: the Greek style is improved, inconsistencies are smoothed over, theological problems are resolved.[2]

Having established the priority of Mark, there is a further question about the relationship between Matthew and Luke. They have a certain amount of material in common that is not derived from Mark, and this might be accounted for in two main ways: either one of the later evangelists has made use of the work of the other, or they are independent of one another and both make use of an earlier source which has since been lost. It is this second hypothesis which has been widely accepted: both Matthew and Luke make use of a source generally designated simply 'Q' (from the German, *Quelle*, 'source'). The problem with the alternative view is that where Matthew and Luke are both editing Mark, their respective modifications have little in common with one another. If Luke was following Matthew, or vice versa, one would expect the other's influence to be apparent in passages derived ultimately from Mark. Not all scholars accept the 'Q' hypothesis, and some wish to argue that Luke has made use of Matthew. However, the majority still think that the hypothesis is the simplest and most satisfactory solution to an extremely complex problem.

On this view of the Synoptic Problem, four main sources are involved: Mark, 'Q', and the material unique to Matthew and to Luke respectively. In the case of the latter two, oral tradition is more likely than a written source. Matthew and Luke compose their Gospels using Mark, 'Q', and their own special material.

TALENTS, PARABLE OF This parable occurs in two versions, in Matthew and Luke, of which Matthew's is the better-known. In this version (Matt. 25.14–30), three servants receive different sums of money from their master to speculate with while he is away. Two of them successfully accomplish this, and are commended on the master's return, whereas the third merely buries the money in the ground and is punished for failing to secure any interest. Matthew probably understands the parable as an exhortation to obey Jesus' commandments before he returns for judgment. But there is more to it than that, and the key to the parable seems to lie in the contrast between the actual generosity of the master and the harshness imputed to him by the unfaithful servant. The faithful servants are both told: 'You have been faithful over a little, I will set you over much; enter into the joy of your master' (vv. 21,23). But the other servant explains his conduct by saying, 'Master, I knew you to be a hard man, reaping where you did not sow, and gathering where you did not winnow' (v. 24); he then returns the money with the words, 'Here you have what is yours' (v. 25). We have here a contrast between two types of obedience. One is an obedience which knows that Jesus' 'yoke is easy, and his burden light' (Matt. 11.30), and that God's giving is always out of all proportion to the service rendered (*see* Matt. 20.1–16, the parable of the labourers in the vineyard).[1] The other is an obedience which regards God as a hard task-master who imposes heavy burdens on his subjects. Those who think like this have a God who corresponds to their view of him; and yet the point of the parable is that this is a complete misunderstanding of the character of God. Understood in this way, the parable is an exposition of one aspect of Jesus' proclamation of God as *Abba* ('Father').[2]

TEMPLE In Jesus' day, the temple in Jerusalem had recently been rebuilt by Herod the Great.[1] The modest structure dating back to the years after the return from Exile in the sixth century BC was transformed into one of the architectural wonders of the world. However, the basic pattern remained unaltered. In the middle stood the central sanctuary, whose interior was divided by a veil into two parts; it was this veil which at Jesus' death was 'torn in two, from top to bottom', according to Mark 15.38. Behind the veil was the 'holy of holies', into which 'only the high priest goes, and he but once a year [on the Day of Atonement] and not without taking blood, which he offers for himself and for the errors of the people' (Heb. 9.7). The central sanctuary stood within a series of 'courts': these were set aside for the use of Jewish women, men and priests respectively. These courts together with the central sanctuary comprised a raised area where only Jews were allowed. Around this was a large area surrounded by colonnades, to which access was unlimited, divided from the raised area by a low wall with notices which threatened Gentiles who passed beyond it with death. Paul was accused of bringing a Gentile companion into the central area beyond this wall (Acts 21.28–29), and it is perhaps referred to in a metaphorical sense in Eph. 2.14, which tells how Christ has 'broken down the dividing wall of hostility' between Jews and Gentiles.[2] In the colonnaded area, the temple's essential commerce took place. Animals and birds for sacrifice could be bought here, and currency exchanged.

In a number of passages, Jesus and the Jerusalem Church are said to have participated in the temple worship (Luke 2.41–43, Mark 14.12, Luke 24.53, Acts 2.46, 5.42); the point here is to emphasize the continuity between the new revelation and the old. As regards Jesus' own attitude, the well-known story in Mark 11.15–18 tells how he 'began to drive out those who sold and those who bought in the temple, and he overturned the tables of the money-changers and the seats of those who sold pigeons'. The older view, which saw this as an attack on commercial activity in a place of worship is probably incorrect: this activity can hardly be regarded as an abuse that needed reform because it was essential for the temple's operation as a place of sacrifice for Jews and Gentile converts from every part of the known world. Jesus' action may perhaps be seen as a symbolic attack on the whole temple system and the view of God associated with it. God has not placed himself in the hands of the temple authorities; it is not his will that they should be the sole legitimate channels of his grace, which they dispense only to those who are willing to pay sufficiently for their services. His will is that everyone should have free access to him: 'Is it not written, "My house shall be called a house of prayer for all the nations"? But you have made it a den of robbers'. Jesus' symbolic action in the temple may be compared with his opposition in word and deed to the Pharisaic interpretation of the law, which he claimed also led to a distorted view of God.[3]

The New Testament writers tend to play down the significance of the temple. In Acts 7.48–50, Luke presents Stephen as arguing that the temple is inessential because (in the words of Isa. 66.1–2), 'Heaven is my throne, and earth my footstool . . .' (see also Acts 17.24–25).[4] Paul sees both the Christian congregation and the individual as 'the temple of God' or 'a temple of the Holy Spirit' (I Cor. 3.16–17, 6.19), which replaces the old temple. John 4.21–24 announces the end of worship in the Jerusalem temple: 'The true worshippers will worship the Father in spirit and truth'. Jesus himself replaces the temple as the true dwelling-place of God (John 2.19–22, see 1.14).

TEMPTATIONS OF JESUS[1] Each of the Synoptic Gospels contains an account of the temptations of Jesus which immediately followed his baptism and the descent of the Holy Spirit. Matthew and Luke are very similar to each other at this point, although the order of the temptations is different. In Matt. 4.8, the devil shows Jesus all the kingdoms of the earth from the top of 'a very high mountain'; Luke 4.5 turns this into a more visionary experience, which took place 'in a moment of time'. Luke 4.6 adds an explanation of the devil's right to give Jesus authority over the world: 'It has been delivered to me, and I give it to whom I will'.

But whatever the minor differences, the two versions of the story are a profound meditation on the nature of Jesus' divine sonship. Temptation is a significant theme elsewhere in the Gospels. Jesus is 'tempted' (or 'tested') by the Pharisees to perform an unambiguous 'sign from heaven' which will prove his claim beyond doubt (Mark 8.11); he is tempted by Satan (speaking through Peter) to renounce the suffering which is God's will for him (Mark 8.33). In the temptation narratives themselves, the same themes are apparent: Jesus is tempted to perform an unambiguous sign (throwing himself from the pinnacle of the temple),[2] and he is tempted to assume the rule of the world as the Messiah should, instead of submitting to suffering which seemed to contradict his messiahship.[3] The other temptation (to turn stones into bread) is rejected with the words, 'Man shall not live by bread alone . . .' (Matt. 4.4). Jesus' messiahship does not mean merely satisfying people's physical needs (see John 6.26–27).

Mark 1.12–13 merely mentions that Jesus was tempted for forty days (rather than *after* forty days, as in Matthew and Luke) in the wilderness, that 'he was with the wild beasts', and that 'the angels ministered to him'. The passage has apparently been influenced by Ps. 91.11,13: 'He will give his angels charge of you to guard you in all your ways . . . You will tread on the lion and the adder, the young lion and the serpent you will trample under foot'. (Strangely enough, part of this passage is quoted by the devil in the account in Matthew and Luke.) A quite different interpretation of Jesus' temptations is given in the Letter to the Hebrews, where they point not to his messiahship but to his humanity: 'In every respect he has been tempted as we are, yet without sin' (Heb. 4.15, see also 2.14–18).[4]

THANKSGIVING Jesus and the early Christians share with Judaism the view that God is to be thanked for all the gifts which sustain and enhance life, notably food and drink. Jesus pronounces a thanksgiving over the loaves that he is about to multiply (Mark 8.6), and over the bread and the wine at the Last Supper (Luke 22.17,19). Paul envisages Christians being able to give thanks even for foods that are forbidden by the law (Rom. 14.6, I Cor. 10.30). I Tim. 4.1–5 opposes those who 'enjoin abstinence from foods which God created to be received with thanksgiving by those who believe and know the truth', and argues that 'everything created by God is good, and nothing is to be rejected if it is received with thanksgiving'.[1] Underlying this is the doctrine of providence: the whole created order is constantly dependent on God, and it is he who is therefore to be thanked for its blessings.[2] The hostility towards the created order felt by Christian gnostics is rejected.

Yet the main cause for thanksgiving is Jesus Christ himself: 'Thanks be to God who gives us the victory [over sin, death and the law] through our Lord Jesus Christ!' (I Cor. 15.57); 'Thanks be to God for his inexpressible gift!' (II Cor. 9.15). If the thanksgiving for food and drink show the dependence of the world on its Creator, these other thanksgivings show the world's dependence on God for salvation. Salvation is his own work just as much as creation is, and the human response is simply to be thankful.

Near the beginning of many of his letters, Paul gives thanks to God for his converts' faith: 'We give thanks to God always for you all . . .' (I Thess. 1.2). This is not mere conventional politeness, but is closely related to the thanksgiving for salvation in Jesus Christ mentioned above. The God who must be thanked for salvation is also the God who ensures that the message of Jesus Christ does not go unheard, but is received in faith by some wherever it is preached; and this too is cause for thanksgiving.[3]

THESSALONIANS, PAUL'S FIRST LETTER TO I Thessalonians is the earliest of Paul's letters, dating from about AD 50 during his stay either in Athens or in Corinth (Acts 18).[1] By comparison with later letters, the theological content is slight, and many typically Pauline ideas have evidently not yet been developed.

1 Paul and the Thessalonians According to Acts 17.1–9, Paul's visit to Thessalonica was marked by the usual pattern: preaching in the synagogue, some successes, Jewish jealousy, intense opposition, and finally expulsion from the city. Although the trouble is said to have been incited by Jews, it is Gentiles ('wicked fellows of the rabble', v. 5) who are apparently mainly responsible for it, and there is nothing specifically Jewish about their objection (in contrast to 18.13): 'These men who have turned the world upside down have come here also. . . ; and they are all acting against the decrees of Caesar, saying that there is another king, Jesus' (vv. 6–7). Paul, Silas (Silvanus) and Timothy therefore have to leave in a hurry (vv. 10,14).

This picture is substantially confirmed in I Thessalonians. Because Silvanus and Timothy are linked with Paul in 1.1, they must have been involved in the founding of the church at Thessalonica.[2] Paul refers to the 'shameful treatment' they had received at Philippi immediately before their arrival in Thessalonica (2.2, *see* Acts 16.11–40), and one of the main themes of the letter is the persecution that immediately threatened to destroy the Thessalonian church. Both Gentiles and Jews were apparently involved in this. Paul writes, 'You suffered the same things from your own countrymen as they [the Judean churches] did from the Jews', but he also attacks the Jews who 'drove us out and displease God and oppose all men, by hindering us from speaking to the Gentiles that they may be saved' (2.14–15).

Expulsion from Thessalonica evidently hurt Paul deeply. He speaks of his grief at being 'bereft' of his converts, his longing to visit them again, and his fear that they should succumb to the persecution and renounce their faith – an anxiety which led him to send Timothy from Athens 'to establish you in the faith and to exhort you' (2.17–3.5). The letter is written in the aftermath of Timothy's return, either to Athens, or, as Acts 18.5 may imply, to Corinth, with 'the good news of your faith and love', and the report 'that you always remember us kindly and long to see us, as we long to see you' (3.6).

2 Problems at Thessalonica It seems that Timothy brought back not only 'good news' of the Thessalonians, but reports of particular problems, and Paul responds to these in his letter.

(i) **Attacks on Paul's Integrity** Despite Paul's relief that the Thessalonians 'remember him kindly and long to see him', in 2.1–12 he is remarkably defensive about his conduct at Thessalonica: 'Our appeal does not spring from error or

uncleanness, nor is it made with guile . . . We never used either words of flattery, as you know, or a cloak for greed, as God is witness; nor did we seek glory from men'. Paul is obviously responding here to accusations made against him by his converts' non-Christian enemies in Thessalonica. Part (perhaps the main part) of the suffering the Thessalonians are having to endure (3.1–4) is verbal rather than physical: their opponents seek to undermine their new faith by attacking the integrity of those who had preached that faith to them, and it is to these attacks that Paul is reponding.[3] According to his opponents in Thessalonica, Paul is a mere charlatan motivated only by self-interest; he is concerned only for his own reputation, or he is after his converts' money, or perhaps he even has sexual designs on them. In being taken in by this confidence trickster, they say, the Thessalonian Christians have only proved their extreme gullibility. Paul protests that his readiness to endure suffering and his blameless conduct prove his integrity. Yet it is not because he is sincere that the Thessalonians can rely on the message he preaches, but because it is not merely the word of men but the word of God (2.13). Ultimately Paul's only defence against the accusations is the witness of the Holy Spirit (1.5).

(ii) **The Christian Dead** Paul had taught the Thessalonians 'to wait for God's Son from heaven, Jesus, who delivers us from the wrath to come' (1.10).[4] In 4.13, he writes, 'We would not have you ignorant, brethren, concerning those who are asleep, that you may not grieve as others do who have no hope', and goes on to explain that Christians who die before the return of Christ will share with 'us who are alive' in the salvation he will bring. The Thessalonians had been so convinced that Jesus would return soon that they believed that none of them would actually die before he did so. When someone did die, this was a severe blow to their faith. Paul assures them that because Jesus died and rose again, so Christians who have died will be raised from the dead (4.14–17).[5] But the Thessalonians are not to concern themselves with the question of when Jesus will return because all we can know is that his return will be unexpected (5.1–11). Ultimately it does not matter 'whether we wake or sleep' (v. 10).

THESSALONIANS, PAUL'S SECOND LETTER TO II Thessalonians shows less concern with the Christians of Thessalonica than I Thessalonians, and if the letter is indeed by Paul, a certain coolness and distance has entered into his relationship with them. However, the interpretation of the letter is closely bound up with the question of authorship.

1 Authorship The main reason why it is often doubted that Paul wrote II Thessalonians is the teaching of II Thess. 2 concerning 'the day of the Lord'. In I Thess. 5, Paul had taught that the day of the Lord would come suddenly and unexpectedly, with no warning or preparation[1]; yet II Thess. 2.3 states that 'that day will not come, unless the rebellion comes first, and the man of lawlessness is revealed, the son of perdition'. In the time immediately leading up to the Lord's return, the Antichrist will be revealed[2]; he will enter the temple and proclaim himself to be God, he will perform miracles and he will deceive many people (2.3–12). Jesus cannot return yet because these events must happen first. This seems completely at variance with I Thess. 5. It cannot be the case that Paul has changed his mind because I Thess. 5.2 and II Thess. 2.5 claim that each of the two views was part of his original teaching at Thessalonica. On the other hand, this discrepancy would only be an argument against Paul's having written II Thessalonians if he were elsewhere an orderly and systematic writer whose thought was always logically coherent. This is not the case; even within a single writing there are often discussions of the same subject that are very difficult to harmonize with each other.[3] The tension between I Thess. 5 and II Thess. 2 is therefore not a sufficient reason for denying that Paul wrote II Thessalonians.

Otherwise, there is no particularly strong reason for denying Pauline author-ship. It is true that he mentions the figure of the Antichrist nowhere else in his letters, but many of his other ideas are discussed only once. It is certainly strange that 2.2 mentions the existence of forged letters ascribed to Paul during his own lifetime. But if II Thessalonians is itself a forgery, it is a particularly blatant one, not only attacking other forgeries (2.2) but claiming that its conclusion is in Paul's own handwriting (3.17) as a guarantee of its authenticity. It seems more likely that it is a genuine letter of Paul's.

2 Circumstances Paul probably wrote II Thessalonians while preoccupied with his missionary activity in Corinth, where he stayed for a year and a half (Acts 18.11). The Thessalonians are continuing to endure suffering (1.4), and Paul speaks of the rest they will shortly enjoy at the return of Jesus and the vengeance that he will then accomplish on their enemies (1.5–12).[4] But the eager expectation at Thessalonica of Jesus' return (evident in I Thess. 4.13–18) has led to a further problem. Someone is claiming that the day of the Lord has already come, and he supports his claim by prophetic utterances and by a forged letter allegedly by Paul. Jesus has already returned – he was perhaps thought to be in Jerusalem because 'the Deliverer will come from Zion' (Rom. 11.26) – and Christians will shortly be assembling to meet him (2.1–2). Some of the Thessalonians have been convinced by this claim, and as a result have abandoned their daily work in order to wait for Jesus' arrival in person. Paul accuses them of 'idleness', and exhorts them to follow the example of his own hard work at Thessalonica, where he had earned his own living (3.6–12). He is aware that the 'idlers' may not accept his authority and may continue to believe that Jesus has already returned to earth (3.14–15). To prevent them regarding II Thessalonians as a forgery and the forged letter (2.2) as genuine, he concludes the letter in his own handwriting: 'I, Paul, write this greeting with my own hand. This is the mark in every letter of mine; it is the way I write' (3.17).

THOMAS
Although Thomas is mentioned as among the twelve disciples in all four of the lists in the Synoptic Gospels and Acts, it is only in John that he achieves any significance.[1] In three of his four appearances, he is referred to as 'Thomas called the Twin'. One of these references (21.2) is of no significance, but in the other three the evangelist seems to characterize Thomas as the pessimist among the twelve. In John 11.16, he expresses the disciples' feeling of foreboding as they accompany Jesus into Judaea: 'Let us also go, that we may die with him'. In 14.5, he expresses their feeling of bewilderment at Jesus' announcement that he is going away. In his most famous appearance, he refuses to believe the announcement of

the resurrection: 'Unless I see in his hands the print of the nails, and place my finger in the mark of the nails, and place my hand in his side, I will not believe' (20.25). Eight days later, Thomas is given the opportunity to do this, and worships Jesus as 'my Lord and my God' (20.26–29).

Here and elsewhere, the resurrection narratives acknowledge that doubt is the natural reaction to the claim that Jesus has risen from the dead. In Luke 24.11 the disciples dismiss the women's report as 'an idle tale'. In the apocryphal ending of Mark they reject the reports of visions to both Mary Magdalene and the two disciples walking in the country. When he finally appears to them, Jesus condemns them 'for their unbelief and hardness of heart, because they had not believed those who saw him after he had risen' (Mark 16.9–14). In Matt. 28.17, it is said that 'some doubted' even when Jesus appeared to them. All these narratives stress the conquest of doubt by faith, but the references to doubt still serve an important function: they point to the resurrection as utterly unprecedented, unexpected, and beyond rational comprehension.[2]

TIMOTHY Acts 16.1–3 tells us that Paul first met Timothy during his second missionary journey, at Lystra. He was the son of a Jewish Christian woman married to a Gentile; II Tim. 1.5 preserves the name both of his mother (Eunice) and of his grandmother (Lois), both of whom are said to have been Christians. Wanting Timothy to accompany him, Paul had him circumcised 'because of the Jews that were in those places, for they all knew that his father was a Greek' (Acts 16.3). Acts presents Paul as a law-abiding Jew even as a Christian, and this may have influenced the narrative here.[1] Later, Acts speaks of Timothy in connection with Beroea, near Thessalonica, and Corinth (17.14, 18.5), and Paul's letters confirm that Timothy preached the gospel in both Thessalonica and Corinth (I Thess. 1.1, II Thess. 1.1, II Cor. 1.19). Elsewhere in Acts, Timothy visits Macedonia (19.22) and accompanies Paul to Jerusalem (20.4).

Paul's letters speak of three important missions on which Timothy was sent. First, he was sent to exhort the Thessalonians to endure the persecution they were experiencing, and to bring Paul news of them (I Thess. 3.1–6).[2] Secondly, he was sent to the Corinthians to remind them of 'my ways in Christ, as I teach them everywhere in every church' (I Cor. 4.17, see 16.10–11). Thirdly, Paul announces his intention of sending him to the Philippians as soon as he knows whether or not he is to be released from prison (Phil. 2.19; Acts 19.22 suggests that this visit did actually occur).[3] Paul speaks of Timothy with exceptional warmth. He is 'my beloved and faithful child in the Lord' (I Cor. 4.17). Paul confesses, 'I have no-one like him who will be genuinely anxious for your welfare', and contrasts him with others who 'look to their own interests, not those of Jesus Christ' (Phil. 2.20–21).

If Paul was not actually the author of the so-called letters to Timothy (as argued below), we know little or nothing about Timothy's later career.

TIMOTHY, PAUL'S FIRST LETTER TO The two letters to Timothy and the letter to Titus form a distinctive group, generally known as the 'Pastoral Epistles'. It is generally accepted that these are unlikely to be genuine letters of Paul.

1 Authorship The three 'Pastoral Epistles' display a similar style, vocabulary and outlook, and they must be considered together in discussing the question of authorship. A detailed comparison of the vocabulary of the Pastoral Epistles and Paul's other letters shows that the former use a very large number of words which are found nowhere else in Paul. Conversely, it also shows that they do not use a large number of words and phrases which are very common elsewhere in Paul. Of course, the vocabulary and style of any writer will change over the years, but it is thought that in this case the difference is too great for this to be a possible explanation.

There are also differences in content between the Pastoral Epistles and the genuine letters of Paul. Paul nowhere else shows any desire to impose an organization of bishops (or presbyters) and deacons on his congregations, as in I Timothy and Titus.[1] Indeed, his conception of the individual congregation as 'the body of Christ', is in tension with such hierarchical ideas.[2] Again and again, the theology of the Pastorals differs from that of Paul. For example, the author of I Timothy reinterprets Paul's doctrine of freedom from the law in an ethical sense: only the good man is free from the law, in the sense that he does not need an external law to tell what to do and what not to do (1.8–10). This is quite different from Paul's real view, which is that the law is the bringer of death and condemnation to its adherents.[3]

Two supposedly prophetic passages also show that the Pastoral Epistles date from a time after Paul's death. I Tim. 4.1–5 predicts that 'in later times' heretics will arise, who forbid marriage and certain foods; and II Tim. 3.1–9 predicts that 'in the last days there will be times of stress'. In the context, it is clear that a situation contemporary with the actual writing of the letters is in mind, which is future only from the fictional position of 'Paul'.[4]

Yet another problem is that the historical references do not agree with any situation in Paul's life known to us from Acts or his letters. They require the hypothesis that after the captivity in Rome described in Acts 28, Paul was released and continued his missionary activity for a time, before being re-arrested and finally executed. There is no real evidence for this hypothesis, however, and it is almost certain that Paul's appeal to Caesar was rejected and that he was executed at the end of the two years of captivity in Rome (Acts 28.30).

2 Circumstances[5] It is necessary to differentiate the fictional circumstances in which I Timothy was written from the real circumstances. The letter is supposedly written to Timothy in Ephesus, to encourage him to oppose heretics, to appoint bishops and deacons, and generally put church affairs in order. Occasional personal notes are part of the fictional setting – for example, the advice recommending the medicinal use of wine for Timothy's stomach complaints (5.23). In fact, the purpose of the letter seems to be to claim the authority of Paul for developments in the church several decades after his death. The author is concerned with the struggle for orthodoxy against heresy, and the development of church order and discipline is a part of this struggle. His argument is, in effect, that orthodoxy as he understands it is the true heir to the teaching of Paul. It may well be the case that those he opposes also appeal to the authority of Paul in support of their own position, like the heretics opposed in II Peter 3.15–17.

The precise nature of this heresy is unclear, but the warning against 'the godless chatter and contradictions of what is falsely called knowledge' (*gnosis*) in 6.20 suggests that it is related to the Gnostic Christianity that we know from later sources. The heretics 'occupy themselves with myths and endless genealogies which promote speculation' (1.4, *see* 4.7). They 'reject conscience' (1.19) – the idea that we possess a natural faculty for distinguishing right from wrong. One result of this is that, inspired by demons, they 'forbid marriage and enjoin abstinence from foods which God created to be received with thanksgiving' (4.2–3). They are 'depraved in mind and bereft of the truth, imagining that godliness is a means of gain' (6.5) – presumably because they require payment for their teaching.

3 Contents Much of the letter is composed of practical instructions about the moral qualities expected of bishops (or elders), deacons, widows, slaves, the rich, and so on. The author is concerned with public opinion: to become a bishop, one 'must be well thought of by outsiders' (3.7); slaves must remain subordinate 'so that the name of God and the teaching may not be defamed' (6.1). The approach is severely practical. Precise rules are laid down about the extent of the Church's financial aid for widows, and for the procedure for disciplining elders; nothing is to be left to the whim of the individual. There is no longer the enthusiastic sense of the Spirit's presence within the congregation that is to be found in Paul, and indeed 'sound teaching' and firm discipline almost seem to make the Spirit superfluous. The return of Christ is no longer thought to be near; it is simply said that it 'will be made manifest at the proper time' (6.15). The Church must therefore accommodate itself to the probability of a much longer existence in the world than had once seemed likely, and organize itself appropriately as an institution belonging to this world as well as the world to come.[6]

This outlook results in an emphasis on the importance of the existing order of things. The state is part of that order, and 2.1–4 urges that prayers and thanksgivings be offered 'for kings and all who are in high positions', so that peace may be preserved. Because women are subordinate to men in secular society, and because their calling is to bear children, it is to be the same for Christian women within the Church (2.12–15). The created order is the work of God and therefore good, and so the heresy which condemns marriage and certain foods is to be rejected (4.1–5). The institution of the family must be regarded as God-given, and providing for one's relatives is therefore a religious duty, neglect of which is a denial of the faith (5.4,8). Knowledge of our place in the created order should moderate our desire for material possessions: 'We brought nothing into the world, and we cannot take anything out of the world' (6.7).

This does not mean that the Church has transferred its allegiance from Jesus Christ to the existing order. On the contrary, the author's view is that respect for the existing order is an expression of loyalty to Jesus Christ, because creation and salvation are the work of the same God. Christ is referred to mainly in solemn credal statements such as 1.15: 'The saying is sure and worthy of full acceptance, that Christ Jesus came into the world to save sinners' (*see also* 2.5–7, 3.16). The Church's faith in Jesus is ultimately a 'mystery' (3.16) that is beyond comprehension, and unlike the heretics with their speculations (1.4), the author is content simply to reaffirm traditional doctrinal statements with no attempt at further exploration and interpretation.

The author implicitly claims that he is offering an authentically Pauline response to the demands of a new situation. Parallels could indeed be found in Paul for the author's social conservatism, his claim that Church life and worship must be orderly, and his concern for the preservation of true doctrine. But in Paul, these characteristics are checked and balanced by others, and this results in the tensions and paradoxes that are often the mark of real creativity. In I Timothy, the paradoxical and exploratory nature of Paul's thought is ignored. Paul, like the author of I Timothy, is concerned that traditional Christian beliefs be preserved and that those who deny them should be opposed; thus, it is the purpose of I Cor. 15 to refute those who deny the traditional doctrine of the resurrection of the dead. But Paul's way of defending the tradition is to explore it further and to work out its implications anew; the author of I Timothy is content to preserve the tradition and to avoid all real debate with those who question it. For Paul, 'heresy' is an opportunity as well as a threat; for the author of I Timothy, it is only a threat.

TIMOTHY, PAUL'S SECOND LETTER TO As II Timothy
shares the language and outlook of I Timothy and Titus, the question of authorship cannot be considered in isolation from these other letters.[1] The general opinion is that all three letters are so far removed from the language and outlook of Paul's other letters that they cannot have been written by him.

1 Circumstances II Timothy differs from the other two 'Pastoral Epistles' in being much more personal in character. I Timothy has little to say about the fictional setting in the lives of Paul and Timothy because its main concern is with the practicalities of Church life in the present. But II Timothy redresses the balance: here, the fictional setting is of the greatest importance. II Timothy professes to be a final, emotional appeal by Paul for the preservation of the truth as he has taught it. The appeal gains its urgency from the imminence of Paul's death: 'I am already on the point of being sacrificed; the time of my departure has come' (4.6). He is in Rome, in chains (1.16–17), unsupported by his fellow-Christians at the first hearing of his case (4.16), and bereft of most of his friends (4.10,20).

But his chief concern is not with himself: he knows that 'a crown of righteousness' awaits him (4.8) and that the Lord will 'save me for his heavenly kingdom' (4.18). His chief concern is with the problem of heresy. In two passages, this is seen as a purely future reality: 'The time is coming [although it has not yet arrived] when people will not endure sound teaching . . . and will turn away from listening to the truth and wander into myths' (4.3–4, see 3.1–9). Elsewhere, however, it is present: 'all who are in Asia' have already 'turned against me, and among them Phygelus and Hermogenes' (1.15, see also 2.17–18). The author wishes to present Paul both as predicting the heresies of his own day, and as combatting earlier forms of the contemporary heresies within his own lifetime.[2] Little is said about what the heretics taught, except in 2.18, where two of them are said to have 'swerved from the truth by holding that the resurrection is past already'. A common source of dissension between the 'orthodox' and the 'heretics' was over the question of the resurrection of the dead: was this a literal and therefore purely future event, or should it be reinterpreted to apply to present experience of Christ? The heretics in II Timothy seem to have held the latter view. The problem for both sides was that in Paul's own thought the two views belong together and are inseparable.

2 The Author's Response Although the author is deeply concerned about the spread of heresy, he knows that in the last resort the truth of the gospel will be preserved by God. 'Paul' is sure that God 'is able to guard until that Day what has been entrusted to me' (the context indicates that this is a reference to the gospel). Although the heretics 'are upsetting the faith of some', still 'God's firm foundation stands' – that is, the foundation of the Church, Jesus Christ as proclaimed in the gospel (*see* I Cor. 3.11).

Yet although the preservation of the truth is God's responsibility, he works through human agents, and Paul encourages Timothy to regard himself as one such agent; Timothy represents the church leaders of the author's own time. He must first be reminded of the contents of the gospel, which he must strive to preserve. In fulfilment of his eternal purpose, God has in Jesus Christ 'abolished death and brought life and immortality to light', and by his grace has called us to participate in this salvation (1.8–10). Timothy must 'remember Jesus Christ, risen from the dead, descended from David, as preached in my gospel' (2.8) – the heretics perhaps denied this view of Jesus, which they may have regarded as too physical and too Jewish. Timothy on the other hand must 'continue in what you have learned and have firmly believed'. But his task is not only to hold fast such beliefs, but also to proclaim them: in contrast to 'deceivers and deceived' (3.13), he is instructed, 'Always be steady, endure suffering, do the work of an evangelist, fulfil your ministry' (4.5). Paul's own example of faithful endurance will encourage him (3.10–11, 4.6–8).

Despite the difference in tone between the two letters, I and II Timothy are complementary. Both are concerned with the preservation of Christian truth and conduct in a situation in which they are under threat. I Timothy concentrates on the often prosaic practical responses which the situation requires; II Timothy provides the motivation for undertaking them – Paul's final appeal that his life's work of contending for the truth should be taken up by others. The fact that the setting is fictional does not alter the effectiveness of the appeal.

TITUS In Gal. 2.1–3 Paul tells how Titus accompanied him and Barnabas to Jerusalem in order to discuss the place of Gentile Christians in the Church. The outcome was that 'Titus, who was with me, was not compelled to be circumcised, though he was a Greek' (v. 3). Titus was presumably the representative of the Gentile Christians (probably at Antioch); Paul must have felt that his chances of persuading the Jerusalem leaders to accept his point of view would be greater if a Gentile Christian was actually present.[1]

Titus next comes into prominence several years later, in the course of Paul's problems with the Church of Corinth.[2] After Paul's authority and integrity had been called in question, Titus was entrusted with the task of conveying a severe letter from Paul to the Corinthians (probably preserved in II Cor. 10–13) and of restoring order. Paul tells us that he had assured Titus that he was confident of success (II Cor. 7.14), but he also mentions his anxious search for him first in Troas (2.13) and then in Macedonia, where Titus finally arrived with the good news of the Corinthians' repentance (7.5–7). II Corinthians also implies that there were two further visits of Titus to Corinth, one before the 'severe letter' visit and one after. Titus was responsible for initiating the Corinthians' collection for the impoverished Christians of Jerusalem, about a year before his second visit (8.5,10, 12.18). He was no doubt one of the 'brethren' who accompanied Timothy to Corinth (I Cor. 16.10–11), responsible for putting into effect the instructions about the collection given in I Cor. 16.1–4.[3] A final visit to Corinth is implied in II Cor. 8.6,16–17,23: immediately after his rendezvous with Paul in Macedonia, Titus is to return to Corinth (presumably bearing Paul's latest letter) in order to help the Corinthians to complete their collection.

TITUS, PAUL'S LETTER TO The letter apparently written by Paul to Titus is the third and briefest of the 'Pastoral Epistles'. It is like I and II Timothy, and for the same reasons, unlikely to have been written by Paul.[1] As in I Timothy the main theme is the need for church order to counter heresy and indiscipline. Thus, the elders (or bishops – the two terms are interchangeable)[2] whom Titus is to appoint are in 1.5–16 specifically opposed to 'men who reject the truth' who 'give heed to Jewish myths' (v. 14). The inadequacies of Titus's Cretan flock make the appointment of the elders particularly urgent. The author quotes a line from Epimenides, a Cretan poet of the sixth to fifth century BC, according to which 'Cretans are always liars, evil beasts, lazy gluttons'; and he adds the curt imprimator, 'His testimony is true' (1.12–13). The references to 'the circumcision party' and 'Jewish myths' (1.10,14) may suggest that the heresy the author opposes is Jewish in origin, but it is more likely that these references are simply intended to provide a convincing setting for the letter within Paul's own lifetime. It was known that his work involved opposition to 'the circumcision party', and so they are mentioned to make the setting of the letter more life-like.

According to 2.13–14, 'our great God and Saviour Jesus Christ' died 'to redeem us from all iniquity and to purify for himself a people of his own who are zealous for good deeds'. Zeal for good deeds is one of the main themes of the letter. Titus himself must exemplify it (2.7), and so must the bishops (1.6–8), older men and women (2.2–5), younger men and women (2.4–6), and slaves (2.9–10). In their different ways, 'all who have believed in God must be careful to apply themselves to good deeds' (2.8), which are far more profitable than 'stupid controversies' over matters of theology (2.9). As well as fulfilling God's purpose in sending Christ (2.11–14, 3.4–7), good deeds render the Church's opponents speechless, because they have 'nothing evil to say about us' (2.8). Here, the goal of the salvation which God has accomplished in Christ is morality – living a godly, sober and upright life, and coming to the assistance of fellow-Christians in need (3.14). The author is perhaps aware that this is a less exciting prospect than the theological debates of the heretics, but he insists that 'good deeds' are far more important (3.8–9).

TONGUES, SPEAKING IN Apart from a single reference in the apocryphal ending of Mark (16.17), 'speaking in tongues' is discussed only in Acts and I Cor. 12.14. A comparison between the views of Luke and of Paul on this subject is instructive.

1 Acts In Acts, people are said to have 'spoken in tongues' only on occasions of exceptional significance in the history of the early Church. Speaking in tongues is the proof of the presence of the Holy Spirit, and the presence of the Holy Spirit is the sign of divine approval of the event taking place. Speaking in tongues is therefore linked with the theme of legitimacy; Luke wishes to show that the major advances in the early history of the Church were not the result of arbitrary human decisions but were planned by God. On the Day of Pentecost, the divine origin of Peter's proclamation is proved by the outward manifestation of the Spirit in speaking in tongues (2.1–13).[1] When Peter is criticized by Christians in Jerusalem for preaching to Gentiles, the criticisms are finally silenced by the fact that the Gentiles spoke in tongues and so proved that God had granted them the Spirit (10.1–11.18, *see* 15.8–9).[2] When Paul arrives at Ephesus to begin his three years of work there, he finds about twelve Christians already there before him; but they only receive the Spirit (manifested in speaking in tongues) when he lays hands on them (19.1–7). The purpose of this narrative is to show that Paul was the true founder of the church at Ephesus – an important point because Luke thinks that his is the only legitimate mission to the Gentiles (*see* 18.24–25, 20.17–35).[3] Thus, speaking in tongues is the proof of the presence of the Holy Spirit, and so guarantees divine approval for the steps being taken: the first preaching of the gospel in Jerusalem, the extension of the gospel to the Gentiles, and the foundation of the church at Ephesus. Luke does not imply that in his view speaking in tongues always accompanies the gift of the Spirit, and it may be that he sees no continuing role for this practice in the Church of his own day.

2 Paul Paul ascribes less significance to speaking in tongues than Luke. In I Cor. 12 his main purpose is to deny the claim made by some of the Corinthians that speaking in tongues is the only sure sign of the Spirit's presence, and as such should be practised by all Christians.[4] For these Corinthians, speaking in tongues is speaking the language of heaven (*see* 13.1); it is a participation in the realm of the exalted Christ (*see* 4.8). In 12.4–13, Paul constantly states that the one Spirit is manifested in a variety of different ways, and the emphasis with which he makes this point suggests that he is opposing the view that the Spirit is manifested in only one way – that is, speaking in tongues. In vv. 14–31, he opposes the divisiveness of this claim, which leads some to feel superior and others to feel excluded. Paul gently mocks the absurdity of these attitudes: the foot may feel excluded from the body because it is not a hand, and the head may think that it has no need of the feet, but in reality they are all part of the same body, utterly dependent on one another. Thus the question, 'Do all speak with tongues?' (v. 30) clearly requires a negative answer: they do not, and it is not God's purpose that they should.

The solution to the divisions the controversy has caused is love (I Cor. 13). Paul returns to the subject of speaking in tongues, however, in I Cor. 14, contrasting it unfavourably with prophecy. As he puts it, 'I want you all to speak in tongues, but even more to prophesy' (v. 5). In this verse, the emphasis does not fall on 'all' for that would contradict the whole point of I Cor. 12. Because Paul is playing down the significance of speaking in tongues, the verse is a concession: 'It is not that I am against all of you who speak in tongues . . .' (*compare* v. 39, 'Do not forbid speaking in tongues'), but he minimizes the importance of this activity on the grounds that it is incomprehensible to the listeners and so contributes nothing to the growth of the congregation (vv. 6–25). It may be of value if someone is available with the ability to interpret (vv. 13,27), but that means that its character as a participation in the heavenly world (*see* 13.1) is denied and its value determined by its ability to communicate rational meaning.

Paul does not go so far as to deny that speaking in tongues may be a gift of the Spirit, but his own criterion for judging alleged manifestations of the Spirit makes its status highly questionable: 'Since you are eager for manifestations of the Spirit, strive to excel in building up the church' (14.12).

–

TRANSFIGURATION OF JESUS

All three Synoptic evangelists tell the story of Jesus' transfiguration. Mark's version (Mark 9.1–8) includes a couple of comments from the evangelist himself, which the other two omit. He states that Jesus' garments were of a whiteness that no earthly bleach could match (v. 3); and he denies that there was any significance in Peter's strange suggestion about making three booths, because in his terror 'he did not know what to say' (v. 6). But, more significantly, it is probably Mark who is responsible for the present context of the story, which determines its interpretation. It follows Peter's confession and Jesus' first prediction of his passion (8.27–33), and marks the beginning of his journey to Jerusalem where he is to suffer and die.[1] The point of the story is that, despite the outward humiliation that Jesus is to endure, he is still secretly the glorious Son of God, to whom the law and the prophets (represented by Moses and Elijah) bear witness.

Luke's version (Luke 9.28–36) makes several interesting additions to Mark. The transfiguration takes place at night, while Jesus is praying and the disciples are asleep (9.28,32,37). The reference to Jesus praying is typical of Luke (*see* 3.21, 5.16, 6.12, 9.18, 11.1).[2] Moses and Elijah are said to have discussed Jesus' death and resurrection with him (9.31); Luke here makes explicit a link that is implicit in Mark. In v. 33 Peter makes his odd remark about the booths 'as the men were parting' – that is, in order to detain them.

There is some evidence that this story was originally told in connection with Jesus' resurrection. Certainly, II Peter 1.17–18 understands it this way, because it regards this as the occasion when Jesus 'received glory and honour from God the Father' (*see also* Heb. 2.9).[3] If this is correct, then the fact that it now occurs in the story of Jesus' earthly ministry is theologically significant: the glory of the Son of God manifested in his resurrection was already his during his earthly life, although in hidden form. In this way, the identity of the earthly Jesus with the exalted Lord is stressed. John 1.14 takes this tendency further by claiming that Jesus' divine glory was manifested throughout his earthly life.

TWELVE, THE[1]

The Synoptic Gospels all claim that Jesus appointed twelve disciples, and the fact that Judas Iscariot was one of their number suggests that this claim must be true because it is hard to imagine the early Church inventing such a tradition. In I Cor. 15.5 Paul reports the tradition about an appearance of the risen Lord to 'the twelve', and this again shows that the concept of 'the twelve' dates back to the earliest period.

However, the four lists in the Synoptic Gospels and Acts are not unanimous about the names of the twelve. There is no problem with eleven of them, who are mentioned in all four, in slightly different orders: Simon Peter, James, John, Andrew, Philip, Bartholomew, Matthew, Thomas, James the son of Alphaeus, Simon the Cananaean [= Simon the Zealot], and Judas Iscariot.[2] However, Mark 3.18 refers to Thaddaeus, and is followed by Matt. 10.3 (although some manuscripts read 'Lebbaeus' here); but Luke 6.16 and Acts 1.13 replace him with Judas the son of James, who is presumably the 'Judas not Iscariot' referred to in John 14.22. It is possible that one of these replaced the other as a member of the twelve because of the other's premature death.

The choice of twelve disciples is obviously based on the traditional twelve tribes of Israel: they are to be the founder members of the renewed Israel. The link between the disciples and the twelve tribes is apparent in the saying reported in Matt. 19.28: 'Truly I say to you, in the new world, when the Son of man shall sit on his glorious throne, you who have followed me will also sit on twelve thrones, judging the twelve tribes of Israel'. The same link is made in Rev. 21.12–14, where the heavenly city has twelve gates on which 'the names of the twelve sons of Israel were inscribed', and twelve foundations, on which were inscribed 'the names of the twelve apostles of the Lamb'.

It is strange that Paul reports a resurrection appearance to 'the twelve' (I Cor. 15.5) because the Gospels report an appearance only to eleven disciples (Matt. 28.16, Mark 16.14, Luke 24.33–43), Judas Iscariot's successor not having been yet appointed (Acts 1.15–26). The phrase 'the twelve' was probably so firmly established in early Christian vocabulary that it could be used even when only eleven of them were actually present.

VIRGIN BIRTH[1] In many ways the nativity narratives in Matthew and Luke are very different from one another, but they are agreed in claiming that Jesus was conceived by the power of the Holy Spirit and that he therefore had no human father (Matt. 1.18–25, Luke 1.26–38). Matthew tells the story from Joseph's standpoint: we learn of his intended response to his betrothed's apparent unfaithfulness, and the angelic annunciation which informs him what has really happened. Luke adopts Mary's standpoint (Joseph is not even mentioned until 2.4), and here the stress is on joy at the fulfilment of the long-awaited promise of redemption, rather than the awkwardness of Joseph's position. The two versions of the story are unrelated to one another, and both of them therefore go back to an earlier belief which preceded the writing of both Gospels.

The virgin birth story is not like the miracle stories relating to Jesus' ministry. None of the later miracles has ever been regarded as indispensable; but the virgin birth, like the resurrection, has traditionally been regarded as a vital component of

Christian faith, one of the beliefs by which the whole structure stands or falls. Like the empty tomb story, it has been understood as significant not so much in itself, but as a sign pointing to a greater miracle – in this case, the incarnation of the divine Son of God. In traditional theology, the virgin birth is the means by which the Son of God assumed human nature.

Yet this belief has been strongly challenged, by people within the Christian Church as well as outside it, on the grounds that it originated at a comparatively late stage in early Christian history. Among the most important reasons put forward for this claim are the following.

(*i*) The story is said to resemble pagan stories in which a god takes the place of a human father in the conception of a child. The reverence of the Gospel narratives of course contrasts with the levity of the pagan parallels, but – it is claimed – the underlying resemblance is unmistakable.

(*ii*) The early Christians believed that Jesus was the Son of God, and some might have understood this to mean that God took over the creative role of the human father in his conception. Thus, Luke 1.35 states that it is because the child is conceived by the Holy Spirit that he is to be the Son of God.

(*iii*) The story may be thought to conflict with the genealogies provided by both Matthew and Luke (Matt. 1.1–17, Luke 3.23–38), which evidently go back to Jewish Christian attempts to trace Jesus' ancestry back to David. In combination with the virgin birth story, the genealogies seem to prove nothing because Jesus was not the son of Joseph and was therefore not a descendant of David. This may suggest that the virgin birth story was a later development which replaced the older belief that he was the Son of David.[2]

(*iv*) Matt. 1.23 quotes Isa. 7.14 in justification of belief in the virgin birth: 'Behold a virgin shall conceive . . .', and so on. The quotation is taken from the Greek Old Testament translation (the 'Septuagint'), in which 'virgin' is an incorrect rendering of the Hebrew *almah*, 'a young woman'. Because Old Testament passages often led to the creation of beliefs about Jesus, this could also be the case here. If so, the belief must have arisen in Greek-speaking circles familiar with the Septuagint, and not in the earliest Jewish Christian tradition.

(*v*) The virgin birth is not mentioned by Paul, Mark and John, and may therefore have been unknown to them. John states that both Nathanael and Jesus' Galilean critics regard him as Joseph's son (1.45, 6.42). Once again, this suggests that this belief was not part of the earliest preaching, and may therefore have originated later.

(*vi*) Later sources also show that it was Jewish Christians who rejected belief in the virgin birth – the very people who would be expected to have preserved the original Jewish Christian traditions. How strong are these arguments? To many, they seem compelling; to others, they are inconclusive. The following points have been made in defence of the traditional view.

(*i*) The New Testament does not elsewhere baptize pagan myths by applying them to Jesus. The pagan gods were regarded as demons, and even the pagans did not take the endless stories of Zeus' affairs very seriously. There is no conceivable reason why such stories should have influenced the Gospel narratives. The parallel which obviously exists was an embarrassment to later Christians, and therefore perhaps already an embarrassment in the New Testament period. There must have been strong reasons for retaining this story in spite of this embarrassment.

(*ii*) The supposed link between the virgin birth and Jesus' divine sonship is not mentioned in Matthew and is not emphasized even in Luke. Its comparative insignificance in the two narratives suggests that it is unlikely to have been the reason for the development of the story.

(*iii*) Matthew and Luke do not regard the virgin birth story as in conflict with the genealogies because they include both. For both evangelists, Joseph is Jesus' adoptive father, and Jesus may still appropriately be regarded as descended from David (*see* Luke 1.32). Joseph and Mary are described as Jesus' 'parents' (Luke 2.27,41,43) and as 'his father and his mother' (Luke 2.33, *see* 2.48). Matthew 13.55 describes him as 'the son of the carpenter' – the phrase is Matthew's own because Mark simply has 'the carpenter' (Mark 6.3). In addition, the claim that the genealogies go back to early Jewish Christian attempts to trace Jesus' ancestry through Joseph back to David is unproved. For all we know, the genealogies may be later than the virgin birth story.

(*iv*) It is true that Old Testament passages have sometimes led to the creation of traditions about Jesus; the claim that he was born in Bethlehem may well be an example of this.[3] However, that belief derived from a passage which was explicitly messianic (Micah 5.2, quoted in Matt. 2.6) and which may have been understood as messianic by pre-Christian Jews (*see* John 7.42). But Isa. 7.14 is clearly not messianic in its original context, and there is no evidence that Jewish tradition understood it as such.

(*v*) The silence of the rest of the New Testament is not a conclusive argument in favour of the late development of this belief. Like other early Christian beliefs, it may have been confined to limited circles (especially during Mary's lifetime?). One reason for this might have been the desire not to provoke the slander that Jesus was conceived as the result of Mary's adultery (an accusation which was nevertheless made, perhaps at an early date).

(*vi*) Some later Jewish Christians did indeed deny the virgin birth; however, others did not. Matthew himself was a Jewish Christian, and Luke too is familiar with and sympathetic towards Jewish Christian traditions. Motives for denying it might have included its defencelessness against slander and its embarrassing affinities with pagan legends.

The arguments in favour of the view that this belief developed at a comparatively late date are of considerable weight, but they do not *compel* assent. Ultimately, whether one believes in the virgin birth may depend not on purely historical arguments, but on one's attitude towards the doctrine of the incarnation. If one cannot believe in the incarnation, or if one wishes to reinterpret it in a looser sense than the traditional one, the virgin birth will appear incredible. The story could then be understood as symbolic rather than literal. Yet if one believes that Jesus was the incarnate Son of God, one may well conclude that the virgin birth is the indispensable sign pointing to that still greater miracle.[4]

WEALTH The issue of poverty and wealth is a central theme in only one of the books of the New Testament: the Letter of James[1]. The author launches into several violent tirades against the wealthy. He attacks the way that even within Christian worship, the man 'with gold rings and in fine clothing' is treated with the utmost deference, whereas 'the poor man in shabby clothing' receives only contempt (2.1–4). This happens despite the fact, well-known from Christian tradition, that 'God has chosen those who are poor in the world to be rich in faith . . .', and despite the fact that it is 'the rich who oppress you' and who 'drag you into court' in their hostility to Christian faith (2.5–7). Later in the letter the author attacks the rich in still more forthright terms: 'Come now, you rich, weep and howl for the miseries that are coming upon you . . . Behold, the wages of the labourers who mowed your fields, which you kept back by fraud, cry out . . . You have lived on the earth in luxury and in pleasure; you have fattened your hearts in a day of slaughter' (5.1–5).

These diatribes against the rich are an extreme example of a prominent element in early Christian tradition: the theme of the overthrow of the great and powerful, and the exaltation of the poor and weak. Examples of this could be multiplied. It occurs frequently in Luke: in the *Magnificat* (1.46–55); in his version of the beatitudes, with its blessings to the poor and woes to the rich (6.20,24); and in the parables of the Rich Fool (12.16–21) and Dives and Lazarus (16.19–31). It occurs also in Paul, who sees God's wisdom in the fact that he has chosen precisely those who are not wealthy, powerful or wise in worldly terms (I Cor. 1.26–29). Frequent comments throughout the New Testament emphasize the spiritual dangers associated with wealth. Rich people have as much chance of getting into heaven as camels have of climbing through the eye of a needle – although because salvation is always a miracle, some of them may yet be saved (Mark 10.23–27). Mammon is a false god whose service is incompatible with that of the true God (Matt. 6.24); indeed its service – 'covetousness' – is 'idolatry', according to Col. 3.5. In the interpretation of the parable of the sower (Mark 4.19), desire for wealth is one of the great dangers to 'the word'. I Tim. 6.10 sees 'the love of money' as 'the root of all evils'. Thus, wealth is condemned both because it results in oppression and because it places its possessors in grave spiritual danger.

Yet the Christian gospel attracted surprising numbers of comparatively wealthy people, and this fact held in check the tendency towards a 'liberation theology' which manifests itself in the Letter of James. In deference to the rich, Matthew's first beatitude commends not 'the poor' (as in Luke) but 'the poor *in spirit*' (Matt. 5.3).[2] Luke too is socially conservative; his work is probably addressed to a wealthy member of the upper classes, and he likes to point to the gospel's success in gaining the patronage of the rich – for example, the women who gave Jesus financial assistance (Luke 8.2–3), and 'not a few of the leading women' of Thessalonica and Beroea (Acts 17.4, 12).

WEDDING FEAST, PARABLE OF Matt. 22.1–14 and Luke

14.15–24 record Jesus' parable of the wedding feast, or, in Luke's version, the 'great banquet' (v. 16). This is an excellent example of the way in which Jesus' parables were expanded and adapted by the early Church to suit new situations.[1] The parable in its earliest form consists of a simple contrast: those who were first invited to the feast all made excuses, and the poor and the outcasts were therefore invited to take their place. Jesus is in the first place criticizing those who might have been expected to respond to his message but who did not. He has in mind not only his Pharisaic opponents, but all who have failed to believe: 'Woe to you, Chorazin! Woe to you, Bethsaida! For if the mighty works done in you had been done in Tyre and Sidon, they would have repented long ago in sackcloth and ashes' (Matt. 11.21). Jesus has therefore been forced to go beyond the bounds of respectable society and appeal to the 'tax collectors and sinners', and these have quite unexpectedly responded to his invitation. In one sense, the great feast is a future entity, but the emphasis lies on its realization in the ministry of Jesus. The Synoptic Gospels repeatedly state that Jesus was criticized by the Pharisees for eating with tax collectors and sinners (Mark 2.15–17, Matt. 11.16–19, Luke 15.1–2), and the parable of the wedding feast (or great banquet) can be seen as a vindication of his conduct in this respect.[2] The feast of the end-time is already present within Jesus' ministry, and he is God's representative as he shares it with those who have responded to his invitation. The choice of guests is admittedly somewhat eccentric, but God has chosen to call them because the guests originally invited have had the bad manners to refuse.

Matthew and Luke adapt this parable in several ways. Matthew turns the householder who gives a banquet into a king who gives a wedding feast for his son, and so relates the parable much more closely to Jesus. Those originally invited do not simply make excuses; they kill the king's servants, with the result that he sends his troops and destroys their city. In this way, Matthew applies the parable to the fall of Jerusalem in AD 70, which he thinks was divine punishment for the Jews' attitude towards God's servants. He also adds an extra passage to the end of the parable, in which the king takes exception to a guest's failure to wear a wedding garment, and has him bound and cast into outer darkness (vv. 11–14). This addition ruins the story because if people are dragged off the streets to a wedding feast they cannot reasonably be expected to dress properly. Its point for Matthew is that one must 'bear fruit that befits repentance' and not rely too heavily on God's mercy and grace.

Luke's version is in general closer to the original form of the story. But here the servant is sent out twice after the initial refusals: once 'to the streets and lanes of the city', and then, when there is still room, 'to the highways and hedges'. Luke has in mind first the calling of the tax collectors and sinners during Jesus' own ministry (see 15.1–2), and second the calling of the Gentiles which he will relate in his second volume. Thus, both Matthew and Luke adapt the parable to their own theological concerns.

WHEAT AND TARES, PARABLE OF[1] The interpretation of this parable is not a problem because Matthew explains in great detail exactly what it means (Matt. 13.24–30,36–43). Christ's Church has been infiltrated by the devil, who has introduced wicked people into the congregation of the righteous. Because it is not always possible to distinguish the good from the bad clearly enough, we can only wait until the coming of Christ as judge. It is he who must accomplish the separation, rewarding the righteous with eternal life and punishing the wicked with hell-fire. The parable is therefore told in opposition to the view that the visible Church on earth can be the pure congregation of the saints. The Church contains sinners as well as saints, and the distinction is in practice so hard to draw that we must simply leave it to God to separate the two in his own good time.[2]

The detailed interpretation has evidently been added to the parable in imitation of the parable of the sower.[3] But in this case, it is not only the interpretation which is the work of the early Church, but most of the parable itself. Matt. 13 is an edited and expanded version of Mark's parable chapter (Mark 4), and the parable of the wheat and the tares occurs where the parable of the seed growing secretly is found in the Marcan original (Mark 4.26–29). On closer inspection, it turns out that the parable of the wheat and the tares is actually an expansion of Mark's parable of the seed. Mark's parable is still faintly visible beneath Matthew's many additions: 'The kingdom of heaven may be compared to a man who sowed good seed in his field . . . The plants came up and bore grain . . . At harvest time [he will] gather the wheat'. The original point of Mark's parable is completely lost, and a new point is made.

WICKED HUSBANDMEN, PARABLE OF In its setting in the Gospel of Mark, this parable refers to Israel's constant maltreatment of God's servants, which is about to culminate in the crucifixion of Jesus (Mark 12.1–11). The threat that the vineyard will be let out to other tenants (12.9) is fulfilled, in Mark's view, by the replacement of Israel as God's people by the mainly Gentile Church. He makes the same point in his passion narrative. Because Israel has put Jesus to death, God shows that he has abandoned his temple by tearing the veil in two; and the new hope for the Gentiles is symbolized by the Gentile centurion's confession of Jesus as Son of God (15.38–39). The replacement of one group by another also occurs in the parable of the wedding feast (or great banquet), where it refers to the tax collectors and sinners who take the places originally allocated to the righteous, who refused to come.[1] It may be that Jesus was making a similar point in the present parable, and that the early Church understood it in allegorical fashion to refer to his crucifixion and the consequent judgment on Israel. But because we possess no independent form of the parable to compare Mark's version with, it is impossible to reconstruct what its original form might have been.

One small alteration made by both Matthew and Luke illustrates the tendency to increase the allegorical element.[2] In Mark 12.8, the tenants first kill the son and then cast him out of the vineyard, whereas in Matt. 21.39 and Luke 20.15, they first cast him out and then kill him. The reason for the change is no doubt that Jesus was first 'cast out' (i.e. rejected) by the Jews, and then put to death.

WISE AND FOOLISH VIRGINS, PARABLE OF[1] This parable is found only in Matt. 25.1–13, and the evangelist probably understands it as an allegory about the situation of the Church as it awaits the return of Christ. The lamp-oil taken by the wise but not by the foolish must stand for the works of obedience that Matthew sees as the criterion at the judgment. The bridegroom's delay refers to the unexpected delay of Christ's return, and the girls' 'slumber' and 'rising' refers to death and resurrection to face the judgment. The harsh exclusion of the foolish who possess no oil means that the unrighteous will be punished. The bridegroom's words, 'I do not know you' (v. 12), recall the words which Christ will utter to the disobedient according to Matt. 7.23: 'I never knew you'.

The parable is thus a thinly-veiled allegory teaching Christian beliefs about the return of Christ. As Jesus told a number of parables about being prepared for the crisis of the full coming of the kingdom of God,[2] it is likely that a genuine parable underlies this allegorical rewriting. But the rewriting has been too thorough to allow us to reconstruct the original.

WOMEN In all four Gospels, women play a comparatively minor role but are generally seen in a favourable light.[1] Thus, in Mark 15.40–41, it is Jesus' women followers who are present at his crucifixion after the men have fled; in John 4, Jesus enters into debate with a woman of Samaria, who despite her murky past attains a fuller comprehension of him than does Nicodemus in John 3; and in the resurrection narratives, it is the women who discover the empty tomb (Mark 16.1–8, etc.).

It is Luke who emphasizes the significance of women most strongly. Luke 1 is dominated by the joyful faith of Elisabeth and Mary as they prepare for the births of John the Baptist and Jesus. Mark 15.40–41 refers to women at the cross 'who, when he was in Galilee, followed him and ministered to him', and so Luke inserts a reference to them into the account of the Galilean ministry: in addition to the twelve, Jesus was accompanied by 'some women who had been healed of evil spirits and infirmities . . . who provided for them out of their means' (8.2–3). The latter phrase suggests financial support from rich, upper class women, and this is confirmed by a reference to Joanna, a member of Herod's court circle. (This passage perhaps shows Luke's concern for the female members of his patron Theophilus' social class; this is again apparent in the references to the conversion of upper class women in Thessalonica and Beroea [Acts 17.4,12].) All the Synoptic Gospels speak of Jesus' favourable attitude towards 'sinners'; but in Luke 7.36–50 the evangelist speaks in the highest terms of 'a *woman* of the city, who was a sinner'. In 22.27–28 it is the women of Jerusalem who weep and mourn as Jesus walks to the place of his crucifixion, in contrast to the men who have condemned him and who will execute him.

In contrast to the evangelists, Paul is often regarded as the arch-misogynist who must bear the chief responsibility for the long history of male oppression of women in the Church. But this is a grotesque caricature. It is true that, for reasons that remain obscure despite his attempted explanation, Paul commanded that women should wear veils as a sign of their subordination to their husbands (11.1–16). And it is also true that he commands women to be silent in church (I Cor. 14.33–35), which contradicts the assumption of I Cor. 11.5 that women will pray and prophesy in public. Another passage which has earned a certain notoriety (I Tim. 2.11–15) occurs in a letter not actually written by Paul.[2] But there are several other points in Paul's view of women which indicate that the usual stereotype is over-simplified.

First, he proclaims that in principle 'there is neither male nor female' in Christ – that is, that the subordination of one sex to the other has been abolished (Gal. 3.28). He is too cautious and socially conservative to put this into practice in a radical way in the life of his churches, just as he never attempts to abolish slavery. Nevertheless, the principle remains.

Secondly, in the admittedly rather unromantic view of marriage in I Cor. 7 ('It is better to marry than to be aflame with passion', v. 9), Paul stresses the mutual nature of the obligations of husband and wife towards one another: 'The husband should give to his wife her conjugal rights, and likewise the wife to her husband. For the wife does not rule over her own body, but the husband does; likewise the husband does not rule over his own body, but the wife does' (vv. 3–4). The whole chapter illustrates Paul's view of the equality of man and woman in Christ.[3]

Thirdly, individual women played an important part in the lives of Paul's congregations. The letter to the Romans is to be conveyed to Rome by 'Phoebe, a deaconess of the church of Cenchreae' (Rom. 16.1). Priscilla is named first before her husband Aquila as a 'fellow worker in Christ Jesus' who risked her life for Paul's sake, and to whom he is therefore grateful (Rom. 16.3). Greetings are sent to 'Mary, who has worked hard among you', to 'those workers in the Lord, Tryphaena and Tryphosa', and to Rufus' mother, 'his mother and mine' (Rom. 16.6,12,13). In Phil. 4.2–3 Euodia and Syntyche are said to have 'laboured side by side with me in the gospel' alongside male colleagues.

WORD[1] Generally in the New Testament, 'the word' refers to the gospel, understood as a spoken message. Thus, in Col. 1.5 'the gospel' is described as 'the word of the truth'. However, in the famous passage which opens the Gospel of John, Jesus Christ himself is described as 'the Word'. The Word existed from all eternity with God, he was God, he was instrumental in the creation of the world, and in the fulness of time he 'became flesh' (John 1.1–3,14). The Greek term, *logos*, was widely used in the philosophical thought of the time. In the Stoic system, the *logos* was the rational principle ordering all reality and preventing it from disintegrating into chaos. This *logos* was expressed most fully in the human mind, and might be identified with God. In the Platonism of the time, there was a tendency to subordinate the *logos* to the supreme God: the *logos* comprised the forms or ideas of all existing realities in the mind of God. This divine mind might be attained by the human mind. Thus, John 1.1, 'In the beginning was the Word, and the Word was with God, and the Word was God', alludes to both neo-Platonic and Stoic ideas. The evangelist's use of this term, however, is diametrically opposed to these philosophical systems because the idea of human participation in the divine realm through the rational faculty is excluded. Christ is the Word in the sense that he alone reveals God: 'No-one has ever seen God; the only Son, who is in the bosom of the Father, he has made him known' (1.18). Although Jesus is never again called 'the Word' in John, he is closely related to his own 'word' – his testimony to his own heavenly origin and his task to bring life to the world.

WORLD In John and Paul, 'the world' is an ambiguous concept, and the ambiguity lies not so much in their own thought as in the object itself. Thus, in John 1.10 the word is used three times with three different meanings: 'He was in the world, and the world was made through him, yet the world knew him not'. 'World' here seems to mean first human society seen in a neutral sense, second the created order, and third human society as hostile towards God. In the statement, 'God so loved the world that he gave his only Son . . .' (3.16), only the first of these meanings is applicable. But when in 12.31, Jesus speaks of 'the judgment of this world' and 'the ruler of this world', the third sense is obviously uppermost.[1] Other cases are ambiguous: in 17.11, Jesus says, 'I am no more in the world, but they are in the world', and any or all of the three senses could be intended.

A similar ambiguity occurs in Paul, although he does not use the term as frequently as John does. The world as divine creation can lead to the knowledge of God: 'Ever since the creation of the world his invisible nature . . . has been clearly perceived in the things that have been made' (Rom. 1.20). But 'world' can also refer to human society organized in opposition to God: in the wisdom of God, 'the world did not know God through wisdom' (I Cor. 1.21).[2]

ZECHARIAH[1] According to Luke, the history of God's accomplishment of salvation through Jesus begins with Zechariah, an elderly, obscure priest, loyal to the law but disappointed at his and his wife's failure to produce children (Luke 1.5–7). While he is serving in the temple, the angel of the Lord appears to him and announces the birth of John the Baptist to him and his wife (1.8–17). Thus, salvation begins with God's initiative, which means a miracle. Zechariah responds with amazement ('How shall I know this? For I am an old man, and my wife is advanced in years' [1.18]), and is temporarily struck dumb as a punishment for his unbelief (1.18–22), until the child is born, when he is suddenly able to praise God in the words of the *Benedictus* (1.64–79). His unbelief has not hindered the fulfilment of God's plan, and he can only respond to God's sovereign action with praise. This suggests that although Luke presents Mary as obediently submitting to God's will (1.38), it is not his view that this obedience is absolutely necessary in order for the incarnation to take place. Had Mary responded with unbelief as Zechariah did, her child would have been born all the same, just as Zechariah's was.

The story of Zechariah and Elisabeth recalls that of another old, childless couple, Abraham and Sarah. Like Zechariah, they too responded to the divine promise with unbelief – in their case, with mocking laughter (Gen. 17.17, 18.11–15). In adopting this traditional theme, Luke is stressing that God's word always speaks of a reality beyond normal, everyday experience, and so is bound to encounter unbelief as well as faith. He will return to this theme in his resurrection narratives, where the disciples at first refuse to believe the women's message (24.11,22–26).[2]

Cross-references

Cross-references

Note There are no separate entries in the main text for terms or names enclosed in square brackets.

ABBA — **1** *See* PRAYER, SPIRIT 1 i; **2** *See* LORD'S PRAYER; **3** *See* PRODIGAL SON, PARABLE OF.

[ABRAHAM] — *See* PAUL 3 iii; COVENANT; GALATIANS; FAITH 5; JAMES, LETTER OF 2 ii.

ACTS OF THE APOSTLES — **1** *See* ASCENSION; PENTECOST; TONGUES 1; PETER v; GAMALIEL. **2** *See* STEPHEN; PHILIP iii, SAMARIA; PAUL 1 i,ii; CORNELIUS. **3** *See* PAUL 1 iii, 2 v; GALATIANS, 1; I THESSAL-ONIANS, 1; I CORINTHIANS, 1; ATHENS; EPHESUS; BARNABAS; SILAS; TIMOTHY; GALLIO. **4** *See* COLLECTION; FELIX; FESTUS; AGRIPPA. **5** *See* COLOSSIANS, 2; I TIMOTHY, 1. **6** On the end of Paul's life, *see* PAUL 2 viii. **7** *See* MARK, 2; LUKE, 2 iv. **8** *See* PAUL 1. **9** *See* STEPHEN. **10** *See* PAUL 1 iii; BARNABAS. **11** On Luke's political views, *see* GALLIO; FELIX; FESTUS; AGRIPPA; CAESAREA; STATE iii.

ADAM — **1** *See* LUKE, 2 iii. **2** *See* PAUL 3 i. **3** *See* I TIMOTHY, 1. **4** *See* WOMEN.

[ADOPTION] — *See* SPIRIT 1 i; PRAYER; ABBA.

[ADULTERY] — *See* DIVORCE.

[AGAPE] — *See* LOVE, LORD'S SUPPER.

AGRIPPA — **1** *See* HEROD AGRIPPA. **2** *See* ACTS, 5; GALLIO; FELIX; FESTUS; CAESAREA.

[ALLEGORY] — On allegorical interpretation of the parables, *see* PARABLES 2, SOWER, TALENTS, WEDDING FEAST, WHEAT AND TARES; WICKED HUSBANDMEN.

[ALMS] — *See* WEALTH; COLLECTION; HYPOCRISY.

ANDREW — **1** On these lists, *see* TWELVE. **2** For John's interest in lesser-known disciples, *see* PHILIP ii; THOMAS. **3** *See* PETER i.

ANGELS   **1** *See* GOD 2. **2** *See* RETURN OF CHRIST. **3** *See* HEBREWS 3 i.

[ANNA]   **1** *See* ZECHARIAH; ELISABETH; SIMEON.

ANNAS   **1** *See* CAIAPHAS; HIGH PRIESTHOOD; SADDUCEES; SANHEDRIN.

ANTICHRIST   **1** *See* I JOHN, 1. **2** *See* II THESSALONIANS, 1. **3** *See* REVELATION, 3 iii.

ANTIOCH   **1** *See* PAUL 1 iii; BARNABAS.

[ANTIPAS]   *See* HEROD ANTIPAS.

[APOCALYPTIC]   *See* RESURRECTION; JUDGMENT; RETURN OF CHRIST, KINGDOM OF GOD; SON OF MAN; ANTICHRIST.

APOLLOS   **1** *See* EPHESUS. **2** *See* I CORINTHIANS, 3 i.

[APOSTASY]   *See* SOWER, SUFFERING, HEBREWS, 3.

APOSTLE   **1** *See* DISCIPLE; TWELVE. **2** *See* RESURRECTION 1; GALATIANS, 3, 4 i. **3** *See* II CORINTHIANS, 1 iv, 2 i. **4** *See* PAUL 1 ii; RESURRECTION 1.

[AQUILA AND PRISCILLA]   *See* APOLLOS, WOMEN.

ARCHELAUS   **1** *See* HEROD; HEROD ANTIPAS; PHILIP i. **2** *See* BETHLEHEM.

[AREOPAGUS]   *See* ATHENS.

ASCENSION   **1** *See* LORD. **2** *See* RESURRECTION 1.

ATHENS   **1** *See* PAUL 2 v. **2** For Paul's own attitude towards Greek thought ('wisdom'), *see* I CORINTHIANS, 3 i.

ATONEMENT   **1** *See* PASSION NARRATIVES; CRUCIFIXION. **2** *See* HEBREWS, 2 iii; HIGH PRIESTHOOD. **3** *See* RESURRECTION 2 i. **4** For the tendency to blame the Jews for the crucifixion, *see* PASSION NARRATIVES 1 iv; 2 iv; 3 iv; 4 iv.

AUGUSTUS   **1** For further examples of Luke's historical inaccuracies, *see* CAIAPHAS; JUDAS THE GALILEAN. **2** *See* ACTS, 5.

[BABYLON]   *See* REVELATION, 3 iv; STATE.

BAPTISM   **1** *See* JOHN THE BAPTIST 1. **2** *See* EPHESUS. **3** *See* JOHN THE BAPTIST 2. **4** *See* SPIRIT.

BARABBAS   **1** For the tendency to blame the Jews for the crucifixion and to exonerate Pilate, *see* PASSION NARRATIVES 1 iv, 2 iv, 3 iv, 4 iv; PILATE.

BARNABAS   **1** *See* GENTILES; CIRCUMCISION; FOOD LAWS. **2** *See* PAUL 2 iii, iv. **3** *See* PAUL 1 i; SILAS.

[BARTHOLOMEW]   *See* TWELVE.

BEATITUDES   **1** *See* SYNOPTIC PROBLEM. **2** *See* WEALTH.

[BELIEF]   *See* FAITH.

[BELOVED DISCIPLE]   *See* JOHN, GOSPEL OF 1 i, ii.

BETHANY	**1** *See* ASCENSION. **2** *See* LAZARUS.
BETHLEHEM	**1** *See* NAZARETH. **2** *See* AUGUSTUS. **3** *See* HEROD; ARCHELAUS.
[BETHSAIDA]	*See* GALILEE.
[BIRTH OF JESUS]	*See* VIRGIN BIRTH; BETHLEHEM; AUGUSTUS; HEROD; ARCHELAUS; SIMEON.
BISHOP	**1** *See* I TIMOTHY, 1, 2.
[BOASTING]	*See* II CORINTHIANS, 2 i; ROMANS, 2 ii.
[BLOOD]	*See* ATONEMENT; HEBREWS, 3 iii.
BODY OF CHRIST	**1** *See* LORD'S SUPPER. **2** *See* TONGUES 2. **3** *See* COLOSSIANS, 2; EPHESIANS, 3 iii. **4** *See* CHURCH. **5** *See* MARRIAGE.
[BROTHERS OF JESUS]	*See* JAMES 2; JOSEPH; MARY, THE VIRGIN; NAZARETH; CAPERNAUM.
CAESAREA	**1** *See* HEROD. **2** *See* FELIX; FESTUS; AGRIPPA.
CAESAREA PHILIPPI	**1** *See* PHILIP i. **2** *See* MARK, 3, 4 ii; PETER ii. **3** *See* DECAPOLIS.
CAIAPHAS	**1** *See* ANNAS; HIGH PRIESTHOOD; SADDUCEES; SANHEDRIN.
CALL	**1** *See* PREDESTINATION.
CANA	**1** On the relation between miracles and parables, compare LAZARUS.
CAPERNAUM	**1** *See* GALILEE. **2** *See* MATTHEW, 3 ii.
[CENSUS]	*See* AUGUSTUS; JUDAS THE GALILEAN.
[CENTURION]	*See* ACTS, 5; CORNELIUS.
[CEPHAS]	*See* PETER.
[CHARISMATA]	*See* SPIRIT 1 iii; TONGUES.
[CHIEF PRIESTS]	*See* ANNAS; CAIAPHAS; HIGH PRIESTHOOD, SADDUCEES; SANHEDRIN.
CHILDREN	**1** *See* ABBA.
CHRIST	**1** For the New Testament's use of the idea of Davidic descent, *see* DAVID; BETHLEHEM. **2** *See* KINGDOM OF GOD iii; EXORCISM. **3** *See* PARABLES 1 iii; PRODIGAL SON; WEDDING FEAST. **4** *See* KINGDOM OF GOD i. **5** *See* PAUL 3 i. **6** *See* MARK, 3, 4 ii.
CHRISTIAN	**1** *See* SUFFERING.
CHURCH	**1** *See* PETER iv; PARABLES 2. **2** *See* BODY OF CHRIST. **3** *See* COLOSSIANS, 2; EPHESIANS, 3 iii.
CIRCUMCISION	**1** *See* GALATIANS. **2** *See* COVENANT. **3** *See* PAUL 2 iii. **4** *See* PAUL 2 iv; BARNABAS; TITUS.
CLAUDIUS	**1** *See* AUGUSTUS.
[CLEOPAS]	*See* EMMAUS.
COLLECTION	**1** *See* II CORINTHIANS, 1; TITUS. **2** *See* ROMANS, 1.

COLOSSIANS, PAUL'S LETTER TO	1 *See* the entry for each letter. 2 *See* PHILEMON. 3 *See* EPHESIANS, 3 ii. 4 *See* BODY OF CHRIST. 5 *See* GALATIANS, 3, 4 i. 6 *See* TITUS, PAUL'S LETTER TO, for another example of this.
[COMMANDMENTS]	*See* LAW; I JOHN, 3 iii.
[COMMUNION, HOLY]	*See* LORD'S SUPPER.
[CONDEMNATION]	*See* JUDGMENT; HELL; LAW 2.
[CONSCIENCE]	*See* ROMANS, 2 i.
[CONVERSION]	*See* REPENTANCE; FAITH; BAPTISM.
CORINTHIANS, PAUL'S FIRST LETTER TO	1 *See* GALLIO. 2 *See* APOLLOS. 3 *See* MARRIAGE. 4 *See* TONGUES 2. 5 *See* BODY OF CHRIST. 6 *See* RESURRECTION, 2 iii.
CORINTHIANS, PAUL'S SECOND LETTER TO	1 *See* COLLECTION. 2 *See* TITUS. 3 *See* SUFFERING. 4 *See* I CORINTHIANS, 3 iv. 5 *See* LAW 2.
CORNELIUS	1 *See* TONGUES 1; GOD 2.
COVENANT	1 *See* GALATIANS, 3, 4; CIRCUMCISION. 2 *See* LORD'S SUPPER. 3 *See* II CORINTHIANS, 2 iii.
CREATION	1 *See* KINGDOM OF GOD. 2 *See* RESURRECTION 2 iii. 3 *See* INCARNATION 1 i.
[CRETE]	*See* TITUS, PAUL'S LETTER TO.
[CROSS]	*See* CRUCIFIXION; ATONEMENT; PASSION NARRATIVES; I CORINTHIANS, 3 i.
CRUCIFIXION	1 *See* ATONEMENT; PASSION NARRATIVES.
[CURSE]	*See* GALATIANS, 4 iii; LAW 2.
[CYPRUS]	*See* ACTS, 5; BARNABAS.
DAMASCUS	1 *See* DECAPOLIS. 2 *See* PAUL 2 ii. 3 *See* PAUL 2 iii.
[DANIEL, BOOK OF]	*See* KINGDOM OF GOD; SON OF MAN; ANTICHRIST.
[DARKNESS]	*See* JOHN, GOSPEL OF, 3 i.
DAVID	1 *See* BETHLEHEM. 2 *See* CHRIST. 3 *See* VIRGIN BIRTH.
[DAY OF THE LORD]	*See* RETURN OF CHRIST.
[DEACON]	*See* I TIMOTHY, 1.
DEATH	1 *See* RESURRECTION 2 iii. 2 *See* JOHN, GOSPEL OF 3 iii; ETERNAL LIFE; LAZARUS.
[DECALOGUE]	*See* LAW; II CORINTHIANS, 2 iii.
DECAPOLIS	1 *See* DAMASCUS: GADARA.
DEMONS	1 *See* EXORCISM; KINGDOM OF GOD; DEVIL; IDOLATRY.
DESCENT INTO HELL	1 *See* HELL.
DEVIL	1 *See* KINGDOM OF GOD; EXORCISM; DEMONS. 2 *See* JOHN, GOSPEL OF 3 i. 3 *See* TEMPTATIONS OF JESUS. 4 *See* ANTICHRIST; REVELATION, 3 iii; II THESSALONIANS, 1; I JOHN, 1.

DISCIPLE	1 *See* APOSTLE; TWELVE.
[DISPERSION]	*See* SYNAGOGUE; I PETER.
DIVORCE	1 *See* MARRIAGE. 2 *See* LAW 1.
[DOCETISM]	*See* I JOHN, 2; II JOHN; HERESY.
[DOUBT]	*See* THOMAS; ZECHARIAH.
[DREAMS]	*See* GOD 2; ANGELS 1.
[DUALISM]	*See* JOHN, GOSPEL OF 3 i.
[EGYPT]	*See* MOSES; BETHLEHEM.
[ELDER]	*See* SANHEDRIN; BISHOP.
[ELECTION]	*See* GOD 3; PREDESTINATION; COVENANT.
[ELIJAH]	*See* TRANSFIGURATION; JOHN THE BAPTIST 1.
ELISABETH	1 *See* ZECHARIAH. 2 *See* JOHN THE BAPTIST 2. 3 *See* SIMEON.
EMMAUS	1 *See* EMPTY TOMB 1 iii.
EMPTY TOMB	1 *See* MARK, 4 iii. 2 *See* MIRACLES 2. 3 The evangelists are divided about whether Mary Magdalene and the others were the first witnesses of the risen Lord as well as of the Empty Tomb; *see* MARY MAGDALENE. 4 *See* JERUSALEM 1; EMMAUS. 5 *See* JOSEPH OF ARIMATHEA, NICODEMUS. 6 On the beloved disciple, *see* JOHN, GOSPEL OF 1 ii. 7 For discrepancies in the names of the women, *see* MARY MAGDALENE.
[END OF THE WORLD]	*See* RETURN OF CHRIST.
[EPAPHRODITUS]	*See* PHILIPPIANS, 2.
EPHESIANS, PAUL'S LETTER TO	1 *See* the separate entries on these letters. 2 *See* BODY OF CHRIST. 3 *See* PAUL 2 iv; GALATIANS, 1. 4 *See* II CORINTHIANS, 2 i.
EPHESUS	1 *See* TONGUES 1. 2 *See* PHILIPPIANS, 1.
[ESCHATOLOGY]	*See* JUDGMENT; KINGDOM OF GOD; RESURRECTION; RETURN OF CHRIST; SON OF MAN.
[ETERNAL LIFE]	*See* JOHN, GOSPEL OF 3 iii; DEATH; RESURRECTION.
[EUCHARIST]	*See* LORD'S SUPPER.
[EVE]	*See* ADAM.
[EVIL]	*See* SIN; FLESH; DEVIL; DEATH.
[EXALTATION OF CHRIST]	*See* ASCENSION; RESURRECTION 1 ii; PHILIPPIANS, 3 i; RIGHT HAND OF GOD.
[EXODUS]	*See* FEASTS; PASSOVER; MOSES.
EXORCISM	1 *See* DEMONS; DEVIL. 2 *See* KINGDOM OF GOD iii. 3 *See* MIRACLES 1.
FAITH	1 *See* GRACE; REPENTANCE; CONVERSION. 2 *See* JOHN, GOSPEL OF 3 iii. 3 *See* PREDESTINATION. 4 *See* SPIRIT 1. 5 *See* JUSTIFICATION;

	ROMANS, 2 ii. **6** *See* HOPE. **7** *See* JAMES, LETTER OF 2 ii.
[FALSE PROPHETS]	*See* ANTICHRIST; REVELATION, 3 iii.
[FAMILY]	*See* CHILDREN; MARRIAGE; DIVORCE.
FASTING	**1** On the presence of the new age, *see* KINGDOM OF GOD iii; PRODIGAL SON; WEDDING FEAST. **2** *See* SABBATH.
[FATHER]	*See* ABBA; SON OF GOD i; SPIRIT 1 i.
FEAR OF GOD	**1** *See* JUDGMENT. **2** *See* I JOHN, 3 iii.
FEASTS	**1** *See* PASSOVER; PENTECOST. **2** *See* HEBREWS, 3 iii.
FELIX	**1** *See* HEROD AGRIPPA. **2** *See* ACTS, 5; GALLIO; FESTUS; AGRIPPA; CAESAREA.
FESTUS	**1** *See* ACTS, 5; GALLIO; FELIX; AGRIPPA; CAESAREA.
FLESH	**1** *See* I CORINTHIANS, 3 iv; RESURRECTION 2 iii. **2** *See* ROMANS, 2 iii. **3** *See* PHILIPPIANS, 3 ii. **4** *See* I CORINTHIANS, 3 i.
FOOD LAWS	**1** *See* MATTHEW, 3 i. **2** *See* CORNELIUS, TONGUES 1. **3** *See* GALATIANS, 1; PAUL 2 iv.
FORGIVENESS	**1** *See* JUSTIFICATION; ROMANS, 3 i; FLESH; JOHN, GOSPEL OF 3 i.
FREEDOM	**1** *See* SLAVERY. **2** *See* I CORINTHIANS, 3 ii; GALATIANS, 4 iv; ROMANS, 1.
[FRUIT OF THE SPIRIT]	*See* SPIRIT 1 ii.
[GABRIEL]	*See* ANGELS.
GADARA	**1** *See* DECAPOLIS
GALATIANS, PAUL'S LETTER TO	**1** *See* JUSTIFICATION; FAITH 3 ii; LAW 2; FREE-DOM. **2** *See* PAUL 2 iv. **3** *See* CIRCUMCISION. **4** *See* COVENANT. **5** *See* ROMANS, 1. **6** *See* LAW 2.
GALILEE	**1** *See* HEROD; HEROD ANTIPAS. **2** *See* NAZA-RETH; CANA; CAPERNAUM. **3** *See* NAZA-RETH.
GALLIO	**1** *See* ACTS, 5; FESTUS; CAESAREA.
GAMALIEL	**1** *See* JUDAS THE GALILEAN. **2** *See* PAUL 1 iv. **3** *See* SANHEDRIN.
[GEHENNA]	*See* HELL; LAZARUS.
[GENEALOGIES OF JESUS]	*See* VIRGIN BIRTH; LUKE, 2 iii.
GENTILES	**1** *See* PAUL 2 iii, iv; CIRCUMCISION; FOOD LAWS. **2** *See* GALATIANS, 3; ROMANS, 1.
[GERASA]	*See* GADARA; DECAPOLIS.
[GETHSEMANE]	*See* MARK, 4 ii; PASSION NARRATIVES 4 iii; JUDAS ISCARIOT iii.
[GIFTS OF THE SPIRIT]	*See* SPIRIT 1 iii; TONGUES.

[GLORY]	*See* TRANSFIGURATION; JOHN, GOSPEL OF 3 ii.
[GLOSSOLALIA]	*See* TONGUES.
[GNOSTICISM]	**1** *See* HERESY; I TIMOTHY, 2; II TIMOTHY, 1; I JOHN, 2; JUDE; II PETER, 2; REVELATION, 2.
GOD	**1** *See* PASSION NARRATIVES 1 ii, 2 ii, 3 ii, 4 ii. **2** *See* SUFFERING. **3** *See* COVENANT. **4** *See* LORD. **5** *See* INCARNATION 1.
[GOLGOTHA]	*See* PASSION NARRATIVES; CRUCIFIXION; ATONEMENT.
GOOD SAMARITAN, PARABLE OF	**1** *See* LOVE; PARABLES; SAMARIA.
GOSPEL	**1** *See* FAITH; APOSTLE.
GRACE	**1** *See* ADAM. **2** *See* SPIRIT 1 iii.
[HADES]	*See* DESCENT INTO HELL; HELL; LAZARUS.
[HAGAR]	*See* FREEDOM.
HEAVEN	**1** *See* ASCENSION.
HEBREWS, LETTER TO	**1** *See* TIMOTHY. **2** *See* INCARNATION 1; PHILIPPIANS, 3 i. **3** *See* HIGH PRIESTHOOD. **4** *See* COVENANT.
HELL	**1** *See* JUDGMENT; LAZARUS; DESCENT INTO HELL.
[HELLENISTS]	*See* STEPHEN; PHILIP iii.
HERESY	**1** *See* I TIMOTHY, 2; II TIMOTHY, 1; I JOHN, 2; JUDE; II PETER, 2; REVELATION, 2.
HEROD THE GREAT	**1** *See* TEMPLE. **2** *See* the separate entries on each of these figures.
HEROD ANTIPAS	**1** *See* GALILEE. **2** *See* JOHN THE BAPTIST 1.
HEROD AGRIPPA I	**1** *See* AGRIPPA; FELIX. **2** *See* ANTIPAS.
HERODIAS	**1** *See* the separate entries on these. **2** *See* JOHN THE BAPTIST 1.
HIGH PRIESTHOOD	**1** *See* SANHEDRIN; SADDUCEES; ANNAS; CAIAPHAS. **2** *See* HEBREWS, 3 iii.
[HOLINESS]	*See* SANCTIFICATION.
[HOLY OF HOLIES]	*See* TEMPLE; HEBREWS, 3 iii.
[HOLY SPIRIT]	*See* SPIRIT.
HOMOSEXUALITY	**1** *See* ROMANS, 2 i.
HOPE	**1** *See* FAITH 3 iii. **2** *See* I THESSALONIANS, 2 ii. **3** *See* SUFFERING. **4** *See* SPIRIT 1 ii.
HUMILITY	**1** *See* COLOSSIANS, 3. **2** *See* PHILIPPIANS, 3 i.
HYPOCRISY	**1** *See* PHARISEES.
IDOLATRY	**1** *See* DEMONS.
[IMMORTALITY]	*See* ETERNAL LIFE; RESURRECTION.
INCARNATION	**1** *See* PHILIPPIANS, 3 i. **2** *See* GOD 4. **3** *See* WORD. **4** *See* SPIRIT 2. **5** *See* SON OF GOD. **6** *See* LORD, GOD 4 for examples of this. **7** *See* JESUS 1.

INSPIRATION	**1** For the use of the OT in Hebrews, *see* HEBREWS, 3. **2** For the use of the OT in Matthew, *see* MATTHEW, 3 ii.
[INTERCESSION]	*See* PRAYER.
ISRAEL	**1** *See* JEWS. **2** *See* ELISABETH; SIMEON; ZECHARIAH. **3** *See* PREDESTINATION.
JAMES	**1** *See* TWELVE. **2** *See* TWELVE; BETHANY. **3** *See* JOHN. **4** *See* MARY, THE VIRGIN. **5** *See* PAUL 2 iv. **6** *See* PAUL 1 iii.
JAMES, LETTER OF	**1** *See* PAUL 2 iv. **2** *See* FAITH 3 ii; JUSTIFICATION. **3** *See* WEALTH.
[JERICHO]	*See* MARK, 3.
JERUSALEM	**1** *See* TEMPLE. **2** *See* CAESAREA. **3** *See* EMPTY TOMB 1 iii. **4** *See* FREEDOM. **5** *See* COLLECTION.
JESUS	**1** *See* VIRGIN BIRTH; INCARNATION; EMPTY TOMB; MIRACLES; RESURRECTION 1. **2** *See* PARABLES 2. **3** *See*, for example, TEMPTATIONS OF JESUS. **4** *See* BETHLEHEM. **5** *See* NAZARETH. **6** *See* BAPTISM 2; JOHN THE BAPTIST 2. **7** *See* JOHN THE BAPTIST 1. **8** *See* FEASTS. **9** *See* GALILEE. **10** *See* EXORCISM. **11** *See* KINGDOM OF GOD. **12** *See* PARABLES 1 iii; PRODIGAL SON; WEDDING FEAST. **13** *See* LAW 1; FASTING; SABBATH. **14** *See* BARABBAS; PILATE; CRUCIFIXION; PASSION NARRATIVES. **15** *See* TEMPLE.
JEWS	**1** *See* ISRAEL. **2** For the tendency to blame the Jews for the crucifixion, *see* PASSION NARRATIVES 1 iv, 2 iv, 3 iv, 4 iv.
JOHN	**1** *See* JAMES. **2** *See* PHILIP iii; SAMARIA. **3** *See* REVELATION, 1; JOHN, GOSPEL OF 1.
JOHN, GOSPEL ACCORDING TO	**1** *See* INCARNATION 1; SPIRIT 2. **2** A Gnostic document from the collection discovered at Nag Hammadi, in Egypt. **3** *See* CANA. **4** *See* INCARNATION 2. **5** *See* FLESH; NICODEMUS. **6** *See* WORD. **7** *See* RESURRECTION 2 ii; RETURN OF CHRIST.
JOHN, FIRST LETTER OF	**1** On the authorship of John, *see* JOHN, GOSPEL OF 1 **2** *See* HERESY; ANTICHRIST. **3**; *see* FAITH; LOVE.
JOHN, SECOND LETTER OF	**1** *See* HERESY.
JOHN, THIRD LETTER OF	**1** *See* BISHOP.
JOHN THE BAPTIST	**1** *See* HEROD ANTIPAS; HERODIAS. **2** *See* PENTECOST. **3** *See* KINGDOM OF GOD iii.

JOSEPH	**1** *See* MARY, THE VIRGIN. **2** *See* VIRGIN BIRTH. **3** *See* JAMES 2.
JOSEPH OF ARIMATHEA	**1** *See* EMPTY TOMB. **2** *See* SANHEDRIN. **3** *See* NICODEMUS.
[JOY]	*See* THANKSGIVING.
[JUDAISM]	*See* PHARISEES; SADDUCEES; COVENANT; LAW; CIRCUMCISION; FOOD LAWS; SABBATH; HIGH PRIESTHOOD; SANHEDRIN.
[JUDAIZERS]	*See* GALATIANS, 2.
[JUDAEA]	*See* JERUSALEM.
JUDAS THE GALILEAN	**1** *See* GAMALIEL. **2** *See* AUGUSTUS. **3** *See* STATE i.
JUDAS ISCARIOT	**1** *See* PASSION NARRATIVES 2 ii. **2** *See* PASSION NARRATIVES 1 i, 2 i, 4 i. **3** *See* PASSION NARRATIVES 4 iii.
JUDE, LETTER OF	**1** *See* HERESY; II PETER. **2** *See* WHEAT AND TARES.
JUDGMENT	**1** *See* PARABLES 1 ii; SHEEP AND GOATS; WISE AND FOOLISH VIRGINS; LABOURERS IN VINEYARD. **2** On the nature of Paul's faith-works contrast, *see* FAITH 3 ii; JUSTIFICATION. **3** *See* JOHN, GOSPEL OF 3 iii. **4** *See* FEAR OF GOD.
[JUSTICE]	*See* JAMES, LETTER OF 2 iii; WEALTH.
JUSTIFICATION	**1** *See* FAITH 3 ii. **2** *See* ROMANS, 2 i. **3** *See* GOSPEL. **4** *See* PEACE.
[KENOSIS]	*See* INCARNATION 1; PHILIPPIANS, 3 i.
[KERYGMA]	*See* GOSPEL.
KINGDOM OF GOD/ HEAVEN	**1** *See* CHRIST 1. **2** *See also* SON OF MAN. **3** *See* CREATION 1. **4** *See* EXORCISM. **5** *See* WEDDING FEAST.
[KNOWLEDGE]	*See* GOD 1; JOHN, GOSPEL OF 3 ii.
LABOURERS IN VINEYARD, PARABLE OF	**1** *See* GRACE; JUDGMENT; TALENTS.
[LAST SUPPER]	*See* LORD'S SUPPER; PASSOVER; JUDAS ISCARIOT ii; PASSION NARRATIVES 1 i, 2 i, 3 i, ii.
LAW OF MOSES	**1** *See* SABBATH; FASTING; DIVORCE. **2** *See* CIRCUMCISION; FEASTS; FOOD LAWS. **3** *See* ROMANS, 2 iii. **4** *See* HEBREWS, 3 iii; HIGH PRIESTHOOD; COVENANT. **5** *See* JAMES, LETTER OF 2 ii.
LAZARUS	**1** *See* HELL. **2** *See* BETHANY.
[LETTER]	*See* II CORINTHIANS, 2 iii; ROMANS, 2 iii.
[LIBERATION, LIBERTY]	*See* FREEDOM.
[LIGHT]	*See* JOHN, GOSPEL OF 3 i.

CROSS-REFERENCES

LORD	1 *See* SON OF GOD ii. 2 For a comparable process in the Synoptic Gospels, *see* INCARNATION 2.
LORD'S PRAYER	1 *See* PRAYER; ABBA.
LORD'S SUPPER	1 *See* COVENANT; PASSOVER; FORGIVENESS. 2 *See* BODY OF CHRIST; IDOLATRY; DEMONS.
LOVE	1 *See* GOOD SAMARITAN. 2 *See* TONGUES 2; BODY OF CHRIST. 3 *See* I JOHN, 3 ii.
[LOWLINESS]	*See* HUMILITY; WEALTH.
LUKE, GOSPEL ACCORDING TO	1 *See* ACTS. 2 *See* AUGUSTUS; CAIAPHAS. 3 *See* JUDAS THE GALILEAN; CLAUDIUS; PAUL 1. 4 *See* SYNOPTIC PROBLEM. 5 *See* SIMEON; ELISABETH; ZECHARIAH. 6 *See* VIRGIN BIRTH; BETHLEHEM. 7 *See* TEMPTATIONS OF JESUS. 8 *See* SYNOPTIC PROBLEM. 9 *See* PETER i. 10 *See* JOHN THE BAPTIST 2. 11 *See* PETER ii. 12 *See* GOOD SAMARITAN; PRODIGAL SON; LAZARUS. 13 *See* TALENTS. 14 *See* PASSION NARRATIVES 3; EMMAUS; ASCENSION. 15 *See* TRANSFIGURATION. 16 *See* PASSION NARRATIVES 3 iii. 17 *See* AUGUSTUS. 18 *See* RETURN OF CHRIST.
[MACEDONIA]	*See* PAUL 2 v; II CORINTHIANS, 1 iii; PHILIPPIANS; I and II THESSALONIANS.
[MAGDALENE]	*See* MARY MAGDALENE.
[MAGI]	*See* BETHLEHEM; HEROD.
[MAMMON]	*See* WEALTH.
[MARANATHA]	*See* LORD.
MARK, GOSPEL ACCORDING TO	1 *See* SYNOPTIC PROBLEM. 2 *See* FOOD LAWS 1. 3 *See* MIRACLES 1; CAESAREA PHILIPPI; PETER ii. 4 *See* PASSION NARRATIVES 1 i. 5 *See* PREDESTINATION. 6 *See* MIRACLES 1, 3. 7 *See* SUFFERING. 8 *See* PASSION NARRATIVES 1. 9 *See* EMPTY TOMB 1.
MARRIAGE	1 *See* I TIMOTHY, 2. 2 *See* DIVORCE. 3 *See* WOMEN.
[MARTHA]	*See* BETHANY; LAZARUS; MARY.
[MARTYRDOM]	*See* SUFFERING; REVELATION, 4 i.
MARY MAGDALENE	1 *See* EMPTY TOMB; WOMEN; RESURRECTION 1.
MARY, THE VIRGIN	1 *See* VIRGIN BIRTH; BETHLEHEM; NAZARETH; JOSEPH. 2 *See* JAMES 2. 3 *See* JAMES 2; PAUL 2 iv.
MATTHEW, GOSPEL ACCORDING TO	1 *See* SYNOPTIC PROBLEM. 2 *See* MARK 2. 3 *See* VIRGIN BIRTH; MARY, THE VIRGIN; JOSEPH; HEROD; ARCHELAUS; BETHLEHEM. 4 *See* JOHN THE BAPTIST; TEMPTATIONS OF JESUS. 5 *See* BEATITUDES; HYPOCRISY;

LORD'S PRAYER. **6** *See* JOHN THE BAPTIST 2. **7** *See* MIRACLES 2. **8** *See* PARABLES 2. **9** *See* LABOURERS IN VINEYARD; WEDDING FEAST. **10** *See* WISE AND FOOLISH VIRGINS; TALENTS; SHEEP AND GOATS. **11** *See* PASSION NARRATIVES 2; EMPTY TOMB 1 ii. **12** *See* PHARISEES. **13** *See* VIRGIN BIRTH; BETHLEHEM; NAZARETH. **14** *See* PETER v. **15** *See* JOHN, GOSPEL OF 1 ii. **16** *See* WHEAT AND TARES.

[MERCY]   *See* GRACE.

[MESSIANIC SECRET]   *See* MARK, 3 i.

[MINISTRY OF JESUS]   *See* JESUS 2.

MIRACLES OF JESUS   **1** *See* MARK, 3. **2** *See* EXORCISM. **3** *See* TEMPTATIONS OF JESUS. **4** *See* MARK, 3 i. **5** *See* PASSION NARRATIVES 2 iii. **6** *See* EMPTY TOMB 1 ii. **7** *See* LAZARUS. **8** *See* INCARNATION 2.

[MONEY]   *See* WEALTH.

[MONEY CHANGERS]   *See* TEMPLE.

MOSES   **1** *See* LAW.

[NATHANIEL]   *See* NAZARETH.

[NATIVITY NARRATIVES]   *See* VIRGIN BIRTH; BETHLEHEM; MARY, THE VIRGIN; JOSEPH; AUGUSTUS; HEROD; ARCHELAUS; ELISABETH; SIMEON; ZECHARIAH.

NAZARETH   **1** *See* BETHLEHEM. **2** *See* JAMES 2; MARY, THE VIRGIN.

NICODEMUS   **1** *See* JOSEPH OF ARIMATHEA.

[ONESIMUS]   *See* PHILEMON.

[ORTHODOXY]   *See* HERESY; JUDE.

PARABLES OF JESUS   **1** *See* the entries for the following individual parables: GOOD SAMARITAN; LABOURERS IN VINEYARD; PRODIGAL SON; SHEEP AND GOATS; SOWER; TALENTS; WEDDING FEAST; WHEAT AND TARES; WICKED HUSBANDMEN; WISE AND FOOLISH VIRGINS. **2** *See* KINGDOM OF GOD iii. **3** *See* JUDGMENT.

[PARACLETE]   *See* JOHN, GOSPEL OF 3 iii; RESURRECTION 2 ii; SPIRIT 2.

[PAROUSIA]   *See* RETURN OF CHRIST.

PASSION NARRATIVES   **1** *See* ATONEMENT; CRUCIFIXION; LORD'S SUPPER; JUDAS ISCARIOT; PETER iii; PILATE; CAIAPHAS; ANNAS; BARABBAS; SANHEDRIN. **2** *See* SYNOPTIC PROBLEM. **3** *See*

LORD'S SUPPER. **4** *See* BARABBAS. **5** *See* MIRACLES 2. **6** *See* LUKE, 2 ii.

PASSOVER — **1** *See* FEASTS. **2** *See* LORD'S SUPPER.

[PASTORAL EPISTLES] — *See* I TIMOTHY; II TIMOTHY; TITUS, PAUL'S LETTER TO.

PAUL — **1** *See* RESURRECTION 1. **2** *See* JAMES 2; PETER v; BARNABAS. **3** *See* LAW 2. **4** *See* GAMALIEL; PHARISEES. **5** *See* ANTIOCH; GENTILES. **6** *See* JAMES 2; BARNABAS; ANTIOCH; CIRCUM-CISION; FOOD LAWS; TITUS. **7** *See* GALATIANS, 1; I THESSALONIANS, 1; I CORINTHIANS, 1; ATHENS; GALLIO. **8** *See* GALATIANS, 2. **9** *See* EPHESUS. **10** *See* PHILIP-PIANS, 1. **11** *See* II CORINTHIANS, 1. **12** *See* COLLECTION. **13** *See* JUSTIFICATION; FAITH 3 ii. **14** *See* LAW 2; ROMANS, 2 i. **15** *See* PHILIP-PIANS, 3 i.

PEACE — **1** *See* the entries for each of these terms. **2** *See* EPHESIANS 3 ii.

PENTECOST — **1** *See* SPIRIT. **2** *See* FEASTS. **3** *See* JOHN THE BAPTIST 1.

[PERSECUTION] — *See* SUFFERING.

PETER — **1** *See* JAMES 1; JOHN. **2** *See* MARK, 3. **3** *See* JOHN, GOSPEL OF 1 ii. **4** *See* JAMES 2.

PETER, FIRST LETTER OF — **1** *See* SILVANUS. **2** *See* EMMAUS. **3** *See* SUFFER-ING.

PETER, SECOND LETTER OF — **1** *See* I TIMOTHY, 1. **2** *See* JUDE. **3** *See* HERESY. **4** *See* TRANSFIGURATION. **5** *See* RETURN OF CHRIST.

PHARISEES — **1** *See* RESURRECTION. **2** *See* LAW, 1; SABBATH; FASTING.

PHILEMON, PAUL'S LETTER TO — **1** *See* PHILIPPIANS, 1, for the evidence of an imprisonment in Ephesus. **2** *See* SLAVERY.

PHILIP — **1** *See* HEROD; ARCHELAUS; HEROD ANTIPAS; HERODIAS; CAESAREA PHILIPPI. **2** *See* also ANDREW; THOMAS. **3** *See* STEPHEN. **4** *See* SAMARIA.

PHILIPPIANS, PAUL'S LETTER TO — **1** *See* EPHESUS. **2** *See* PAUL 2 v. **3** *See* TIMOTHY. **4** *See* INCARNATION 1, LORD. **5** *See* JUSTI-FICATION; FAITH 3 ii; GALATIANS, 2.

[PHILOSOPHY] — *See* I CORINTHIANS, 3 i; GOD 1; WORD.

PILATE — **1** *See* STATE. **2** *See* PASSION NARRATIVES 1 iv, 2 iv, 3 iv, 4 iv. **3** *See* BARABBAS.

[POVERTY] — *See* WEALTH.

PRAYER — **1** *See* LORD'S PRAYER; LUKE 2 ii.

[PREACHING] — *See* GOSPEL.

PREDESTINATION — **1** *See* GRACE. **2** *See* SPIRIT 1. **3** *See* CALL. **4** *See* ISRAEL. **5** *See* JUDGMENT.

[PRE-EXISTENCE OF CHRIST]	*See* INCARNATION 1 i; CREATION 3.
[PRESBYTER]	*See* BISHOP.
[PRISCA AND AQUILA]	*See* APOLLOS; WOMEN.
PRODIGAL SON, PARABLE OF	**1** *See* PARABLES 1 iii. **2** *See* JOHN, GOSPEL OF 2. **3** *See* WEDDING FEAST.
[PROMISE]	*See* PAUL 3 iii.
[PROPHECY]	*See* SPIRIT 1 iii; TONGUES.
[PROSELYTES]	*See* GENTILES.
[PROVIDENCE]	*See* GOD 2.
[Q]	*See* SYNOPTIC PROBLEM.
[QUIRINIUS]	*See* AUGUSTUS.
[RANSOM]	*See* REDEMPTION.
[RECONCILIATION]	*See* PEACE.
REDEMPTION	**1** *See* ATONEMENT.
REPENTANCE	**1** *See* CONVERSION; FAITH; BAPTISM; GOSPEL. **2** *See* CORNELIUS.
RESURRECTION	**1** *See* EMPTY TOMB; ASCENSION; MARY MAGDALENE; JOSEPH OF ARIMATHEA; THOMAS; EMMAUS. **2** *See* PHARISEES; SADDUCEES; SANHEDRIN. **3** *See* EMPTY TOMB. **4** *See* EMPTY TOMB 2. **5** *See* ASCENSION. **6** *See* PAUL 1 ii. **7** *See* EPHESIANS, 3 i. **8** *See* HOPE; SUFFERING. **9** *See* RETURN OF CHRIST. **10** *See* JOHN, GOSPEL OF 3 iii. **11** *See* I CORINTHIANS, 3 iv.
RETURN OF CHRIST	**1** *See* RESURRECTION 2 ii. **2** *See* LUKE, 2 iv.
[REVELATION]	*See* SPIRIT 1; ROMANS, 2 i; JOHN, GOSPEL OF 3 ii.
REVELATION, BOOK OF	**1** *See* JOHN. **2** On the authorship of the Gospel, *see* JOHN, GOSPEL OF 1. **3** *See* HERESY. **4** *See* EPHESUS. **5** *See* RETURN OF CHRIST. **6** *See* DEVIL; ANTICHRIST. **7** *See* STATE iv.
[RICHES]	*See* WEALTH.
[RIGHTEOUSNESS]	*See* JUSTIFICATION; ROMANS, 2 ii.
[RIGHT HAND OF GOD]	*See* LORD; ASCENSION.
[ROME]	*See* STATE.
ROMANS, PAUL'S LETTER TO	**1** *See* JAMES 2; GALATIANS, 2. **2** On Rom. 9–11, *see* ISRAEL. **3** *See* COVENANT. **4** *See* JUSTIFICATION. **5** *See* COVENANT. **6** *See* II CORINTHIANS, 2 iii. **7** *See* SIN ii.
SABBATH	**1** *See* LAW 1. **2** For another example of the same procedure, *see* FASTING.
[SACRIFICE]	*See* ATONEMENT; HIGH PRIESTHOOD; HEBREWS, 3 iii.

SADDUCEES	**1** *See* HIGH PRIESTHOOD; SANHEDRIN; PHARISEES; RESURRECTION.
[SAINTS]	*See* SANCTIFICATION.
SALVATION	**1** *See* REDEMPTION; GRACE.
SAMARIA	**1** *See* GOOD SAMARITAN; JOHN; PHILIP iii; SIMON MAGUS.
SANCTIFICATION	**1** *See* CONVERSION; BAPTISM; JUSTIFIC-ATION.
SANHEDRIN	**1** *See* SADDUCEES; HIGH PRIESTHOOD; PHARISEES. **2** *See* the individual entries on these figures.
[SARAH]	*See* ELISABETH; ZECHARIAH.
[SECOND COMING]	*See* RETURN OF CHRIST.
[SERMON ON THE MOUNT]	*See* MATTHEW, 2 iii, 3 i; LUKE, 1 iv; BEATI-TUDES; LORD'S PRAYER; HYPOCRISY; SIN i.
SHEEP AND GOATS, PARABLE OF	**1** *See* JUDGMENT; HELL; PARABLES 1 ii; WISE AND FOOLISH VIRGINS; WHEAT AND TARES.
SILAS/SILVANUS	**1** *See* PAUL 1 iii. **2** *See* I THESSALONIANS, 1. **3** *See* I PETER, 1.
SIMEON	**1** *See* ELISABETH; ZECHARIAH.
SIMON MAGUS	**1** *See* PHILIP iii; SAMARIA.
SIN	**1** *See* LAW. **2** *See* HYPOCRISY. **3** *See* PAUL 3 i; ROMANS, 2 i, iii.
SLAVERY	**1** *See* PHILEMON. **2** *See* CALL.
[SON OF DAVID]	*See* DAVID; BETHLEHEM.
SON OF GOD	**1** *See* INCARNATION. **2** *See* ABBA. **3** *See* LORD. **4** *See* PHILIPPIANS, 3 i.
SON OF MAN	**1** *See* KINGDOM OF GOD. **2** *See* RETURN OF CHRIST. **3** *See* CHRIST 2; MARK, 4 i.
SOWER, PARABLE OF	**1** *See* PARABLES 2. **2** *See* PREDESTINATION.
SPIRIT/HOLY SPIRIT	**1** *See* PENTECOST. **2** *See* GOSPEL. **3** *See* ABBA. **4** *See* LORD. **5** *See* TONGUES; BODY OF CHRIST. **6** *See* JOHN, GOSPEL OF 3 iii. **7** *See* INCARNATION.
STATE	**1** *See* PASSION NARRATIVES 1 iv, 2 iv, 3 iv, 4 iv; PILATE; BARABBAS. **2** *See* JUDAS THE GALI-LEAN. **3** *See* the individual entries on these figures. **4** *See* ANTICHRIST.
STEPHEN	**1** *See* SANHEDRIN.
SUFFERING	**1** *See* MARK, 4 ii. **2** *See* I THESSALONIANS, 1, 2 i. **3** *See* I PETER, 2 iv. **4** *See* HOPE.
SYNAGOGUE	**1** *See* LAW 1. **2** *See* GENTILES; CIRCUMCISION.
SYNOPTIC PROBLEM	**1** *See* MATTHEW, 2; LUKE, 1. **2** *See*, for example, EMPTY TOMB 1 i–iii; PASSION NARRATIVES 1–3.

[TABERNACLES, FEAST OF]	*See* FEASTS.
TALENTS, PARABLE OF	**1** *See* separate entry. **2** *See* ABBA.
[TAX-COLLECTORS]	*See* JESUS 2 v; PARABLES 1 iii; PRODIGAL SON; WEDDING FEAST; KINGDOM OF GOD.
TEMPLE	**1** *See* HEROD. **2** *See* EPHESIANS, 3 ii. **3** *See* LAW 1; TALENTS; LABOURERS IN VINEYARD. **4** *See* STEPHEN.
TEMPTATIONS OF JESUS	**1** *See* DEVIL. **2** *See* MIRACLES 1; MARK, 4 i. **3** *See* MARK, 4 ii. **4** *See* HEBREWS, 3 i.
[THADDAEUS]	*See* TWELVE.
THANKSGIVING	**1** *See* I TIMOTHY, 2. **2** *See* CREATION 1. **3** *See* GOSPEL.
THESSALONIANS, PAUL'S FIRST LETTER TO	**1** *See* PAUL 2 v. **2** *See* SILVANUS; TIMOTHY. **3** *See* SUFFERING. **4** *See* RETURN OF CHRIST. **5** *See* RESURRECTION 2 iii.
THESSALONIANS, PAUL'S SECOND LETTER TO	**1** *See* I THESSALONIANS, 2 ii. **2** *See* ANTI-CHRIST. **3** *See*, for example, ISRAEL. **4** *See* RETURN OF JESUS.
[THEUDAS]	*See* JUDAS THE GALILEAN; GAMALIEL.
THOMAS	**1** *See* also ANDREW; PHILIP ii. **2** *See* ZECHA-RIAH.
TIMOTHY	**1** *See* PAUL 1 iv. **2** *See* I THESSALONIANS, 1. **3** *See* PHILIPPIANS, 1.
TIMOTHY, PAUL'S FIRST LETTER TO	**1** *See* BISHOP. **2** *See* BODY OF CHRIST. **3** *See* LAW 2. **4** *See* II PETER, 1 iv. **5** *See* HERESY. **6** *See* RETURN OF CHRIST.
TIMOTHY, PAUL'S SECOND LETTER TO	**1** *See* I TIMOTHY, 1. **2** *See* I TIMOTHY, 1.
TITUS	**1** *See* PAUL 2 iv. **2** *See* II CORINTHIANS, 1. **3** *See* COLLECTION.
TITUS, PAUL'S LETTER TO	**1** *See* I TIMOTHY, 1. **2** *See* BISHOP.
TONGUES, SPEAKING IN	**1** *See* PENTECOST. **2** *See* CORNELIUS. **3** *See* EPHESUS. **4** *See* BODY OF CHRIST.
TRANSFIGURATION OF JESUS	**1** *See* MARK, 3. **2** *See* LUKE, 2 ii. **3** *See* II PETER, 2.
[TRIAL OF JESUS]	*See* SANHEDRIN; CAIAPHAS; ANNAS; PILATE; BARABBAS.
[TRINITY]	*See* SPIRIT 2; INCARNATION.
[TRUST]	*See* FAITH.
[TRUTH]	*See* JOHN, GOSPEL OF 3 i.
TWELVE, THE	**1** *See* DISCIPLE; APOSTLE. **2** *See* the separate entries for PETER; JAMES; JOHN; ANDREW; PHILIP; THOMAS; JUDAS ISCARIOT.

[UNBELIEF]	*See* THOMAS; ZECHARIAH.
[UNLEAVENED BREAD, FEAST OF]	*See* PASSOVER; FEASTS.
VIRGIN BIRTH	**1** *See* MARY, THE VIRGIN; JOSEPH. **2** *See* DAVID. **3** *See* BETHLEHEM. **4** *See* INCARNATION.
[VOCATION]	*See* CALL.
WEALTH	**1** *See* JAMES, LETTER OF 2. **2** *See* BEATITUDES.
WEDDING FEAST, PARABLE OF	**1** *See* PARABLES 2. **2** *See* JESUS 2 v; PARABLES 1 iii; PRODIGAL SON.
WHEAT AND TARES, PARABLE OF	**1** *See* RETURN OF CHRIST; JUDGMENT; SHEEP AND GOATS; WISE AND FOOLISH VIRGINS. **2** *See* MATTHEW, 3 iii. **3** *See* SOWER.
WICKED HUSBANDMEN, PARABLE OF	**1** *See* WEDDING FEAST. **2** *See* PARABLES 2.
[WISDOM]	*See* I CORINTHIANS, 3 i; CREATION 3.
WISE AND FOOLISH VIRGINS, PARABLE OF	**1** *See* RETURN OF CHRIST; JUDGMENT; PARABLES 2. **2** *See* PARABLES 1 ii.
WOMEN	**1** *See* MARY MAGDALENE; MARY, THE VIRGIN; ELISABETH. **2** *See* I TIMOTHY, 1. **3** *See* MARRIAGE.
WORD	**1** *See* INCARNATION 1; JOHN, GOSPEL OF 3 ii.
[WORKS]	*See* FAITH 3 ii, 5; JUSTIFICATION.
WORLD	**1** *See* JUDGMENT. **2** *See* I CORINTHIANS, 3 i.
[ZEALOTS]	*See* JUDAS THE GALILEAN.
ZECHARIAH	**1** *See* ELISABETH. **2** *See also* THOMAS.

THE WORLD OF THE NEW TESTAMENT